D0915889

"A ROOF OVER MY HEAD"

"A ROOF OVER MY HEAD"

Homeless Women and the Shelter Industry

Jean Calterone Williams

University Press of Colorado

© 2003 by the University Press of Colorado

Published by the University Press of Colorado
5589 Arapahoe Avenue, Suite 206C
Boulder, Colorado 80303

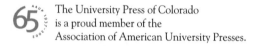 The University Press of Colorado
is a proud member of the
Association of American University Presses.

The University Press of Colorado is a cooperative publishing enterprise supported, in part, by
Adams State College, Colorado State University, Fort Lewis College, Mesa State College,
Metropolitan State College of Denver, University of Colorado, University of Northern
Colorado, University of Southern Colorado, and Western State College of Colorado.

The paper used in this publication meets the minimum requirements of the American National
Standard for Information Sciences—Permanence of Paper for Printed Library Materials. ANSI
Z39.48-1992

Library of Congress Cataloging-in-Publication Data

Williams, Jean Calterone, 1966–
  "A roof over my head" : homeless women and the shelter industry / by Jean Calterone
Williams.
    p. cm.
Includes bibliographical references and index.
  ISBN 0-87081-731-0 (hardcover : alk. paper)
  1. Homeless women—Services for—United States. 2. Single mothers—Services for—United
States. I. Title.

HV4505 .W53 2003
362.83'086'942—dc21

                                                                              2002155958

Design by Daniel Pratt

12   11   10   09   08   07   06   05   04   03   10   9   8   7   6   5   4   3   2   1

For Cass and Shane

CONTENTS

ACKNOWLEDGMENTS

This study would not have been completed without the support and assistance of many people. I owe a great debt to the shelter residents and staff who gave so generously of their time and shared their thoughts with me. Particularly for the homeless and battered women, who had many other pressing details to attend to and problems to address, I deeply appreciate their participation. Theresa Grates, director of My Sister's Place, along with the shelter staff and residents, were especially central to the study.

Matthew Crenson, Toby Ditz, Sue Hemberger, Richard Katz, Laury Oaks, Danny Walkowitz, Edward Williams, and Nancy Williams read all or parts of the book. Their questions and suggestions for clarification were essential in shaping its direction. Discussions with the students in my Gender, Welfare, and Homelessness class at Arizona State University—many of whom were low income and currently or formerly received welfare benefits—also helped to develop the connections made between homelessness and poverty. Krista Hornaday and Matthew Edling provided expert, careful research assistance at different points in the writing process. Thanks to Cal Poly, San Luis Obispo, for a grant that provided much-needed research time to revise the book in the fall of 2001.

The support and enthusiasm of my editor at the University Press of Colorado, Kerry Callahan, was incredibly helpful. I am grateful for her encouragement and expertise, and her attentiveness to the book and its subject matter certainly facilitated the project's completion. As an anonymous reviewer, Donileen Loseke provided thorough and thoughtful suggestions, many of which I incorporated into the book.

Finally, in addition to providing expert reading of portions of the book, Cass Russett deserves thanks for his vital support during the course of this project. His help, advice, and emotional support have been central to its completion.

"A ROOF OVER MY HEAD"

INTRODUCTION

During the 1980s and 1990s, the steadily rising number of people living on the streets and in shelters in most U.S. cities was accompanied by increased scholarly and public attention to homelessness. Particularly noteworthy were the statistics citing women and children among the fastest-growing segments of the homeless population. Women were seen as a surprising subset of the "new" homeless; few women were among the hobos and itinerant workers of the late nineteenth and early twentieth centuries. And in part because homeless women often have children with them, women's homelessness introduced new concerns and understandings about what it means to be on the street.

This study features homeless women's perspectives about why they become homeless, so it addresses the causes of homelessness in homeless women's own voices. Women's homelessness results from a complex interweaving of multiple issues. Both men and women suffer from a lack of low-income housing, low wages, and sporadic employment, but women also contend with domestic violence and the traditional responsibility of caring for children. It is difficult to capture the interaction of these multiple reasons for homelessness without sustained and intimate knowledge of homeless women's lives. Statistics tell only part of the story; poverty rates, unemployment rates, and welfare rates cannot fully describe women's homelessness. For these reasons this project relies on the rich and detailed information revealed through homeless women's personal narratives. These narratives highlight the importance of poverty and domestic violence in understanding women's homelessness.

In addition to the causes of homelessness, I also question the *meanings* of homelessness through homeless and housed people's perspectives. That is to say, homelessness refers to the lack of a dwelling considered standard in our society, the literal lack of a roof over one's head. But homelessness also symbolizes, in a very visceral way, all the things we as a society attribute to poor people—it represents the lack of personal responsibility, the loss of a work ethic, and a general disassociation from the norms and trappings of middle-class society. In analyzing these deeper meanings of homelessness, which both homeless and housed people help to create, this study also looks at how such meanings of homelessness affect the kind of help homeless people are offered.

Homelessness is analyzed in this book through three separate, although interconnected, components. First, to understand the meanings and experiences of homelessness, I interviewed both homeless women and housed people in Phoenix, Arizona; these two sets of interviews represent two prongs of the study. The third prong analyzes shelter services, philosophies, and policies because ideas about homelessness are both created and reflected in the shelter system.[1] Shelters are important because they often serve as housed people's only representation of homelessness. They give clues about how to understand homelessness, transmitting meanings of homelessness and representations of homeless women. By making many aspects of their programs mandatory, for instance, shelters give the impression that homeless people will not take the initiative on their own to look for work or housing, enroll their children in school, or keep their living spaces clean. They must be forced to do so. By mandating budgeting classes, shelters suggest that people become homeless in part because they are irresponsible with their money. It is in a sense a symbiotic relationship: shelter programs influence the ways housed people think about homelessness, and the views of the housed public—whether ordinary citizens or policymakers—affect the formation of shelter programs and how such programs treat homeless people.

Thus a description of homeless women's lived experiences appears alongside a consideration of homeless and housed people's interpretations of why people become homeless, what kinds of people constitute the homeless population, and the best policy responses to homelessness. This study reflects the processes by which homeless and housed people—in their attempts to make sense of poverty and homelessness as these issues impinge upon their daily lives—participate with shelter employees, homeless advocates, and policy-makers in shaping the meanings of homelessness.[2] By relying on the words of ordinary homeless and housed people to provide the majority of the data for this book, I suggest that to understand the politics of poverty and homelessness, one needs to examine the ways people in multiple social locations engage in constructing meanings for homelessness and the identity of "the homeless."

METHODOLOGY

For two years in the mid-1990s I talked with, ate with, walked with, and listened to homeless people talk about their lives. For many women I became a shoulder to cry on, an ally to laugh with, and a willing listener to stories of shelter staff disrespect—as well as caring work—for homeless women. My own perspectives about homelessness and my attitude toward homeless people underwent a major change. Instead of the sometimes uncomfortable mix of sympathy and revulsion I had felt for the seemingly incomprehensible life of a homeless person, I now feel empathy, respect, and awe that anyone emerges from homelessness and from the shelter system with self-respect, hope, and humor intact.

During a two-year period I visited fifteen homeless shelters, battered women's shelters, and antipoverty agencies in Phoenix, Arizona, and interviewed and spent extended time with homeless women in five of those shelters. In-depth, semistructured interviews occurred with thirty-three homeless women and two homeless men—discussing family and work histories, education, income, violence, mental illness and substance use, as well as how they felt about homelessness and what it meant to them. Interviews ranged from one to four hours. I had ongoing contact with many of these women—meeting their friends or family members, visiting their jobs, accompanying them on errands, and having extended talks over a meal or a cup of coffee. Participant observation took place with an additional 100 homeless men and women. Ongoing interactions with some of these shelter residents provided much of the same information as the in-depth interviews.[3] Finally, I also interviewed shelter directors and caseworkers, usually professional social workers, hired to work with the homeless.

To provide additional breadth to the interview data, I reviewed fifty randomly chosen confidential case files at the Lighthouse, one of the family homeless shelters featured in the study. The files provide less depth than the interviews, but the information they contain on work, education, and family history helps to support my findings with statistical information. They also offer a different kind of information than was gained from the homeless interviews and participant observation. Specifically, the files are notes written by a staff equipped with distinct categories of "the deserving and the undeserving"[4] homeless, through which residents are filtered. In this sense they provide another set of data on staff attitudes, beliefs, and practices. In addition, I worked for a year as a part-time paid caseworker at one of the battered women's shelters. Exposure to staff and residents as a caseworker versus as a companion to the residents brings a different perspective on the difficulties inherent in both living and working in a shelter and on the meanings of homelessness.[5]

Although the various interviews and sources present a complex weave of multiple perspectives on homelessness, the experiences and points of view of homeless women remain central. My wish to describe homelessness from the standpoint of homeless women means that the portrayal of shelter staff tends to be more negative than positive. Indeed, in comparison to other studies of homelessness, the portrait of shelter staff often seems to miss the caring and empathetic work many do for the homeless.[6] Further, in contrast to the depiction of homeless people, the staff seems much more one-dimensional. This is the case because although I interviewed caseworkers and directors of shelters, I self-consciously depict staff words in the context of how homeless women experience them. A shelter resident does not simply listen to a caseworker describe homeless people as "dysfunctional" and in need of basic "life skills" training but understands that those beliefs translate directly to decisions about assistance (or lack of assistance) that deeply affect the possibility of becoming housed. Thus staff attitudes and beliefs—often a mix of objective distance and paternalistic concern[7]—are described from homeless women's, not staff members', perspectives.

Individual caseworkers wield exceptional power over individual homeless women, who are dependent upon the shelter to meet basic needs. Many caseworkers labor valiantly to assist homeless women in a socioeconomic context of diminishing real wages, job stability, and availability of public assistance. But because the shelter staff serves as the most direct representative of a stingy and bureaucratic system, homeless women may blame them for inadequacies the staff cannot control. These representatives of the system, even when they provide real assistance to the residents, also personify the seemingly endless regulations and personal intrusions homeless women have to accept to get housing. Homeless women often do not perceive caseworkers as full human beings or note the times they have been helpful and caring because homeless women experience staff help in the context of their own powerlessness. The goal, then, is not to depict caseworkers' experiences and viewpoints but to show life from the standpoint of homeless women and to emphasize their voices, so conspicuously absent from much scholarly research.

My ability to gain the trust and confidences of women had to do in part with being a female researcher. In the largely sex-segregated world of family homeless shelters, women often congregated to discuss housing, their children, and jobs; the conversations would wind their way casually around a number of topics. Men did not share in these conversations, and had I been a male researcher, I probably would have had great difficulty engaging in participant observation. Likewise in the two battered women's shelters, all the staff members were women, as were the residents. Although male volunteers were allowed and even welcomed by some residents, most women assumed that I could better relate to their experiences of battering and abuse in part because I am a woman.

Similarly, my race impacted the interviewing process. Race and class are charged topics at the shelters, although conflicts tend to remain just under the surface and are rarely openly addressed. As a middle-class white woman I look much like the majority of staff people and social service workers omnipresent in homeless women's lives. I feared my questions would be interpreted as just one more intrusion in a context where requests for personal information from the staff cannot be refused. Although I worked hard at not appearing to be aligned with the staff, spending much more time with the residents, my race—as well as my class, gender, and age—certainly impacted how women spoke to me and what they chose to reveal.

Not surprisingly, Latina and African American women seemed particularly suspicious of me. At the beginning of the study, before I had engaged in much participant observation and therefore was an unfamiliar face at the shelters, Latina and African American women tended to avoid me more than white women did. As I became a more familiar presence and conversed regularly with many shelter residents, the racial composition of residents agreeing to interview gradually changed. By the end of the study period, my interviews roughly correlated to the overall family shelter population in terms of race and ethnicity.

Indeed, after I had overcome their initial reluctance to talk, many women eagerly poured out their stories. Women in the family shelter system are constantly asked to talk about their lives, and often these are less requests than demands with benefits attached for acquiescing. Once women realized that the interview process allowed them to share their stories without judgment or strings attached, many described how cathartic it was to tell their stories and how important it was to have someone listen to them and take their perspectives seriously.

As I conducted interviews and began to write, I struggled with whether and how to identify women racially. First, I did not want to reify the notion that racial categories are somehow biologically based or "real" as opposed to being social constructions. Second, given the number of women interviewed and the largely qualitative data I gathered, it is impossible to make generalizations based on race regarding access to programs, length of shelter stay, or even education or family structure. Everything I observed at the shelters indicated, however, that the caseworkers' distrust of homeless women—the suspicion that they were lying about their reasons for homelessness, were using drugs or alcohol, were not really battered—was worse for women of color. Although subtle, white women perhaps were defined as deserving of assistance more often than Latina or African American women because a largely white staff had been schooled in stereotypes about the lazy welfare queen, a woman of color in most representations.[8] Thus the shelter system provides an interesting window into the process by which race—although a social construction rather than a biological category—comes to have real, ongoing, serious material meanings and consequences for people.

The disavowal of African American, Latina, and Native American women's deservingness can also be seen in the interviews with homeless women. White homeless women repeatedly used whiteness to argue or confirm that they were part of the deserving poor. Their whiteness itself was used as proof of honesty, thrift, and a work ethic. White women's often successful use of whiteness (the shelter staff accepted it as a marker of deservingness) exemplifies the ways that even homeless white women are in a sense privileged through their ties to the dominant culture. It was for this reason that I chose to identify women by race (along with age and number of children). Race and ethnicity—in particular, categories of white, black, and Latino—were central to white women's representations of homelessness.

The homeless interviews were conducted with residents from two homeless shelters, the Lighthouse and the Family Shelter; two transitional housing programs, People in Transition and Endowment for Phoenix Families; and two domestic violence shelters, La Casa and Rose's House; and they were combined with participant observation in three of those programs and in one homeless camp in the desert.[9] Interaction varied from simply spending time talking with residents, eating lunch together on and off the shelter grounds, and occasionally driving people on errands to participating in an adult recreation program and women's support group at People in Transition. Because this study examines the contexts and meanings of women's homelessness, particularly the connections between domestic violence and homelessness, most of the interviews—thirty-three of thirty-five—were conducted with women. As a result, although participant observation occurred with both men and women, the generalizations made here pertain most directly to women's encounters with emergency shelter programs.

I was interested in discovering how women experience and interpret their own lives and struggles, how they describe living in shelters, and how—if they are able—they resist dominant understandings of homelessness. Within the boundaries of my questions, then, homeless women (and a few men) formulated their own narratives of their homelessness, relating stories of becoming homeless that made sense to them. These stories are mediated by the author to the extent that I asked certain questions and not others and have the power to frame their stories in a specific context. The homeless women's narratives, however, remain their own in the sense that they decided which events and information explain their homelessness and, by exclusion, what does not count as an explanation of why they lost housing.[10] Thus this study does not provide a pure or unadulterated view of homelessness, nor should women's interviews be interpreted as "authentic" or pure. Rather, this study provides a representation of homelessness dominated by homeless women's views and stories. Rich in paradox and contradiction, these stories indicate a great diversity in personal experience. Thus I do not claim to offer the "homeless point of view"; rather, these voices are multiple and conflicting.[11]

Women's representations of their histories and current living conditions reveal much about how homelessness is understood as a "public problem" in the United States and about the relationship of homelessness to American culture.[12] As the interviews will indicate, certain kinds of explanations for and solutions to homelessness have more cultural resonance than others. In other words, homelessness can only be explained by placing it in the specific cultural context of the late-twentieth-century and early-twenty-first-century United States, where the dominant view of poverty focuses on individual rather than structural explanations and divides the poor into categories of deserving and undeserving. Homeless women's stories intersect with these notions of the deserving and the undeserving poor. Moreover, shelter residents' experiences as homeless people and housed people's personal interactions with the homeless actually contribute to the process by which categories of deservingness are constructed. In this way the interviews with sixty-five people who were not homeless become an important tool to analyze meanings of homelessness. Housed people with no formal or direct connection to homelessness understand and interpret the existence of homelessness from their specific social locations, using shared cultural constructions of homelessness and poverty.

Housed participants came from a wide range of organizations and workplaces, including, but not limited to, schools, an art gallery, a construction company, a law firm, an actuarial company, a counseling center, and a real estate office. Those who might be considered more politically active than the norm were also sought out and included National Service Program employees, as well as Democratic, Republican, and Libertarian activists and members of the National Organization for Women. Although the majority were middle class, low-income and upper-income people also participated. The interview asked for opinions about why people become homeless, how homelessness can be addressed, what feelings and responses homelessness evokes, personal experience with homelessness in the past, and definitions of homelessness.[13]

ETHNOGRAPHY

Relatively few studies of homelessness focus on women, and even fewer are ethnographies that allow homeless women themselves to define their homelessness.[14] Ethnographic studies of homeless people typically use participant observation, focusing on how and where homeless people live and considering the issues and problems they face while living in shelters or on the streets. Such studies build on a long line of urban ethnographic explorations of the lives and material struggles of people in low-income communities.[15] The best of these ethnographies capture the myriad ways the people interviewed make sense of their lives, helping to create meanings for homelessness and poverty.[16]

Ethnographic research supplies depth and contextual information that help to make sense of homeless women's experiences. It is only through in-depth interviews and long-term participation in at least some aspects of homeless women's lives that the political and cultural meanings of homelessness surface and the relationship between personal experiences and the cultural construction of homelessness is revealed. Sherry Ortner points to the "immediacy" and "power" of relating people's stories, although at the same time she cautions against ethnography's tendency to portray a group as static and homogeneous—failing to capture "the multiple subject positions," the diverse and sometimes contradictory voices, and the dynamism of the people studied. Nevertheless, Ortner argues that "America is overanalyzed and underethnographized" and suggests that we look to ethnography as a way of knowing rather than a "kind of text":

> Ethnographic knowledge is knowledge of the lived worlds of real people in real time and space, and while we may be able to do without ethnograph*ies* as we have known them, we cannot do without ethnography. And although there is a significant body of ethnographic work on America, much of it quite good, the ratio of knowledge derived from this work to knowledge derived from polling, statistics, media analysis, and journalism is radically out of whack.[17]

Indeed, the literature on homelessness contains a significant number of books that rely on survey or other kinds of research, with the authors sometimes never speaking to a homeless person at all. Even though homeless people are living with homelessness, they are not presumed to have significant specialized knowledge about why it occurs and how to address it. Their presumed "deviance" means they are incapable of being experts on homelessness or of sharing inside knowledge to explain the process of becoming homeless.

Analyses of homelessness also tend to divide people into groups, arguing that a certain percentage are homeless as a result of drug use, another group is mentally ill, and still another is homeless because of the structure of the economy.[18] Although categorization usually represents the first step in calculating how many people are homeless and why and how government and private agencies can best respond to them, Peter Marcuse criticizes the practice. He argues that it is symptomatic of a reliance on "specialism, or calling a general problem the sum of a number of different special problems."[19] Rather than focus on the systemic or structural roots of homelessness, specialism both reflects and encourages a cultural understanding of homelessness as merely a "mental health, substance abuse, or criminal justice problem."[20]

Although survey research has been important in extending understanding of why homelessness occurs, use of this particular methodology tends to rely on specialism, resulting in explanations for homelessness that categorize people based on the *one* reason they lost housing. In addition to the other problems inherent in specialism, such categorization precludes a focus on the *process* of becoming homeless—on how, for example, domestic violence, drug use, and poverty actually intertwine to lead to homelessness.[21] Ethnography lends itself more easily to an emphasis on the process of becoming homeless and in that sense has affected the results of this study. Participant observation and in-depth interviews are more likely to find the multiple and interconnecting factors that affect housing status.[22] My interviews showed that women became homeless as a result of a combination of events and reasons that intersected and often depended on one another, that occurred in a specific time and place to a particular person. Such particularities reveal themselves only through the ongoing and intense interaction possible with in-depth interviews and participant observation.

THE SHELTERS

The shelters discussed in this book house as few as five families to as many as 100 individuals; all have cumbersome sets of rules and significant client and staff contact. Previous literature on homelessness has often focused on people literally living on the street[23] or in large armory-style shelters[24] rather than on people living in stricter shelters, in long-term transitional living programs, or doubled up with friends or family. The studies of people on the streets and in armory shelters have greatly increased our understanding of homelessness.[25] Homeless families and individuals living in the smaller shelters and transitional living centers, which often exercise more control over residents, however, may have somewhat different reasons for becoming homeless or different experiences while homeless.

Studies of people literally living on the street may miss homeless adults who have children with them—most of them women—as the majority are in some form of shelter rather than living in the woods, in the desert, or under a freeway overpass. Children are likely to be taken from their parents and placed in state-run crisis child care if they are discovered living on the street. Similarly, literature focusing on armory-style shelters may skew attention toward those homeless people who are mentally ill or heavy substance abusers because they are probably the least likely to obey stricter shelter rules. In contrast to the shelters in this study, armory-style shelters tend to have fewer rules and expectations of residents and to be less well staffed. Often homeless people must apply for a bed on a night-by-night basis, people may sleep together in a large room rather than have their own spaces, consumption of alcohol off the shelter premises may be fairly unrestricted, and people must exit the shelter early in the morning and not return until evening.

By contrast, smaller, more tightly controlled shelters offer more privacy and amenities than the armory-style shelters, such as individual rooms for each family and fewer clients per caseworker. Although the more comfortable living environment is accompanied by more stringent regulations, these shelters are almost always full, and many homeless people find it difficult to gain admission to them. Generally, such shelters do not permit residents to use alcohol or drugs on or off the shelter premises. Before the staff considers accepting a person with a history of drug or alcohol use, he or she must have been clean for some time before having sought shelter or be willing to attend counseling once in the shelter. Moreover, caseworkers tend to accept those homeless people who appear most "motivated" or most likely to succeed in finding a home within the three months they live at the shelter. This may exclude mentally ill women, although those who have been "stabilized" on medication are sometimes accepted. This practice may also favor those with more skills or job experience, since they are the group most likely to become stably housed within three months.

The definition of homeless people as deviants tends to dominate in these smaller, more tightly controlled shelters. Most Phoenix shelters are short term, offering no more than three months of housing, and they are staffed primarily by social workers. Assigning the problem of "fixing" homeless people to social workers tends to individualize and psychologize the reasons people become homeless, since social workers as social deviance experts not only advocate for shelter residents with housing programs or other social service agencies but also argue that they need to help homeless people eradicate "dysfunctional" behaviors.[26] Under the direction of social workers, the services these shelters offer differ from those that might be available if job training programs or housing developers had primary responsibility for confronting homelessness. Perhaps the response would not center around temporary, emergency shelters offering life skills classes but would focus on building permanent low-income housing or generating entry-level jobs outside the service sector.[27]

Consonant with the emphasis on homeless deviance and dysfunction, shelters employ complex sets of rules, mandatory "work programs," and curfews—all geared toward social control of residents. Although more true for homeless than battered women's shelters, attempts to micromanage residents' lives suggest that social control is often viewed as the only acceptable response to the "intractable" problem the homeless represent. Lee Rainwater argues that since the 1960s,

> Political and public discussion has seldom concerned itself with poverty as a basic condition of the life of a significant group in American society. Instead debate has focused on the social problems associated with poverty—thus we have issues of the welfare crisis and welfare reform, street crime, crack cocaine, poor schools . . . births to unmarried teenage mothers, infant mortality, homelessness. . . . Each problem has its own diagnosis, its own therapy, and its own professionals hungry for funding. Poverty and the poor as a class get lost in the scramble for social problem definition and control.[28]

As Rainwater suggests, the first step in "fixing" the homeless is to divide them into distinct categories based on their particular dysfunction. Thus drugs, alcohol, laziness, teen pregnancy, and hopelessness can be addressed with the appropriate responses and therapies.

Relatedly, within the context of social control, Phoenix shelters tend to categorize homeless women into discrete groups. In general, each directs its services toward one subpopulation of the homeless—such as abused and neglected teens, drug addicts, homeless women, or battered women—to the exclusion of others similarly without housing. This propensity extends in particular to the construction of separate identities—and therefore different services—for battered women versus homeless women.[29] Battered women's shelters and homeless shelters each create a different set of eligibility criteria that corresponds to a specific identity. Shelters refuse to provide services to women who do not conform to the criteria that supposedly define the particular group the shelter program targets. Yet according to women seeking shelter, neither battered women's shelters' nor homeless shelters' eligibility criteria fully reflect women's lives and experiences. Thus those who do not clearly fit into either the battered woman or the homeless woman identity have great difficulty locating a program to assist them or may redefine their experiences to correspond more closely to the shelter staff's expectations.

The decision to include in this study women from both homeless and domestic violence shelters resulted from their strikingly similar reasons for seeking emergency housing. In particular, many told stories about abusive partners in discussing their past histories and paths to both kinds of shelters.[30] Although I began this research by concentrating exclusively on women in homeless shelters, I extended the interviewing to include women in domestic violence shelters when I discovered the centrality of abuse in homeless women's stories. Interviews and participant observation reveal that a woman with a history of having been battered may enter a homeless shelter after spending some time at a domestic violence shelter. She may also go directly from her battering relationship to a homeless shelter because, among other reasons, the domestic violence shelters are full. Other women may prefer the attention paid to housing and job needs at Phoenix homeless shelters. The women's stories in this study indicate that many seek assistance for multiple problems but learn to emphasize one and conceal another to gain acceptance into a particular shelter. They also suggest that the distinctions between "battered woman" and "homeless woman" are not straightforward or absolute.

To meet residents at both homeless and battered women's shelters, I had to get the permission of a sometimes reluctant shelter staff. Some shelters such as La Casa, a battered women's shelter featured in this study, have policies generally prohibiting researchers from interviewing residents on the grounds that doing so violates client privacy. Others want to encourage residents to spend their time pursuing housing, employment, and other goals rather than answering interview questions, and residents may not be readily accessible because they are working on these goals. Moreover, a dearth of public, community space at the shelters made it difficult for me to become familiar to residents, a key element in relieving the uneasiness that may initially accompany an interview request.

All homeless people who agreed to interviews did so voluntarily. At the Family Shelter and Rose's House where I spent a good deal of time talking with residents, accompanying people on errands, or assisting with child care, I initially set up interviews by attending resident meetings or gatherings, explaining my research, and passing around a sign-up sheet for those who wanted to participate. In this way people could decline to interview without having to face me directly, a position I assumed would be more comfortable for them than a face-to-face refusal. In time I met other shelter residents through women who had participated in those initial interviews, while visiting in women's rooms, or when talking with people in the public community area. Similarly, at the Lighthouse, initially the caseworker put a sign-up sheet on the door of the shelter that described the study and had specific times for people to sign up. I then met other people while I was in the shelter to conduct the initial interviews; sometimes I approached people, and other times women would express interest in being interviewed. At People in Transition I spent time talking casually with people, and I helped organize and participated in recreational trips and an off-and-on women's support group. I then asked people individually if they wanted to participate.

At La Casa, unlike at the other shelters, the caseworker set up the interviews herself. Her concern was not to select the women to be interviewed so much as to ensure that they could decline without discomfort, thereby avoiding the possibility that some women might feel pressured to participate. In this sense La Casa offered me the least access to shelter residents. In addition to the caseworker's control over interview arrangements, she did not allow me to spend time interacting with residents on the shelter grounds. As a result, Rose's House figures more prominently than La Casa in the discussions regarding domestic violence shelters.

HOMELESSNESS AND WOMEN'S POVERTY

In her article on gender and homelessness, Jan Hagen emphasizes the significance of poverty for intensifying the risk of homelessness:

> While the lack of affordable, safe housing has been well-documented, relatively little attention has been given to the relationship between poverty or low income and homelessness. Over the past decade, the relative value of incomes generally has declined and public assistance benefits particularly have failed to keep pace with inflation. . . . Those especially at risk are mother-headed families who depend on public assistance benefits. . . . The much discussed and documented "feminization of poverty" and the more recent attention to the "pauperization of children" indicate that women and their children are at a particularly high risk for homelessness resulting from poverty and once homeless, for difficulty in locating affordable housing.[31]

Thus women's poverty leads to women's homelessness by numerous paths. The trends Hagen notes show no signs of reversal, suggesting that women will continue to be disproportionately poor and an ever-growing percentage of the homeless population.

In addition to concerns specific to women and families headed by a single mother, women have also felt the effects of an increasing gap between rich and poor. From 1979 to 1995 the poorest 20 percent of U.S. families saw their incomes decrease by 9 percent, whereas the richest 20 percent experienced a 26 percent increase in family income.[32] The poverty rate for both two-parent and single-parent families in which at least one adult worked increased from 7.8 percent in 1978 to 10.1 percent in 1999.[33] And the poor became poorer: those below 50 percent of the poverty line rose from 29.9 percent of all poor persons in 1975 to 39.3 percent of those in poverty in 1999.[34] In particular, the percentage of low-income African Americans below 50 percent of the poverty line increased from 32.1 percent of all black people in poverty in 1975 to 42.8 percent in 1999.[35]

Even given the difficulty many two-parent families have staying out of poverty, single-parent families headed by women are much worse off than married couples. For example, in 1979, 30.4 percent of female single-parent families were poor compared with 5.4 percent of married-couple families.

Little had changed by 1999, when 27.8 percent of families headed by a single mother were poor, as were 4.8 percent of two-parent families.[36] Breaking the percentage down by race indicates that black and Latina single mothers are disproportionately poor. Whereas 22.5 percent of all white, single-parent, female-headed households were poor in 1999, 39.3 percent of African American and 38.8 percent of Latina female-headed families were below the poverty line.[37] A look at the poverty of female single-parent families as a percentage of all families in poverty is also telling: the percentage of single-mother families rose from 23.7 percent of all families in poverty in 1960 to 48.5 percent of families in poverty in 1999.[38]

Data from the U.S. Department of Housing and Urban Development and the U.S. Conference of Mayors suggest that the gendered and racialized aspects of poverty are reflected in the composition of a homeless population that has grown younger and more female and is increasingly made up of disproportionate numbers of people of color. In 2000 the U.S. Conference of Mayors surveyed twenty-five cities' yearly reports on hunger and homelessness and reported that African Americans make up 50 percent of the homeless population, whites are 35 percent, and Hispanics constitute 12 percent.[39] Homelessness provides an opportunity to see the ways class and race are linked. Blacks in particular are significantly overrepresented in the homeless population; racial discrimination and a generally immobile class system intersect to create persistent poverty, which itself is linked to homelessness. The fact that the class structure in the United States is made static in part by the persistence of racism suggests that blacks will continue to be overrepresented in the homeless population.[40]

Likewise, homelessness reflects the feminization of poverty. Just as women who head families are more likely than men to be poor, so homeless families are more likely to be headed by a single woman than by a single man or by two parents. The U.S. Conference of Mayors reports that in 2000, 63 percent of homeless families were single-parent families, with ten cities reporting that 80 to 96 percent of homeless single-parent families were headed by women.[41] A study by the Institute for Children and Poverty found that 95 percent of homeless families are headed by women, based on aggregate data across ten cities.[42] As a proportion of the homeless population, families grew from 27 percent in 1985 to 36 percent in 2000.[43]

As the economy grew in the second half of the 1990s, poverty, by some measures, decreased, yet homelessness did not decline. According to the U.S. Conference of Mayor's report, the demand for emergency shelter increased every year from 1985 to 2000, through periods of both economic stagnation and growth.[44] These statistical measures, along with this study's findings, indicate that homelessness persists even in periods marked by a relatively healthy economy, when unemployment is low.

As the discussion of women's reasons for becoming homeless will support, economic growth does not necessarily translate to a decrease in the homeless population. Much of the persistence of homelessness is explained by complex, intersecting factors like the shortage of low-income housing, low wages associated with service-sector employment, and diminishing welfare benefits. Homelessness is linked to poverty in both complex and straightforward ways and has much to do with the differential educational, occupational, and housing options and opportunities available to the rich and the poor. Women's poverty additionally is associated with their traditional responsibility for the care of children, lower wages, and separation from family support systems as a result of past or present violence. As Leslie Kanes Weisman argues, because of the growth in women's poverty in the past twenty years, it has become increasingly important for studies of homelessness to focus on the unique sets of issues and problems women's homelessness presents: "Single women and women heading families are burgeoning among the homeless as a result of government cuts in disability benefits, rising housing costs, an increase in divorce rates, domestic violence, teenage pregnancies, and increasing poverty caused by unemployment, low-paying jobs, and wage discrimination."[45] Women interviewed in Phoenix shelters emphasized the impacts of these family disruptions, financial responsibilities, and economic difficulties on their paths to homelessness.

Notwithstanding the complex story each woman tells when asked what events led her to seek temporary shelter, the Phoenix data indicate a clear pattern: most women were poor prior to becoming homeless. Poverty often combined with domestic violence and low-rent housing shortages to create a crisis situation. Just as Mark Rank discovered in his interviews with people receiving government assistance, most of the Phoenix women and their families managed to survive for some time barely getting by and precariously housed. When financial difficulties occurred—problems like a car breakdown that would not cripple a middle-income family—no surplus money was available to meet unexpected needs.[46] Many of the women's parents and current circle of friends were low-income as well but had not experienced homelessness. These friends and family members lacked the resources needed to assist their homeless relatives with substantial amounts of money or long-term housing.

It is additionally important to probe the issue of women's homelessness to unearth the ways gender ideology shapes responses to homelessness. A homelessness policy dominated by "shelterization"[47] and social control is gendered on several levels. In the shelter, staff attitudes, rules, and acceptance policies combine to articulate appropriate (largely conventional) gender roles. First, homeless women are more likely than their male counterparts to appear to meet shelters' demands for docile, appreciative clients. In this sense they are more likely to be defined as deserving of help and to be accepted into shelters. Relatedly, caseworkers feel comfortable approaching a largely female clientele—defined as weak, passive, and dependent—with paternalistic and controlling measures.

On the other hand, even if women—in particular white women—are more likely to be defined as "good" clients, women are under more pressure to appear deserving of help because they have fewer options than men. The vast majority of homeless adults who have children in their care are women. They cannot stay on the street without risking losing custody of their children. Moreover, even for single women, the risk of rape and other violence makes living on the street extremely dangerous. Thus women have few alternatives to the controlling environments of the shelters.[48]

OVERVIEW

These issues figure prominently in both Chapter 1 and Chapter 2. In Chapter 1 women recount their paths to homelessness, describing a complex set of interlocking reasons for the loss of housing. For the women interviewed in Phoenix shelters, poverty, domestic violence, and low-rent housing shortages most often lead to homelessness. Within the context of the narratives in Chapter 1, Chapter 2 describes the physical environments of the shelters and the relationships between the staff and residents within the shelter system. Social workers closely monitor homeless shelter residents' daily lives and minute aspects of their behavior, primarily by controlling public and private space within the shelter. Although battered women's shelters are less controlling than homeless shelters, many of the same tactics are found in both types of shelters.[49] Women resist social worker surveillance and regulations they find onerous or unfair in a variety of ways. Because they rely on the shelter to meet basic needs like housing and food, however, resistance is often covert and individual.

Chapter 3 brings housed people into the story, plumbing their interview responses for clues to the ways homelessness is understood in U.S. society. Their attitudes about poverty, personal interactions with homeless people, and charitable impulses reveal much about the multiple meanings of homelessness. Likewise, Chapter 4 argues that cultural definitions of the term *homeless* are layered with multiple ideological and material connotations, such that to call a person "homeless" conveys much more about her than that she simply lacks housing. By focusing again on homeless women's interviews, this chapter allows homeless women to, in a sense, answer housed people's conceptions of the homeless.

Finally, Chapter 5 compares domestic violence and homeless shelters. Although women in both groups share strikingly similar life stories, the shelters themselves differ in many ways. Whereas homeless shelters assist residents with job and housing needs, domestic violence shelters emphasize emotional healing. The programs and services offered by the two types of shelters significantly affect women residents both materially and in terms of their understandings of themselves and of poverty and homelessness. Staff caseworkers play a key role in delineating meanings for the identities of "homeless woman" and "battered woman." These institutional definitions help to create and sustain distinctions between residents in the two types of shelters.

CAUSES OF HOMELESSNESS
Homeless Women Speak

Women enter homeless and battered women's shelters for a variety of reasons. The process of becoming homeless is often a long one; the causes of a woman's homelessness may have been building for a significant period before she actually has to enter a shelter. Moreover, multiple factors intersect to affect a woman's housing stability, such that it is impossible to find *one* reason to explain each woman's homelessness. At the same time, women's stories reveal striking similarities in their experiences, most notably in terms of persistent poverty, gendered violence and abuse, and low-income housing shortages. In this chapter each woman's narrative appears in a separate section on, for example, single parenthood, drugs, or housing. But because the women's stories so strongly suggest that reasons for homelessness are multiple and interdependent, such categories are rudimentary and imperfect, used more for organizational purposes than to label the women. Indeed each woman's words weave a complex, multifaceted portrait of poverty and homelessness.

DOMESTIC VIOLENCE

Women's stories underscore the importance of a focus on abuse from spouses, boyfriends, parents, and other relatives to understand and interpret the reasons for women's homelessness. Particularly for women who apply to emergency shelters, battering is intertwined with poverty and homelessness. Yet most homelessness studies fail to address seriously the role of domestic violence in women's homelessness.[1] Likewise, battering is often decontextualized from an examination of women's social locations and the economic systems in which they participate. Homelessness and battering continue to be viewed as separate issues.

In the face of this tendency to distinguish between battered and homeless women, the Phoenix interviews suggest that homelessness, poverty, and violence are woven together; so dense and intricate is the pattern that it becomes difficult to discuss one—homelessness—without accounting for the others—domestic violence and poverty. In other words, domestic violence is not a direct or single "cause" of women's homelessness but helps to create the circumstances that make low-income women more susceptible to homelessness.[2] Because of the extensive resources a woman who leaves a battering relationship needs to support herself and her children, the shelter presents one of the few choices available to low-income women. A significant amount of money is needed to avail oneself of other options, such as staying in a hotel, renting an apartment alone, or moving to another city.

The vast majority of women who enter domestic violence shelters in Phoenix are poor, as are those in homeless shelters. They have few personal resources such as savings, significant education and job training, or family or friends who can take them in for any period of time. Whereas women at homeless shelters decry the lack of attention to domestic violence, those in battered women's shelters have critical housing and job needs that are overlooked. Rather, the domestic violence shelter is designed principally to shield women from danger and to offer counseling and emotional healing in hopes that women will not return to their relationships. Although many shelters assume that women leaving an abusive relationship need psychological counseling or are in serious physical danger, low-income women primarily look to shelters to provide housing and support in their quest for economic stability. Tensions result when women's needs collide with shelter objectives.

Kimberlé Crenshaw maintains that these tensions particularly impact low-income women of color. In her study of battered women's shelters in Los Angeles, Crenshaw reveals the dynamics of "structural intersectionality" as they play out in the lives of low-income African American, Latina, and Asian American battered women—arguing that women of color suffer multi-layered subordination based on race, gender, and class. Crenshaw suggests that persistent poverty and its attendant issues of housing shortages and underemployment are particularly important in considering the experiences of battered women of color:

Economic considerations—access to employment, housing, and wealth—confirm that class structures play an important part in defining the experience of women of color vis-à-vis battering. . . . Shelter policies are often shaped by an image that locates women's subordination primarily in the psychological effects of male domination, and thus overlooks the socioeconomic factors that often disempower women of color. Because the disempowerment of many battered women of color is arguably less a function of what is in their minds and more a reflection of the obstacles that exist in their lives, these interventions are likely to reproduce rather than effectively challenge their domination.[3]

Just as Crenshaw argues, African American, Latina, and Native American women interviewed in the Phoenix shelters face significant financial obstacles in leaving abusive relationships, contending with racial discrimination in the past and present that makes their journeys to stable housing more difficult. Although the dynamics certainly differ for women of color—who are disproportionately low income—my interviews revealed that Crenshaw's reasoning provides a way to understand the situations of most women in the shelters, regardless of race or ethnicity. The economic factors Crenshaw noted—"employment, housing, and wealth"—are paramount in explaining why the vast majority of women seek shelter.

Betsy,[4] a thirty-one-year-old white woman with three children, describes the part domestic violence played in her past. Abuse was partly responsible for her need to stay in the homeless shelter where she currently resides. Betsy begins the story of how she became homeless when she ran away from home at fifteen, saying, "I guess I've been homeless from fifteen to twenty-one, but I didn't think of myself that way then." For those six years Betsy supported herself through sex work and as a relief driver for truckers, riding back and forth across the country with truckers who paid her a penny a mile to drive while they slept. She had to sleep on the streets only twice during those years, but supporting herself through sex work was difficult; her voice lowers to a whisper and she cries when she talks about it.

For a few years in her twenties, Betsy worked alternately as a live-in housekeeper and as a cashier in a retail store. She then met her husband, Ron, and had her first child, who was four years old at the time of the interview. Because the couple had difficulty living on the money Ron made at his appliance repair business, they were repeatedly evicted when they were short on rent. In the four years prior to Betsy's arrival at the shelter, they had moved twenty-two times. During the past year, cocaine played an increasing role in their marriage, and Ron became increasingly violent. As the couple became more involved in using drugs, Ron's violence escalated, and he grew less interested in and committed to working. Betsy blames Ron for their homelessness, arguing that "the main reason I'm homeless is that Ron didn't want to work." Because Ron did not want Betsy to work and three births in four years kept her at home for some months with each baby, the family's financial problems intensified. The last time they were evicted, the landlord would not return what was left of their security deposit for fourteen days, and the family had no money to pay for a motel or another apartment.

Betsy had tried to leave her husband some months earlier, after his drug use and the violence had spiraled "out of control." She asserts, however, "The only place I had to go was my father's house. I was trying to quit using drugs, but he's an addict too, and they would knock on my bedroom door at night saying, 'Betsy, do you want to get high with us?' I knew if I didn't get out of there I wouldn't be able to quit using." With three children in tow, her friends were not willing to take her in or were unable to spare the room or the funds to feed and house her and the children, so Betsy returned to her husband. She tried for the next two weeks to get into Rose's House, a battered women's shelter, but either the shelter was full or the staff did not think Betsy's "problem was domestic violence because I wasn't defining it that way. I didn't understand that was the issue." It is unclear why the staff initially refused to admit Betsy, but battered women's shelters make much of a perceived distinction between battered women and those whose primary issue is homelessness. Eventually, Betsy went to an organization called Community Resources, which assists with rent and utility payments to try to prevent people from becoming homeless and directs those who have become homeless to area shelters. Community Resources helped Betsy get into Rose's House the following day by emphasizing her battering relationship. She stayed there for the next six weeks, then went to the Family Shelter, a homeless shelter.

It is difficult to point to the one reason Betsy became homeless. Even before she and Ron began using cocaine, neither had the education or skills that translated to jobs that paid enough to adequately support their children and themselves. The couple faced great difficulty finding low-income housing. Their repeated evictions meant yet another obstacle to stable employment, as they were constantly moving from one apartment to another—sometimes a fair distance from their former residence and jobs. Nor did they own a car to facilitate travel to work. Ron tried to start his own appliance repair business, working out of their apartment, but continual moves made it difficult for customers to locate him. Both Betsy and Ron had cultural expectations that a husband would take care of "his" family, expectations that made Betsy reluctant to work full-time and Ron less likely to encourage her to do so. Thus they had to forego a badly needed second income. On the other hand, with three children the cost of child care during work hours would have demanded a large portion of their second income. Ron's violence created even less stability in their household, and Betsy's inability to rely on a family she had fled at age fifteen created few options for her when she attempted to leave him.

Latanya's story contains many of the same elements as Betsy's. A twenty-six-year-old African American woman, Latanya grew up in a family with eight children, with a father who was an alcoholic and abusive to both her mother and the children. Like Latanya, most of her sisters have also had violent relationships, and she remains close to only one sister who also lives in Phoenix. Latanya had her first child at age seventeen, dropped out of high school, and lived with her son's father for five years. When she left him, Latanya moved with her son to an apartment subsidized by the U.S. Department of Housing and Urban Development (HUD). With subsidized housing, jobs in a fast-food restaurant and cleaning houses, and some help from her sister, she managed to support herself and her child.

Two years later Latanya met her current boyfriend, Emil. After two years together the couple had a son, and she gave up her subsidized housing a year later to move into his home. Over the past year Latanya left Emil several times and stayed with her sister when he became violent toward her. Finally, she said she decided to leave him "for good" and called the shelter: "My sister wanted me to stay with her, but I wanted counseling, so I went to Rose's House." Although she claims she is not "really" homeless because she has the option of living with her sister, Latanya's sister's husband already works three jobs to support the family, and three more people would strain their resources. Latanya has applied for subsidized housing again, but she faces a long delay in obtaining such housing because of a two-year waiting list.

Since public housing assistance and private low-income housing are so difficult to secure, women often apply to longer-term transitional housing programs that also offer other kinds of services and support. The differences in Ella's current situation, compared with Latanya's or Betsy's, indicate the benefits for women involved in such programs. But much of her story closely resembles Latanya's and Betsy's. A forty-three-year-old white woman with three children, Ella left her husband five years ago. By the time she left, the violence in their eighteen-year marriage had escalated to the point that her husband, Jim, routinely threatened her with knives and guns. She believes that if she had stayed longer he eventually would have killed her, and as a result Jim still does not know where she lives. During their marriage the couple was homeless off and on, at one time sleeping for four months in the woods and for two years in their camper, getting most of their food from dumpsters. Ella worked sporadically as a waitress and her husband in construction, but they primarily lived isolated lives in rural areas. Ella notes that the poverty and violence escalated simultaneously over time, to the point that in the last year and a half of their marriage they rarely bought groceries:

"One time, we lived off canisters of candy thrown away by the supermarket for one month. We lived off chicken thrown away from the supermarket deli. I would have to pick off the dirt and mop strings before serving it."

The violence in Ella's marriage made a fragile economic situation worse and contributed to her need for social services or a shelter when she left. She needed a supportive shelter or program to ensure her and her children's safety and allow her time to finish school and find employment. Women like Ella who leave violent partners are much like other homeless women who are estranged from family members or whose families are too impoverished to offer them many resources. Because an abuser often isolates his partner from friends and family and a woman's shame over the beatings encourages her to remain isolated, women fleeing violence may lack a network of friends and family upon whom to rely for housing, money, food, or clothing. Moreover, low-income women who wish to leave such a relationship generally have little money saved with which to support themselves until they find employment. Others cannot find a job that pays a living wage. Even a woman leaving a middle-class home may have earned a salary well below her husband's and may find it difficult to live on her income alone. Although Ella possessed a high school diploma, during her marriage she "felt like there was no way out . . . that it was possible only to get waitressing and fast-food jobs" that she did not think would support herself and her children. At the same time, however, she began to realize that she could obtain assistance from social service organizations (she and her husband would occasionally get food boxes) without her husband, and she saw that as providing an escape from the marriage. In fact, Ella learned as much as she could about how to access social service agency benefits as a single mother, ensuring that she could support herself and her children when she eventually left her husband.

After she left Jim, Ella stayed at Rose's House for two months and was subsequently accepted by the Endowment for Phoenix Families (EPF), a transitional program for homeless families. Ella has participated in their two-year program and recently applied and was awarded three more years in a second program, also run by EPF, whose goal is to help people become financially secure enough to leave government-subsidized housing permanently. In the three-year program families find their own housing and pay a portion of their incomes to the landlord for rent; HUD pays the balance with a voucher. They continue meeting with a case manager from EPF.

Ella currently juggles a full-time university schedule (she has a 4.0 grade point average), part-time employment as a case manager counseling and advocating for elderly men and women, and raising her three children, ages nine, ten, and thirteen. In addition to subsidized housing, she receives a Pell grant and some welfare benefits, as her work at the hospital is an unpaid internship, a requirement for her graduation. Despite all her accomplishments, Ella and her children continue to live in constrained economic conditions. Their old, sparsely furnished house has torn window screens, and the carpet is worn through to the concrete floor in several places. Ella explains, "We still run out of almost all food except beans and rice by the end of the month."

Like Ella's, Marta's story provides an expression of the ways domestic violence and poverty may intersect and create the very elements that lead to homelessness. A forty-year-old Latina, Marta was staying with her five children at the Family Shelter when I met her. Because she only recently learned that shelters existed, Marta had tried leaving her twenty-year marriage several times in the past without going to a shelter. She once lived in her car with her youngest child for five months while attempting to become financially independent of her husband, Bob. Unable to make the transition from the car to housing, she returned to live with her husband for a few months to gain more work experience, obtain a higher-paying job, and save money so she could leave permanently. During a fight between Marta and Bob that resulted in a fire in the house, the police were called, and they provided Marta with a list of battered women's shelters. She applied to Rose's House and was accepted within a week, staying for a month before moving to the Family Shelter.

Marta's story provides a glimpse into the practices many battered women employ. Although they are involved in violent relationships, women often work simultaneously to free themselves from abuse, remaining in a relationship while incorporating a "vast array of personalized strategies and sources . . . to end the violence in their lives."[5] Such strategies may entail remaining in the relationship for a period of time while trying to negotiate an end to the abuse, save money, or finish school or job training so they can leave with more resources. Asking family networks to pressure the abuser to end his violence or turning to social service agencies for assistance are other strategies.[6]

The day I met Marta, she had only two weeks left in the shelter before her ninety days expired. When she spoke about her search for housing or another program for her family, her face clouded with worry: "I have too many children to get into the Endowment for Phoenix Families. Other people have found me eligible, but no one has a place open." Further, Marta could not find an apartment building that would accept her, even though she had enough money saved to pay her deposit. As soon as the managers learned that she had five children, lived on an income of $561 per month in welfare benefits (excluding food stamps), and had a bad credit history, they refused to rent to her. The caseworker at the Family Shelter was pressuring Marta to ask her husband for money to help support their children. Indeed her stay at the shelter for the next two weeks was contingent on her demanding money

from her husband. Marta did not want to involve Bob in her financial difficulties, believing a request for his assistance would be the first step in returning to her husband. In thinking about her options, Marta remarked, "I'm in
a position now where I will remain homeless or go back with my husband."
She did not want to live with Bob again, saying she had spent a weekend
with him and saw his "old behaviors coming up" and felt it was "dark and
tense" at his apartment.

In the ensuing weeks, shelter staff allowed Marta to stay beyond their
usual ninety-day limit, but she still could not find housing. She spoke with
increasing anxiety about her inability to find a place to live and spent hours
sitting by the phone in the community area, making calls and checking
messages repeatedly to see if an apartment manager or program director had
returned her calls. When Marta's extensions at the shelter had run out, she
refused to return to her husband. A month after the first interview she was
sleeping in her car next to her children, who were sleeping in a tent trailer
behind an acquaintance's home.

Marta's story provides a sharp indictment of the shelter system. First,
her experience makes obvious the extent to which homeless shelters ignore
the existence and ramifications of domestic violence. Clearly, Marta suffers
when the Family Shelter discounts her abusive history and demands that she
contact her husband for financial support. Second, given that most shelters
provide only three months of housing, women are pressured to find housing
in a relatively short time in a market where little low-income housing exists.
Three-month emergency shelters like the Family Shelter are organized to
assist "families," yet their emphasis on finding work and the assumption that
housing can be secured in three months is more plausible for a single adult or
a couple with no children than for a single parent with several children.
Encouraging Marta to find work when she could not support a family of six
from earnings even significantly above minimum wage seems counterpro-
ductive if the goal is to keep her from becoming homeless again. Yet her
welfare benefits, at approximately $12,000 per year including food stamps,
put her nowhere near the poverty level—closer to $20,000—for a family her
size.

A shelter system based primarily on three-month emergency housing is
more a stopgap than a real solution for homeless women or men. For homeless women, though, who are likely to have children with them, the system is
set up in a way that makes it highly unlikely that they will become stably
housed. Although not all will leave the shelter for their cars or the streets,
like Marta did, many will continue to experience eviction and precarious
housing situations. Given the emphasis on individual and behavioral explanations for homelessness, within the explanatory framework provided by the
shelter system Marta is seen as having failed.

WELFARE BENEFITS

In 1996 Aid to Families with Dependent Children (AFDC), the primary cash benefit program for poor women, was replaced with Temporary Assistance to Needy Families (TANF). The new welfare law repealed the entitlement status of AFDC, replacing the previous program's unlimited federal funds with a block grant. New federal guidelines focused on mandatory work, tightened eligibility requirements, and limited the amount of time a recipient can remain on the welfare rolls. Many of the problems experienced by poor and homeless women on welfare exist under both programs. Indeed, given the nature of reforms, many of homeless women's specific difficulties in dealing with the welfare system were exacerbated by the reforms. For the women in this study, the most troublesome and immediate obstacle was often insufficient income with which to pay for rent, utilities, and food. Not surprisingly, in some cities as many as 60 percent of first-time homeless women with children are receiving welfare benefits when they become homeless.[7]

Arizona's welfare benefits, as in all fifty states, are significantly below the poverty line. Although the 1999 poverty level for a family of three was $13,290,[8] Arizona's maximum benefit for the same size family was $347 per month, or $4,164 annually. Adding food stamps brings the amount to $7,416 per year.[9] (This differs little from the median state's maximum yearly benefit of $5,052 for a family of three, excluding food stamps.) From 1970 to 1995 the value of the benefit a family of three received from AFDC fell 47 percent, adjusted for inflation, and fewer low-income working families were eligible for AFDC benefits.[10] This trend continued after 1995. From 1994 to 2000 Arizona, for example, saw a 10.7 percent decrease in the real value of benefits.[11] This was in keeping with other states. Only six states showed no drop in the value of benefits; the median state benefit declined 10.5 percent.[12]

The women in this study represent the poorest of the poor, at least among women and single, female-headed families. Their reliance on welfare benefits is often episodic, but for many, welfare represents a safety net utilized with some regularity, often interspersed with low-wage work or periods of reliance on a husband's or boyfriend's income. Although welfare benefits have provided a way for some women to avoid homelessness, as Veronica's story indicates, benefit amounts are so low that women have to pair them with some other form of income to survive. Reliance on benefits usually means the barest form of survival, particularly because of the high cost of housing.

Veronica is a twenty-five-year-old Latina with two children, ages two and four. She is staying in La Casa, a battered women's shelter, in part to escape her boyfriend, who has abused her for the past six years. It is clear that Veronica needs the shelter not only because she is battered but in large part because she relies on welfare benefits that are insufficient to pay for rent, utilities, food, and clothing. She explains why she came to La Casa:

> I came to the shelter yesterday. I was living with my boyfriend on and off for six years. . . . I left him before and stayed with my mom. I went back because I didn't get along with my mom [and she ended up throwing me out], and I didn't have anywhere else to go. The last time he beat me up I called the cops for the first time—he's in jail now. I was tired of the abuse, and I felt like if he didn't care about me, if he could do that to me, I shouldn't care about him.

Veronica receives $347 in cash benefits and $300 in food stamps per month for herself and her two children. With an eighth-grade education, she possesses few marketable skills. She says she lied to the welfare department, saying she was not living with her boyfriend, José, in order to receive benefits. Even with benefits, however, she and José survive only because his father took them in and accepts $150 per month for rent and utilities, which, according to Veronica, "was nothing compared to getting your own place." She had attempted to rent her own apartment: "I tried to get a place on my own, but I couldn't keep up with the electricity payments, so I went back to my boyfriend." Another time, Veronica tried to leave her boyfriend and live with her father, who eventually made Veronica move out because his new wife objected to her and her children living in the house.

Veronica hopes the La Casa staff can help her find housing and pursue her general equivalency diploma (GED) and computer training. She remarks sadly, "My boyfriend used to threaten me that if I left him he'd come find me. Now he says he beats me because he *wants* me to leave." Clearly, Veronica is not happy in her relationship. She has repeatedly tried a number of options, including living with her mother, who eventually threw her and her children out; living with her father, where she is not welcome; and living on her own, which she cannot afford. At least with José and his father she can provide for her children, and José's father attempts to control his son's abuse of Veronica.

Many women, like Veronica, cannot survive on welfare benefits alone; most need additional income from another source. A study by Kathryn Edin examined the extent to which welfare recipients rely on unreported money from work, boyfriends, or other family members.[13] Of the fifty women Edin interviewed, all stated that they supplemented their welfare checks with other income. Despite regulations that mandate reporting such income, only four of the women reported any portion of their extra earnings. Edin and Jencks describe the sources of income:

> Only 58 percent of their income came from food stamps and AFDC. Of the remaining 42 percent, just over half came from absent fathers, boyfriends,

parents, siblings, and student loans, while just under half came from unreported work of various kinds. Seven mothers held regular jobs under another name, earning an average of $5 an hour. Twenty-two worked part time at off-the-books jobs such as bartending, catering, babysitting, and sewing, earning an average of $3 an hour. Four sold marijuana, but even they earned only $3 to $5 an hour.[14]

Others earned money from occasional sex work. Edin and Jencks argue that those women who worked or received money from relatives without reporting their income did not live luxuriously. Rather, even with their extra earnings, forty-four were judged to do "without things that almost everyone regards as essential."[15] For most, welfare benefits and supplemental earnings were not enough to pay for safe, adequate housing, telephone service, a car, or fresh fruit. TANF makes the option of combining welfare and off-the-books work less viable as a relatively long-term strategy for financial support, since no individual can receive welfare for a total of more than five years throughout her lifetime.

Like Veronica, most women who receive welfare benefits report difficulty meeting rent and utility payments consistently. Coupled with the low value of benefits is the shortage of low-rent housing. HUD defines housing as affordable if it costs no more than 30 percent of a household's monthly income. According to this standard, even in the low-cost rental market Veronica would encounter prices above her means. For example, given her income, she might be in the market to rent an apartment at the 20th percentile, where 80 percent of existing rental units would be more expensive than the apartment she rents. Such an apartment would fall into the $250 to $375 range.[16] But Veronica and her two children receive $7,764 per year in benefits, including food stamps but excluding Medicaid. Thirty percent of her income would be $194 per month in rent. For Veronica and the 7.6 million people nationwide whose annual incomes fall below $10,000, only 4.4 million rental units exist that are cheap enough to allow them to pay 30 percent of their incomes for rent. For the 2.8 million households whose annual incomes are below $5,000, only 1.1 million units rent for $125 per month or less.[17]

The figures provide a graphic example of the extent to which housing costs influence the ability of low-income women to remain afloat financially. Even with the modest savings some have accumulated while staying at the shelter, most women leaving the shelter for apartments rely on churches or other charitable organizations to augment their own funds to pay the first month's rent and security deposits. In some cases apartment managers ask the churches to guarantee payment of rent if the homeless woman cannot pay in the future. As several women's stories will illustrate in the next section on low-income housing, locating an affordable apartment is difficult in Phoenix, as in most cities.

HOUSING

Many studies have emphasized the effect of the low-rent housing shortage on people's vulnerability to homelessness.[18] Like so many other low-income people, most women in Phoenix domestic violence and homeless shelters reported difficulty consistently meeting rent and utility payments for several years before they became homeless. Once women lost housing through eviction or leaving an abusive partner, they faced an arduous search for another low-income unit. Some "doubled up" with friends or family for several weeks after they had been evicted, and many became homeless when such quarters became too crowded or the host family was no longer able to support another family. Others sought emergency shelter after a lengthy but fruitless search for low-cost housing. Still others applied for subsidized housing through HUD but found themselves on two-year waiting lists.

Low-income households, whether employed or receiving benefits, spend a disproportionate amount of their earnings on housing. Data from the American Housing Survey[19] indicate that nationally, median monthly housing costs (rent and utilities) for "extremely low-income" renters equaled 70 percent of their incomes in 1999.[20] In Arizona 46 percent of renters paid more than 30 percent of their incomes for rent in 2001.[21] As the following stories indicate, many people pay such a high portion of their income for housing because their wages, like Veronica's welfare benefits, are significantly lower than those necessary to pay even cheap rents. Paying more than 30 percent of one's income for housing, of course, critically increases vulnerability to homelessness.

Studies on affordable housing indicate that since the 1970s the low-cost housing stock has declined all over the country, while the number of low-income people has grown. Peter Marcuse argues that the "spatial restructuring" taking place in many U.S. cities has followed the twin paths of abandonment and gentrification.[22] Property owners converted low-income housing, including single-room occupancy hotels (SROs), to more profitable higher-income housing in areas close to downtown and near parks or waterfronts and abandoned other low-income housing in less profitable areas:

> The spatial restructuring, of which gentrification is a part, is not inconsistent with abandonment; it is rather the opposite side of the same coin. Gentrification increases land values and demand in certain areas of the city. . . . Demand inevitably declines elsewhere, causing prices to fall, maintenance to be reduced, living conditions to deteriorate, and, at the extreme, whole buildings to be abandoned. Government policies follow and accentuate this process of

differentiation. They support gentrification with tax abatements, low cost loans, and infrastructure improvements. They withdraw services and facilities from declining areas.[23]

Like many cities, Phoenix's downtown recently underwent a "revitalization" accompanied by gentrification and abandonment. Of the thirty-three SROs in Phoenix's downtown twenty years ago, only three remain. Even as the downtown area has seen construction of high-rises and parks and the upgrading of low-cost housing into condominiums or other higher-priced units, in outlying neighborhoods much of the low-income housing has been abandoned. Even with rehabilitation of all existing low-income housing, however, the affordable housing stock in Phoenix would still not meet the demand.[24]

A Center on Budget and Policy Priorities study confirms that from the mid-1970s to the late 1980s, many U.S. cities lost unsubsidized, privately owned low-rent housing to the abandonment and gentrification Marcuse describes. Although the supply of government-subsidized low-rent units increased by 900,000—from 1.1 million units in 1973 to 2 million nationwide in 1989—the number of private, unsubsidized units contracted by 2 million nationwide during the same period.[25] By 1993 nationwide there were 11.2 million low-income renters and just 6.5 million low-rent apartments.[26] This gap proved particularly critical for extremely low-income renters by 1999, when 7.7 million households competed for just 4.9 million rental units in their income range.[27]

Janet and her husband, Carl, both white and in their early thirties, moved to Phoenix several years ago with Janet's two children from a previous marriage. Janet described the difficulties they experienced trying to find an affordable apartment, the rapid loss of control over their finances that occurred when their expenses increased slightly, and their subsequent eviction: "We had a really nice apartment that was beyond our means. Carl is a carpenter, but he wasn't working consistently, then our car broke down and [the cost of repairs] put us out on the street." After they were evicted, the family became so occupied with daily survival—in particular finding a place each night for their children to sleep—that their financial situation seemed hopeless. Janet explained:

> We panhandled every day. We'd put the kids in school, or they'd stand with us on the weekends. We'd make enough every day to stay at Motel 6. We don't do drugs, always dressed nice, we're decent people, and people could tell so they gave us money. . . . If my husband went to work . . . he wouldn't get paid for two weeks. We needed the money to get a motel room that night. My husband would go with his tools to the street corner and ask for daily pay. Sometimes he'd get work.

For three weeks Janet and Carl panhandled, trying to make money for a motel and food that day and to save enough to make a deposit on an apartment again.

Finally, the family found a week-to-week rental they could afford, but a few months later they learned they had to move again when the landlord increased the rent substantially in anticipation of the arrival of winter travelers. Thousands of people living in colder climates make the yearly trek to the desert in October or November, staying until their East Coast cities have begun to thaw. During the period October through March, Phoenix apartment availability decreases and rents increase. With three weeks' notice, Janet and Carl were again unable to find an affordable apartment. They finally decided to apply to the Family Shelter, even though they thought it would be dangerous: "Our experience with shelters was like an armory place, with drunks and druggies; we didn't want to go to a shelter." They were accepted, but the shelter had no opening for two weeks, so they panhandled every day again until the shelter had space for them.

Like Janet and Carl, both Angela's and Kristen's homelessness resulted most directly from eviction and their subsequent inability to find affordable housing. I spoke with both of them during their separate stays at the Lighthouse homeless shelter, and even though they did not know each other, they shared remarkably similar stories. A single mother with a two-year-old son, Angela is twenty-four years old. She had been living in a low-cost apartment, all she could afford while working as a housekeeper for $200 per week. The theft of food from her apartment eventually led to her eviction. Angela's resources are so limited that she carefully divides her income for necessary expenses each month to the last dollar. When she had to purchase more food to replace the stolen groceries, she did not have enough money left for rent:

> The maintenance people gave my key to two [neighbors] and they stole everything—food, jewelry. You put all your money into food, you can't afford to pay rent! I said, I'll let you take me to court [for not paying my rent] because Legal Aid wouldn't help me until I got sued. I never got the court papers, and I got evicted. I stayed with my cousins, but after awhile I felt like a nuisance. . . . My uncle found this place for me to be in.

Once she had been evicted from her low-rent apartment, Angela could not find another with equally affordable rent: "I've been on my own since I was seventeen and was always able to support myself. It's hard to get a second job if you have a child and your first job's ten hours a day. . . . From here I'll be able to get into a decent apartment because I can save money here. You can get a decent apartment for cheap if you have enough money down."

Like Angela, Kristen lost her low-rent apartment, and within a few weeks her housing options had narrowed to a homeless shelter. Kristen, a white woman in her early twenties with a young son, was renting an apartment for $165 per month. Because she did not qualify for subsidized housing, Kristen had previously experienced difficulty finding an affordable apartment, usually sharing places with friends or renting a room in someone's house. Although she had lived in the latest apartment for only seven months, Kristen considered it "the only long-term place I had on my own, ever." When the owner decided to sell the complex and the tenants had to leave, she could not find anything in her price range.

Kristen stayed in a motel room for two nights, then with a friend for a few nights, and then with her mother, who after one night threw Kristen and her son out. She explained why living with her mother or other relatives is impossible: "I became a ward of the state at fifteen, basically lived in shelters all my life. . . . My mom's a drug addict and alcoholic, very abusive." Like Angela, Kristen's combined income for her jobs as a temporary employee and at a fast-food restaurant provided wages too low to afford most rents on her own, and again like Angela, she did not receive housing assistance from the government.

Angela's, Kristen's, and Janet's stories suggest that minimal housing assistance on a monthly basis would make it easier for many low-income families to find apartments in their price ranges. But low-income families in the 1990s faced great difficulty acquiring housing assistance.[28] According to the American Housing Survey, almost two-thirds of the poor households in a typical metropolitan area were receiving no federal, state, or local housing assistance.[29] Families who need housing assistance face long waiting lists. Nationwide, delays typically average sixteen months for public housing and twenty-three months for subsidized housing through the national low-income housing program, Section 8.[30]

Many people cannot get on a Section 8 waiting list because the lists become so long that some housing authorities stop accepting new applications. Therefore the figures of 1.4 million households on waiting lists for privately owned subsidized housing and 900,000 on waiting lists for public housing in the mid-1990s[31] do not include the many families unable to get on a list. In 2000, 40 percent of cities surveyed by the U.S. Conference of Mayors had stopped accepting applications for one or more housing programs because the waiting list was already so long.[32] In 2000 Phoenix reported an average wait of forty-eight months for Section 8 certificates and twelve months for public housing.[33] On a national basis, housing authorities were able to meet the needs of just 29 percent of those eligible for subsidized housing in 2000 through placing families in public housing and granting Section 8 certificates and vouchers.[34]

Several problems exacerbate the low-cost housing deficiency. First, women described much of the low-rent housing and apartments that accept Section

8 subsidies as dangerous and sometimes centers for drug dealing. Although Angela desperately wanted a low-rent apartment, she maintains she felt unsafe in her former residence: "I was just as glad to get out of [my apartment building, which housed a lot of people on] Section 8 because there's a lot of drugs there." Moreover, much low-rent housing is physically deficient. According to HUD's definition, units may be deemed "deficient" if they lack such essentials as hot or cold water, a flush toilet, or electricity or have repeated problems with heating. Nationwide, 14 percent of poor households lived in deficient housing in 1995.[35]

SINGLE MOTHERHOOD

The end of a relationship for women in every income bracket often means a lower standard of living. Particularly for low-income women, who often manage to remain just above the poverty line when both wife and husband work, a divorce may lead to homelessness. Responsibility for children adds to a woman's financial burden. Among the shelter residents interviewed, women who had recently divorced or become separated from male partners retained primary financial responsibility for their children in every case.

Gloria and her two children became homeless after her divorce. A thirty-five-year-old African American woman, Gloria has education and skills many other homeless women lack, and yet she still has difficulty supporting her children without the help of her husband's second wage. Gloria described her experience with homelessness:

> As I became a single parent through divorce, I dropped a lot financially. It took me years to get to a place where I can actually do this by myself without my "ex" or federal or state agencies. . . . When we got divorced, the kids and I were living in a place we couldn't afford on just my income. It's been two years now since I was evicted. . . . I had resigned from [my job] because I was being harassed by my boss. I did eventually get unemployment, but only after a battle.
>
> When I was evicted, I had nowhere to go. My brother who lives in town was living in HUD housing, and the rules are you can't have other family members stay with you. We stayed there, but it put his housing in jeopardy. When the stress and strain got too much—he had a three-bedroom place with five kids and a wife—I went to my church to see if they could help. [The church] helped me stay in a motel for a week. The Ministry for Families Shelter took us in after five days in the hotel—they were full until then.
>
> I stayed at Ministry for three weeks. I had already applied at EPF, but like anything it's a process. I had to go through a very grueling interview. People get rejected for reasons they really shouldn't be—they actually could be a success in the program. I had been eliminated from my first interview because I think they thought I was homeless through my own fault. They looked at me and thought, "How could a woman who's intelligent and articulate and has [years of work

experience] have become homeless?" Luckily, through my own persistence I got another interview and was accepted.

Although Gloria had significant resources, she still had difficulty maintaining housing following her divorce. A major obstacle to stability was her friends' and family members' inability to offer her long-term assistance. Her brother, for example, had little disposable income and, as Gloria described in her narrative, lived in HUD housing. Her mother had no contact with the family, and her father had sexually abused Gloria as a child. After two years of doubling up with family members and living at a shelter, Gloria has a job, is supporting her children with the help of the EPF program, and "can see light at the end of the tunnel."

Like Gloria, Dee Dee's single parenthood made her more susceptible to homelessness. A forty-year-old white mother of a teenage girl, Dee Dee did have family members with the resources to help her stay out of a shelter, but they refused to offer assistance. Sitting in the Lighthouse shelter she remarked of single parenthood, "For female single parents, this is where you end up if you don't have a support system." After a serious car accident that left her bedridden for months, Dee Dee had no other adult on whom to rely during the time she could not work. She described the events of the past year:

A year ago I was involved in a car wreck and almost died. The lesson I've learned is that your life may be supersuccessful, and some series of events occur that are beyond our volition, and even an educated person can't control things. . . . When I had my accident, I went on AFDC. When I got out on my own [after staying with my mother for a few weeks before my daughter and I were kicked out], it wasn't enough to pay the rent. I wasn't recuperated, so I couldn't work. I should have still been in rehab, but my mom forced us out on our own.

One of the few women at the Lighthouse with a college degree and professional work experience, Dee Dee's reasons for needing a shelter conform to the stereotypical "deserving" homeless person's story. In that story a middle-income person who has long embodied "middle-class values" by working and paying taxes suffers a medical emergency over which she clearly has no control. Dee Dee's history, however, differs from the vast majority of other people living at the shelter. Most shelter residents would probably have been homeless much sooner had they experienced Dee Dee's accident. Indeed, as the next section suggests, women with fewer resources than Dee Dee had might face a serious financial crisis after an illness lasting only a week or two.

MEDICAL EMERGENCY

Julie and her husband, Alex, are a white couple in their mid-twenties. Their experiences attest to the ways a medical emergency, even when not life threatening, can create grim economic difficulties for those engaged in low-wage, hourly work. I interviewed Julie, as her young daughter, Laura, played around us, in her room at the Family Shelter. She traced the beginning of their problems to three and a half months before, when her gall bladder "went out." Although she and her husband had never been well-off, they had managed to live fairly stably in the past.

Alex had just lost his job working in a nursing home kitchen, cooking and feeding meals to residents. That same week Julie—pregnant with twins—went to the hospital in extreme pain: "I miscarried because my gall bladder was so swollen, and poison from it is leaking into my system. They released me without taking it out because I don't have insurance, and they said it's not an emergency until it bursts." Julie found a job shortly after her release from the hospital but lost it in a week and a half because she had to be rushed back to the hospital, again in extreme pain caused by her gall bladder. Again the hospital refused to remove it until the gall bladder actually burst. Julie was hospitalized repeatedly over the next three months and just as regularly found positions and lost them when she had to go to the hospital again. None of her jobs offered sick leave or vacation days. Compounding their problems was her husband's drug use, long an issue in their relationship. They had moved to Phoenix from California a year ago so both could "get away from drugs." Julie complained that after Alex lost his job in the nursing home "he was lazy about finding another job; he started using drugs again and hanging out with his friends."

Since neither Julie nor her husband was working regularly during this period and the couple had no financial reserves to call upon, they paid rent only sporadically and were eventually evicted. She called her church, but unlike some of the other homeless women whose churches helped them for a few days, the minister at Julie's church said "maybe living on the streets would teach them a lesson." The family stayed with another couple in a small apartment that charges by the week. The host couple, Julie learned, lived by stealing clothes and appliances and then returning them to stores for money, and they pressured Julie to participate. She returned some clothes for them but felt unhappy about it: "I couldn't do it. . . . I couldn't get myself to steal. I didn't want to live like that. I felt like every time we did something bad, we went down."

Rather than have to cooperate in stealing merchandise to pay the rent, Julie and her husband and daughter left the apartment but had nowhere to go. She looked away and her voice dropped to a whisper as she recounted how they slept behind a convenience store and panhandled for a day: "We were freezing and starving. Laura had a cold stare; she wouldn't let anyone touch her. I stood on a corner with a sign [asking for money] with Laura. I never thought I'd do that. . . . If it was just me I don't know if I'd be fighting this hard. I have my daughter as a responsibility, my priority. If I didn't have her I might be living like the people at the kitchenette, day by day." Worried about Laura's "cold stare," the next day they went to Community Resources to ask for help. Julie explained to the receptionist that they were homeless but was told that the caseworkers' schedules were full. They would be unable to see Julie for another week. "I told the receptionist I had a baby, but she said she didn't care. So I raised hell, and we got seen the next day." Community Resources paid for a motel for them for two days until the Family Shelter had an opening.

Since she arrived at the Family Shelter less than two weeks ago, Julie has had to return to the hospital in extreme pain from her gall bladder. The shelter caseworker intervened with the hospital administration on her behalf and arranged for Julie to have her surgery in the next few days. She is pregnant again and stands to have another miscarriage if the gall bladder is not removed soon.

DRUG USE

Although Julie's story shows how medical problems may deeply affect a low-income family, her husband's drug use unquestionably added to the family's difficulties. Her case and others indicate that drugs tend to make a bad situation worse by exacerbating existent financial difficulties stemming from low wages and sporadic evictions. If drug use alone explained homelessness, middle-class drug users would end up on the street more regularly. Rather, the interviews suggest that substance abuse often works in tandem with other issues or crises or simply with poverty to produce homelessness.

María, a thirty-five-year-old Latina with three children, has been married for ten years. She and her husband, Diego, lived happily the first seven years, but he began using crack during the past year and a half, and she also used drugs sporadically. Diego lost his job, at which he had made enough for the family to live relatively comfortably while María stayed home taking care of the children. With no money or jobs, they lived for a year and a half moving back and forth between relatives' homes.

María left her husband several times during that period, staying with her family each time. She described how his crack use increased his tendency to be violent toward her: "Ten years ago my husband hit me and went to jail for domestic violence. Since then he didn't hit me until a year and half ago." At one point she left her husband for two months, lived with her parents, and worked at a department store. She was not making enough to pay for food, rent, and utilities on her own. Eventually, María returned to her husband. Because of their drug use and his violence, "My family used up all their patience with me and wouldn't let us stay anymore." The next time María wanted to leave her husband, she called Rose's House. At the shelter María participated in a drug treatment program and started divorce proceedings, and her children received counseling. She wants to "become independent," which for María means no longer relying on welfare benefits. She argues that she needs more education and skills to separate emotionally and financially from her husband. Accepted into a high-profile and exclusive program to help women become financially secure and avoid having to depend on welfare benefits, María currently lives with her children in a Section 8 subsidized apartment and is attending school and job training.

Public discourse on homelessness tends to distinguish those who are homeless because of drug or alcohol addiction from the "situationally homeless," who become homeless, for example, because they have been laid off or experienced a calamity beyond their control. The easy separation between those on drugs and others suggests that drug users are homeless through their own fault or are so mired in drug and alcohol addiction that their lives center around finding the next drink or fix. María's story shows that no easy separation exists. On one hand, she has partial responsibility for her homelessness because of her past actions and choices. On the other hand, she represents the model "successful" client at Rose's House in the sense that she is motivated, hardworking, and is currently living independently with her children.

Academic and community-based studies, in their attempts to estimate the number of people who have become homeless as a result of crack or other drugs, often imply that a distinct category of the "drug-addicted homeless" exists. Although efforts to gauge the seriousness of drug use as a reason for homelessness are important, figures on how many homeless use drugs are often cited without explaining how drug or alcohol use has actually affected people's lives. More significant, drug or alcohol use may be named as the only reason for homelessness, but in fact, substance abuse is usually just one of several issues and circumstances that lead in concert to the crisis of homelessness. On the other hand, in the family shelters focused on in this study, heavy drug users—for whom drugs as a single-factor explanation for homelessness may be more fitting—are probably less likely to be present than in other types of facilities for the homeless. Christopher Jencks cited a Cuomo Commission study that found that of the adults in New York City's "general purpose" shelters who chose to participate anonymously in drug testing, 66 percent tested positive for cocaine. Just 16 percent of those in family shelters tested positive.[36] In the in-depth interviews conducted for this study, eight of the thirty-three women said they had previously used drugs fairly consistently.[37]

Ann's story is in many ways similar to María's. A twenty-one-year-old white Lighthouse resident, Ann believes, like María, that her and her husband's drug use led to their homelessness. Whereas María, however, seems in many ways the picture of the hardworking and appreciative "deserving poor," Ann comes closest of any woman I interviewed to the stereotype of the homeless person for whom homelessness is part of a "lifestyle" that includes drugs, alcohol, and crime. Ann and her husband began using crack a year ago. They soon lost their jobs, then their apartment, and finally were forced to live in their car with their two daughters, ages two and four. Ann stole food, liquor, and clothing from local stores, which she then sold on the street, returned to another store for cash, or traded for drugs. Kenny, Ann's husband, sold drugs on the street. In this way they managed to support themselves and their drug habits for several months. The police eventually arrested Ann for theft, and she went to jail for two weeks; Kenny disappeared, apparently having left the state. When Ann was released, she and her children went to live with her parents; she secured a job as a telemarketer and stopped using crack.

Living with her parents was not easy for Ann, as her relationship with her mother had been strained since her childhood. Ann began drinking alcohol at age eight and says she was an alcoholic until age sixteen, when she joined Alcoholics Anonymous and quit drinking. Ann's brother had molested her from ages five to sixteen, and she "has never really forgiven" her mother for not believing the abuse was taking place when Ann went to her as a child. She had repeatedly tried to run away as a child, but with her father a prominent minister in their small town, she felt she had nowhere to hide. As a result, Ann felt very uncomfortable living with her mother, and when Kenny returned to Phoenix she happily left her family's home with him.

Kenny and Ann started using drugs again, and Ann was fired from her job. Again they lost their apartment and this time had no car to live in. For four days they alternated sleeping at homes of friends and sitting in a diner all night. Ann's parents had taken her children, and she had nowhere to sleep; she began to call shelters, and the Lighthouse was the only one she found with an opening. Within a few days of their arrival at the shelter, the staff caught Kenny using drugs and kicked him out. Subsequently, the police arrested him for drug dealing, and he will serve six months in jail. Ann remains at the shelter with her youngest daughter while her parents care for her older child.

Even though Ann and Kenny's decision to engage in drug dealing and theft distinguishes them from many other homeless women interviewed for this study, certain elements of Ann's story have been repeated elsewhere. As mentioned earlier, because of past abuse, Ann experienced considerable stress when living with her parents—stress compounded by the knowledge that with her eight-dollar-an-hour salary at her telemarketing job she would have great difficulty supporting herself and her daughters without her parents' assistance. Unlike María, who wanted to separate from her husband because of his violence and was able to stop using crack when she entered a rehabilitation program through the shelter, Ann does not want to separate from her husband. Each time they are together, her crack use escalates.

MENTAL ILLNESS

Like alcohol and drug use, mental illness works in tandem with other problems to increase the likelihood of homelessness, particularly for women with limited resources. If the illness is severe, however, it can reduce even middle-class women to life on the streets, especially if they lack family and community support. Sharon's story shows how mental illness may lead to homelessness for a woman of any income level. A thirty-two-year-old African American woman, Sharon described her year-and-a-half ordeal with mental illness that continues to leave her with many unanswered questions:

> In the spring of 1994 I began to get serious headaches. Before the headaches I was working 80 to 100 hours a week during the busy season at my job [working with computer databases]. By July I was taking forty to fifty aspirin a day, but I put off going to the doctor because I was in the busy season at work. On July 10 I had a very severe headache and woke up with very little memory. I woke up in a motel and didn't know how I got there. I went to the hospital, but they couldn't find anything wrong physically. I can't remember where my apartment is—I never have been able to remember.

While she was in the hospital Sharon's doctors discovered she was suicidal, so she remained there several weeks for psychiatric care. She had come to believe that "living was wrong" and had planned her suicide and funeral in detail, even sending her last check from work (which she received while in the hospital) to a funeral home in advance payment for her burial. Although at the end of several weeks Sharon continued to contemplate suicide, the hospital released her to the People in Transition shelter where she has resided for the past year.

Sharon continues to have trouble remembering much of her past. She does know she grew up in a lower-middle-class home, attended college, and married shortly after she graduated. Her husband died, and she had a long-term relationship with another man but did not remarry. Although her psychiatrist has told her that her thoughts and behavior are typical of someone who has suffered rape or incest, Sharon cannot remember any such abuse. Rather, she remembers a comfortable childhood with her family, a close-knit group heavily involved in charity work through their church. Sharon does remark that in retrospect she can see that the mental problems that now afflict her started a long time ago, but she never addressed them.

A month after I interviewed Sharon, she got into subsidized housing supported through a city psychiatric organization and continues to see her psychiatrist there. She tried to go back to her old job while still at the shelter, but her headaches continued. Moreover, the company expected her to work ten- to twelve-hour days, which Sharon could not fulfill if she were to make it back to the shelter on the bus before curfew. As a result, she had quit her job long before moving to her own housing. Although Sharon has many resources on which she can draw, including a supportive family, the possibility of a job with a good salary, and salable skills, the severity of her mental illness precludes her from working and makes it difficult for her to live independently. A well-furnished apartment and a career in computers mean little to a woman who cannot remember where her apartment is located, and it is questionable whether she will be able to work as consistently as her past employer expected she would. Sharon's story indicates that unless one is extremely wealthy or lives with a caretaker, mental illness may lead to homelessness as easily for a working-class or middle-income person as for a low-income woman.

Like Sharon, Frances also suffers from mental illness, but she is poorly educated and has a history of low-income jobs. A white woman with no children, Frances has trouble distinguishing between her dreams and reality; she hears voices and has contemplated suicide since childhood. Unlike all but one or two of the women I interviewed, Frances looks like the stereotypical homeless person. She appears much older than her forty-eight years, and although on some days she is bright, alert, and clean, she is usually unkempt and unwashed—wearing several layers of clothing even when the temperature is warm. Frances's story is marked by a cycle of relationships filled with abuse and violence alternating with periods when she worked alone to stabilize herself, only to begin another relationship.

When she was quite young, Frances was in a car accident that left her with head injuries—including a fractured skull—and sharp, shooting pains in her legs. Her father did not seek medical attention for her, and Frances claims her current doctors believe her head injuries may have contributed to her lifelong struggle with mental illness. She married her first husband, Dan, at age sixteen to escape sexual abuse by her uncle and a brother. She also wanted to distance herself from her "dominant father," who raised Frances and her brothers by himself in the rural Midwest: "My father tried to teach me to be submissive, not to ask 'why' about anything."

After five years of marriage, when Frances was twenty-one, Dan died. The suicidal thoughts that had plagued her as a child worsened, and Frances tried to shoot herself, injuring her leg. Notwithstanding her depression or perhaps because of it, she remarried shortly after Dan's death. Although she had been relatively happy and financially secure with Dan, she and her second husband were neither happy nor secure. Eventually, they lost the house Frances and Dan had bought together, and she left him and moved out of the state. For ten years Frances worked anywhere she could—in a laundry, putting up drywall—and saved her money. She managed to purchase a car and began to make payments to buy the trailer in which she lived. She calls herself a "workaholic" during this time, living in relative isolation.

Frances's seclusion ended when she went on what was to have been a short trip to attend an aunt's funeral in Phoenix but ended up staying in the city when she met Tim: "I spent three days with him, and we fell in love; his kids started calling me Mommy. He would hit me, but I stayed because of the kids. It got to the point where he was threatening to kill my family, tying me up and torturing me. I found out he killed his wife later, when I went to the police." Frances left Tim after just six months, but by that point she had suffered significantly both emotionally and financially. When she went to the police after she left, she discovered Tim had written thousands of dollars in bad checks in her name. Frances had a "nervous breakdown" and lived with her father for a few months while she tried to recuperate, then she worked for the next two years as a drywaller and a prostitute, trying to clear her credit: "In that type of work [prostitution] it's very depressing. I hated it 'cause I hated sex." Depressed and still feeling the effects of her breakdown, Frances started using heroin and drinking with the woman out of whose house she worked as a prostitute.

Fearful that her drug habit had gotten out of control, Frances checked herself into a rehabilitation program at the county hospital in Phoenix. When the hospital released her, she went to a homeless shelter: "By this time I was too insecure to even fill out a job application. I had been real successful with my drywalling business and even owned a trailer. I was always good at living simple and saving money." Finally, Frances found a job through the state taking care of a paraplegic: "He told me he was a psychologist, so I opened up to him about my sexual dysfunction. He told me I needed to be with his friends to get over it; I believed him." Eventually, someone in the state office that had assisted Frances in securing her job discovered the situation and sent her to a domestic violence shelter. Although she says the week spent in the shelter "helped me a lot," Frances also contends that "the stress there was high," and she was evicted for "misuse" of her medication for her ongoing depression. Once again Frances checked herself into the hospital, this time because she had become increasingly depressed and suicidal. The hospital referred her to People in Transition, where she currently lives.

In listening to Frances tell her story, one becomes overwhelmed by the constant and recurring violence and despair in her life. Although her lack of education and reliance on physical labor to support herself aggravate her troubles, the cycle of abuse and isolation in her adult life is most striking. Talking with Frances leaves no doubt that she continues to be mentally unstable. No amount of subsidized housing, supportive friends willing to have her stay in their homes, job training, or disability benefits will solve Frances's problems. It is clear that the shelter cannot offer her the daily— even hourly—support, supervision, and counseling she needs. Indeed at one point the staff at the shelter had to require that Frances enter the hospital for crisis psychiatric care when she began overdosing on her medication and was unable to function.

AGE

For nearly seventy years social programs passed as part of the Social Security Act of 1935 have provided social insurance as well as public assistance for the aged. Such programs, along with Medicare, have significantly decreased the poverty rates of the elderly. Notwithstanding the general improvements in elderly poverty, unemployed workers between ages fifty-five and sixty-two—those not yet old enough for Social Security payments—may experience difficulty supporting themselves. Particularly at risk are those with experience working in factories, laundries, construction, or other jobs demanding physical stamina and skill—in part because employers in such fields are reluctant to hire workers nearing age sixty. Additionally, some aging workers may be unable to do the tasks for which they were trained because of disability or simply because the work has become too difficult.

In her study on elderly homeless women under age sixty-five, Sandra Sue Butler connects their vulnerability to poverty less to unemployment than to the severing of familial relationships: "Those who have been socialized to be homemakers and to be dependent on their husbands' income may become destitute at mid-life because of separation, divorce, or widowhood. . . . Mothers who depended on Aid to Families with Dependent Children while bringing up their children no longer receive support once their youngest child reaches 18."[38] As Butler points out, life changes that sometimes occur with aging affect the elderly, in particular elderly women. In general, however, the older women interviewed for this study had consistently worked at low-wage, often manual labor for most of their adult lives. They became homeless as a result of a loss of income when they could no longer secure employment. As with the families and younger single women interviewed, unemployment often intersected with other circumstances and choices to lead to homelessness.

A fifty-nine-year-old white woman with a long history of jobs in the unskilled, manual labor market, Susan exemplifies the quandary manual laborers face as they age: employers often perceive them as too old to complete physically challenging tasks easily and quickly, and job training programs target younger people. Susan came to People in Transition after being fired from her position as a housekeeper at a supervisory care home for mentally disturbed people. The stress and long hours demanded of her as a live-in employee, Susan claims, exhausted her to such an extent that each night after finishing her cleaning responsibilities she would fall into bed and sleep until she had to begin work the next morning. Although Susan disliked the stress at her job, she had refused to quit: "I'm the type of person that once I get a job I will hang onto it, regardless. That's not wise—healthwise it can kill you."

Since her arrival at the shelter six months ago, Susan has looked for work every day, concentrating her efforts on laundry jobs or dishwashing. With work experience as a presser and sorter in a laundry, a housekeeper, and a waitress, Susan's options are limited to positions requiring physical stamina she fears she no longer has: "I did want something better, but I don't think I'll be able to accomplish it. I don't want to go back into manual labor, but I've got to survive. I wanted to go into creative writing or be a gunsmith, but until I can get a job to get started, I can't do anything."

Susan is clearly motivated to work, and her self-worth is closely connected to her ability to support herself. But her job search is stymied by her limited skills, advancing age, and current status as a "homeless person":

> I'm willing to work eight hours a day. I don't care if it's 11 P.M. to 7 A.M. . . . . I'd take a job for $3.25 [an hour]. . . . I don't want to be a freeloader. What I want is a job.
>
> The public views us as bums, [saying], "You don't want to work, so you go to a shelter." That's not usually the case. I do want to work. I want to get out of here. I don't think they view us even as second-class citizens. Even lower than that. People don't realize there are complications to getting out of the shelter— you need a job and an apartment. A lot of people don't want to do anything to correct [homelessness]. People won't hire you if you're living in a shelter. I don't tell people who I'm applying to [that I live at People in Transition] because I'm afraid a lot of people will turn me down because of it.
>
> I heard on TV that a program that's giving jobs to homeless people is costing too much. Well, then they complain about welfare. It's got to be one or the other. The only way to get off welfare is to get a job. How stupid that is—if there were more companies [that would hire homeless people] there wouldn't be homeless people.

Although Susan now asserts that she would be willing to work for $3.25 an hour—significantly less than minimum wage—when she first arrived at the shelter she looked for a job paying more than minimum wage. As she has watched the months pass, however, rejected in her attempts to secure job after job, she has become desperate. At this point Susan would probably accept any kind of employment, even if it threatens her health or pays very little, to get by for two more years until she can collect Social Security. Six months after the first interview she still had not secured employment, although she continued to pursue leads almost daily.

Susan's dilemma resonates with the choices Frances faced. Although Frances is more than ten years younger than Susan, she looks older, having had three strokes in the past few years and having battled mental illness most of her life. Frances described her own difficulties finding work, experiences that echo Susan's:

> With women my age, we have no work skills; we were told when we were growing up that we were supposed to be housewives. It's hard to make it on minimum wage, hard to even get a job at minimum wage at my age. I could do drywall, but then you have to have a vehicle. Then [you don't make much money, so] you have to get an apartment in a dangerous area.
>
> Job Corps is just for eighteen- to twenty-three-year-olds. It's scary to think about getting a GED or going to community college at my age. We think we can't keep up with the young kids. . . . People my age, we need to get more job skills or have the minimum wage increased so we can do more than barely exist.

Although Frances mentioned that she "could do drywall," for which she has been trained and has substantial past experience, her delicate frame, failing health, and mental illness suggest otherwise. Historically, both she and Susan were able to support themselves on work that paid minimum wage or slightly above. But the real value of the minimum wage has declined substantially since the 1970s. Moreover, advancing age makes strenuous physical work impossible while also preventing Susan and Frances from relying on strategies that helped them survive in the past, such as working longer hours or taking a second job to make ends meet. The probability that these women will be able to provide for themselves seems dim.

Like Susan and Frances, Angie supported herself through low-paying jobs for thirty-five years, but she has become physically unable to fill any position requiring even the slightest physical strain. Angie is a sixty-year-old white woman whose only daughter is deceased, and she had been living at People in Transition for a year when I met her. With severe arthritis in her hips, knees, and hands, Angie has trouble walking or standing for longer than a few minutes and walks with a marked limp even when she uses her cane or walker. Friendly and open, she and several other older men and women regularly sit outside in the sun and read and chat with one another. In answer to my question about how she came to live at the shelter, Angie tells a story about her life that begins more than ten years ago:

> Before I got divorced I worked for Woolworth for twenty-five years. Then I came out here, got divorced, and met this other guy, Rich. I wanted to make a new life for myself, so I bought a used mobile home. I worked at K-Mart out on the patio. One night [at K-Mart] a man walked out with a cart of stuff he hadn't paid for, and [the manager] thought I was in on it, so they fired me. [At that time] my arthritis wasn't so bad, so I was able to work there.

Soon after she lost her job Angie also lost her mobile home when she could no longer pay the costs associated with it, and Rich disappeared: "I had owned my mobile home but couldn't keep up with the space rent. They called out the sheriff and auctioned it off to pay for the back space rent. . . . From there I was on the street for a month and a half. I walked the street twenty-four hours a day. I was never sure if I'd be alive the next morning. The man upstairs was on my side. I stayed by myself—I was afraid to hook up with anyone."

After a month and a half of walking the streets and occasionally sleeping in laundromats, Angie found a job cleaning apartments; when the woman for whom she worked discovered she was homeless, she allowed Angie to sleep in empty apartments. Three months later Angie was hired as a residential caretaker for elderly people, working and living in their homes for several years. Eventually, she began to rekindle her relationship with Rich. By this point Angie's arthritis had worsened to the point that she could no longer easily keep up with the work required of her as a caretaker. She quit her job, and the couple moved into a motel, supporting themselves on the little money Angie had managed to save during the past few years and by charging room rent on her credit cards. Eventually, the money ran out, and Rich decided to move out of state to live with his daughter. He took Angie to a church to see if they could assist her with housing, and the church staff helped her get into People in Transition.

Angie now receives close to $500 a month in disability benefits. But her credit card bills, run up while she stayed in motels with Rich, were consuming $160 a month and left her with insufficient money for housing, food, and other necessities. After staying at the shelter for a year and paying as much as possible on her bills, Angie has reduced them to a more manageable sum that would allow her to live independently on her disability payments if she found subsidized housing. She has been on the waiting list for housing since her arrival at the shelter a year ago.

A few months after I interviewed her, Angie's name reached the top of the waiting list for subsidized housing in a city north of Phoenix where she wants to live. Meanwhile, however, she had begun a romance with an elderly man named Frank who also lives at the shelter. Because she had applied for housing as a single woman, Frank could not move in with Angie without jeopardizing her ability to stay in the apartment. So Angie and Frank came up with a different plan: they would leave People in Transition to camp in national forests and state parks around Arizona with Frank's sister. Since both Frank and Angie receive disability benefits—Angie for her arthritis and Frank because he recently underwent triple bypass surgery—Frank reasoned that if they camped for a year, between their two incomes they could save enough money to eventually afford housing together. Instead of accepting the apartment, then, Angie decided to attempt to live with Frank and his sister in the tent and car they had lined up for the excursion.

Angie and Frank left feeling hopeful about their plans and happy to be able to share a tent after living consigned to separate men's and women's dorms at the shelter. After just ten days, however, Frank brought a depressed and discouraged Angie back to the shelter. In that short time her arthritis had worsened significantly from sleeping on the cold ground: "After ten days my arthritis was so bad I could hardly walk, so I had to come back. I wanted Frank to come back with me, but I guess I didn't figure a blood relative, that he would choose his sister over me." Although ostensibly it was her arthritis that forced her to concede that she could not cope with living outdoors, Angie clearly had not enjoyed many aspects of her ten days in the state park. She described sleeping in a tent, cooking by campfire, and other aspects of outdoor life with some distaste: "We got our drinking water from the town near where we were and boiled water from the creek to wash our dishes in. But we couldn't shower or wash our hair, and I couldn't stand that. The first weekend we woke up and it was 29 degrees. I was shaking."

Notwithstanding her aversion to camping, Angie maintains that she would have stayed if she could have physically withstood outdoor life, such was her desire to live free of the dormlike atmosphere and shared living space, curfew, and other rules at People in Transition. A mature woman who has lived on her own for many years, Angie misses the simple freedoms that come with one's own living space: "I can't wait to get out of here. I had a taste of freedom [while we were camping]. Not that I'm not grateful [that I'm able to stay in the shelter], because I am. But [in my own place] if I want to watch TV all night I can, or [I can] come out of the shower and not have to worry about getting dressed right away." Six months after I interviewed Angie, she got her wish. Although not with Frank, she did manage to move out of the shelter; she and a woman friend found an apartment together and are currently living in Phoenix.

SOCIAL NETWORKS

Homeless women in this study generally had strong, extended social networks made up of friends and sometimes family members who were also low-income. By the time a woman arrived at a shelter, she usually had called upon these people repeatedly. Friends and family helped as much as they could, and women often turned to the shelter system when they had exhausted their social networks.[39] Although some women did not have contact with their families as a result of past arguments or abuse, most still had friends they could rely on, if only for a short time. Those women who lacked a support network generally had recently moved to Phoenix and did not yet have many friends who would help with rent or with whom they could double up.

Rita's history provides a telling example of the part social networks play in homeless women's lives. After moving to Phoenix several months earlier with her husband and three children, Rita and her family stayed with friends while searching for an apartment. Although both she and her husband were working, they needed time to save enough money to pay the first month's rent and security deposit: "We looked for apartments, but we had an eviction from when my husband got Valley Fever [and was unable to work for a short time], so that's going against us. Plus they say we need a three bedroom with three kids, and we can't afford it." Some friends welcomed them into their apartment, and between the two families, twelve people lived in a three-bedroom dwelling for several months.

Although Rita still considers the family to be friends, the strain of so many people living in close quarters and both families' financial insecurity eventually created conflict. Rita explained, "Every time we got some money saved up, they needed it because their electrical was getting turned off or something. [Finally], we moved out into a motel right up the street. It would take my whole week's check to pay for a week there. We went to Community Resources, and they . . . got us an appointment with the Family Shelter." Rather than a family disassociated from others, Rita and her husband had friends who were willing to allow them to live in their apartment in spite of overcrowded conditions and their own financial difficulties. Rita calls the experience "pretty hectic" and hopes not to have to return to such a situation. Even though she works full-time as a nurse's aide and her husband works twelve hours a day as a plumber, she has yet to locate an affordable apartment.

Tracy's story provides another example of assistance provided by friends, even friends who have little disposable income themselves. A nineteen-year-old white woman with two children—an infant and a two-year-old—Tracy was one of the youngest homeless people at the Family Shelter, where she had come after getting evicted from her subsidized housing. The management asked her to leave because they caught her boyfriend using drugs, and the couple's constant yelling and fighting disturbed other tenants. Shortly thereafter, a pregnant Tracy lost her job at a convenience store because she "was too big to do some of the work," and she broke up with her boyfriend because he wanted her to give their baby up for adoption.

After the apartment manager evicted Tracy, she and her young daughter moved back and forth from hotels to friends' homes:

I would have been on the street if it hadn't been for friends taking me in. . . . I was pregnant, going from hotel to hotel; friends were paying for it. Then I moved [out of state] but moved back. Friends paid for both. We stayed with a friend in Phoenix for the last two weeks before I had the baby, then . . . again until the baby was eight weeks [old]. It was too crowded with me and two kids there; too much was going on. So I stayed with different friends again. I moved in with one friend, but it was too stressful 'cause he worked 'till 1:00 in the morning, then the kids got up at 8:00 and woke him up. He'd get mad, and there was lots of stress.

Finally, Tracy went to Community Resources to apply for rent assistance. The caseworker suggested she apply to shelters, where she could spend time gaining financial stability so she had "less of a chance of [eviction] happening again." The Family Shelter accepted Tracy but had no immediate openings, so she placed her children in a crisis child care center through Child Protective Services until the shelter had room for them.

Although Tracy maintains contact with her parents, she does not feel comfortable asking for their help. She ran away from home at age thirteen, living in abandoned buildings or sleeping on rooftops until she was fifteen. She was then sent to live with her uncle, from whose home she also ran away. Without family assistance and in the last stages of pregnancy, unable to engage in the kind of activity demanded by her previous jobs as a waitress or in a convenience store where she had to lift boxes, Tracy believed her only choices were to rely on her friends for support or turn to a shelter. Because she had never wanted to resort to a shelter, explaining "my ego is too big—I wouldn't be here except for my kids," Tracy tried to stabilize herself financially without help from social service agencies. With a newborn infant and crowded housing conditions, however, she finally decided she could not stay with friends any longer.

Notwithstanding the inconveniences involved in living with another family in an apartment designed for fewer people, both Tracy's and Rita's friends provided them with a place to stay. Unlike them, however, recent émigrés from other states and women hiding from abusive spouses or other family members usually have fewer friends on whom to rely. Lisa's story, among others, indicates that there are instances when homeless women, even those considered "situationally homeless," are relatively isolated. Lisa, a white woman in her late thirties, came to Phoenix with her two children, ages eight and four, to hide from a fiancé she describes as "paranoid and abusive." When she realized that her fiancé, William, would try to track her down if she left him, Lisa decided to move to a state where she had no family or friends so William would be less likely to find her. She and her children arrived with no car, no employment lined up, and little money. After two weeks in Phoenix, during which time Lisa states she "hadn't had a full meal," she resigned herself to the need for assistance and applied for welfare: "People always say that getting on AFDC is a cop-out. The easy way would have been to stay with William, but it took more integrity to leave and get on assistance."

Unable to afford an apartment on her AFDC allowance, she rented a room for herself and her children in a house owned by a mentally disabled woman and her emotionally disturbed young son. The mother and son's constant physical fighting caused Lisa and her children considerable stress. Moreover, the woman began locking the phone and answering machine in her room, both of which were crucial in Lisa's efforts to find a job. The family moved to the home of an older woman who seemed relatively stable, but Lisa soon learned she was a "closet" alcoholic. Complaining that the family was home too much, after a month the woman was no longer willing to rent to them. After leaving her house, Lisa and her children moved from one problematic housing situation to another. The stress and constant moving caused their health to deteriorate; Lisa and the children became ill with chronic bronchial infections.

By this time Lisa had made a friend who owned his own business in Phoenix and arranged for her and her children to sleep in his office until they were able to find better housing. They slept on the floor in the unheated office during December and January (even in Phoenix's desert climate the temperature can dip below freezing at night), piling on blankets supplied by Lisa's friend to try to stay warm. Lisa finally decided to look into shelters, although she feared a drug-infested and unsafe environment. She met with a caseworker from the Family Shelter who, she asserts, had to convince her to come to the shelter: "I thought a shelter would be so unsafe that I'd rather be on the street than there. I agreed to go because of rules like no drugs or alcohol, people have to sign in and out, and no one's allowed in the rooms." Surprised by the structure and support offered at the Family Shelter, Lisa moved her children there in early March. From there, EPF accepted her, and she now lives in an apartment that costs her one-third of her adjusted income (paid to EPF). Analyzing her struggles over the past year, Lisa asserts that women's ability to leave abusive partners "all comes down to economics": "So many women stay in abusive situations for economic reasons. . . . I tried for a year to get on my feet, but you can't do it without a stable living environment. . . . It was a blow to my pride and self-esteem to end up in a program like this, but I don't mind the case management. I've been through so much, it's helpful to meet with a case manager." Lisa believes she "might have made some bad decisions" that undermined her tenuous financial position and housing problems, and she thinks her biggest mistake lies in her failure to accumulate any savings.

Describing her life before moving to Phoenix as a combination of generally stable periods alternating with tumultuous intimate relationships, Lisa has been married twice, both times to abusive men. After her children were born and Lisa had divorced her first husband, she completed a college degree while holding down a job. Although she had some difficulty supporting her family during those years, since completing her degree five years ago, Lisa has managed to live a relatively comfortable lower-middle-class life. With her college degree she worked as a freelance desktop publisher, which did not afford her a consistent or wholly reliable income. Still afraid that William will find her, since moving to Phoenix Lisa has contacted only one family member, her sister, although even she does not know where Lisa lives.

Rita's, Tracy's, and Lisa's stories seem inconsistent with the conventional wisdom that most homeless people are exceptionally isolated prior to becoming homeless. In public discourse, homeless people often represent the extreme of disconnectedness, referred to as the "dispossessed" or the "displaced." Peter Marin, writing about homeless people in Santa Barbara, California, provides an example of how the language of isolation is used to define some homeless people as living in "*self-imposed* exile":[40]

> Yes, many of those on the streets could be transformed, rehabilitated. But there are others whose lives have been irrevocably changed, damaged beyond repair, and who no longer want help, who no longer recognize the *need* for help, and whose experience in our world has made them want only to be left alone. . . . Having been stripped of all other forms of connection, and of most kinds of social identity, they are left only with this: the raw stuff of nature, something encoded in the cells—the desire to be free, the need for familiar space.[41]

Homeless people in this description are deprived of characteristics considered essential to humanity, such as the need for human connection and even rudimentary private living space. Although Marin is careful to refer to only a small subset of homeless people, this representation often extends to all homeless people in public discourse. Although homeless families are sometimes portrayed as less separated from the mainstream than other homeless people, the attention to disassociation and isolation tends to frame all of the homeless as mentally unstable or at least different than others.

In interviews with housed people in Phoenix, such cultural understandings of the "rootless" homeless person surface, providing a common thread in explanations for homelessness that otherwise vary greatly from one another. For example, Patty, a twenty-five-year-old white housed woman, argued that people become homeless through a variety of factors including "economic racism and classism," periodic downturns in the economy, drug and alcohol addiction, and choice. Despite her assertion that homelessness results most often from economic racism and classism, her strongest point of reference for homelessness suggests a fundamental difference in homeless people's humanity: "When I picture a homeless person, he or she is usually unclean, unkempt, sometimes psychologically unstable. When I was younger I had this image of the homeless I saw as never having had a childhood—I could not imagine them as children." The homeless are unimaginable as children because their presumed disaffiliation marks them throughout their lives as fundamentally disconnected from other people. A person so isolated from others is difficult to picture ensconced in any kind of family formation presumably necessary for a child's upbringing and survival.

It is early research into homelessness that provided both an intellectual foundation for analyzing homelessness and popular cultural representations of the homeless based on the notion of disaffiliation. Such studies found high degrees of isolation and disassociation from others. For example, in their study of homeless people in a Boston shelter in the early 1980s, E. L. Bassuk and colleagues found that "74% of the overall sample had no family relationships and 73% had no friends to provide support."[42] This was not reflected in the women's interviews for the present study. Sixty-one percent of the people staying at the shelter Bassuk studied, however, had been diagnosed as mentally ill, a much higher percentage than that found at the Phoenix homeless and battered women's shelters. Principally because the family homeless shelters have stringent rules regarding work, curfews, and behavior, caseworkers may screen out many mentally ill people because they anticipate that their presence will cause disorder at the shelter. They also may fear that mentally ill women will not be able to participate in all mandatory facets of the program.

Yet the differences between the kinds of shelters profiled in the two studies does not fully explain the disparity in results. Indeed I argue that evidence of social networks among the homeless may be ignored or misunderstood precisely because of the strength of the notion of disaffiliation. This becomes clearer by reevaluating another study of homeless and housed women, also carried out in Boston. In this study Ellen Bassuk and Lynn Rosenberg assert that part of the explanation for why women seek housing in shelters can be found in their fragmented social networks. A high incidence of childhood abuse and physical or emotional distance from families of origin mean that social networks are fragile or nonexistent, making low-income women more susceptible to homelessness. When Bassuk and Rosenberg compared female-headed families living in Boston homeless shelters with low-income female-headed families primarily residing in public or private subsidized housing, the authors found that of the forty-one homeless women willing to answer a question about abuse, seventeen—or 41 percent—stated that they had been abused as children, compared with 5 percent of the housed women. Housed women relied on an extended network of family members who lived in close proximity, whereas homeless women had fewer family and female supports. Indeed only 26 percent of the homeless women could name three adult supports, whereas 74 percent of housed women could; 22 percent of homeless women could name no supports.[43] The authors argue that although the housed women had many of the same financial difficulties and lack of work experience as homeless women, they had managed to secure subsidized housing in part because of a significant network of friends and family: "The nature and extent of a family's support network play an important role in determining whether it will need emergency shelter."[44]

The Phoenix interviews sustain Bassuk and Rosenberg's contention regarding the importance of a strong social network but differ in finding that homeless women often did have networks they had relied upon for assistance and housing. Women often sought shelter after friends and sometimes family members had offered all the aid they could afford. Indeed 85 percent of the women living in homeless shelters in the Bassuk and Rosenberg study had come to the shelter from a "doubling-up" situation, in other words, from shared living space with another family. The authors mention but do not seriously consider this as confirmation that homeless women had supportive friends and that their tendency to name fewer adult supports than housed women may have been an *effect* of their homelessness and pursuant need to double up, thereby perhaps straining the limits of friendship with other low-income people. A number of women in Phoenix shelters described the tension that resulted from doubling up, stress that sometimes became severe enough to lead them to seek emergency shelter. Indeed, of the housed women interviewed by Bassuk and Rosenberg, 23 percent were doubled up at the time of the interview, suggesting that the next step for these families could be a homeless shelter as well.

It would appear then that evidence of homeless women's social networks may become lost in a more generalized—and widely accepted—argument about isolation. Marcia Cohen and David Wagner analyzed the extent to which this concept of disaffiliation has permeated studies of homelessness: "Homelessness has frequently been linked to a process of social disaffiliation in which the homeless are defined as socially deviant as a result of attenuated family, friendship, and institutional ties. Theodore Caplow defined homelessness as 'a condition of detachment from society characterized by the absence or attenuation of the affiliative bonds that link settled persons to a network of interconnected social structures.'"[45] Cohen and Wagner argue that such a characterization of homeless people ignores the intricate social networks and burgeoning collective social protest that exist among the homeless. The authors developed this perspective in the course of conducting interviews with a group of men and women who had participated in a month-long "tent city protest" in Maine. The homeless group organized the demonstration to demand year-round shelter and greater access to social services and benefits, and their efforts resulted in the growth of a local homeless movement.

The participants in the Cohen and Wagner study contrast sharply with the construction of homeless people as disaffiliated and rootless, with over

80 percent reporting that they were currently married or in long-term intimate relationships. Although fewer had relationships with families of origin (almost half stating that they had been abused or in foster care as children), 87 percent could name three or more close friends on whom they relied for support. The disparity between these findings and those in Bassuk's studies may be explained in part by the participants in Wagner and Cohen's study. They were clearly more politicized than the norm. Perhaps those involved in organized protest are able to develop a greater sense of efficacy and unity based on their experiences with political organizing; this sense of unity also enables some homeless people to embrace the homeless label with a sense of pride. Cohen and Wagner suggest that homeless women may have more difficulty than men finding pride in the "homeless" label, however, citing the "romanticized image of the tramp"[46] as a historic male image that provides a positive basis for identity construction for homeless men, whereas women experience more social and cultural pressure to maintain a connection to "home."

These findings are consistent with the stories told by women in Phoenix. Although most had strong social networks, few expressed identification with or pride based on their role as "homeless person." Indeed the connection of homelessness to social disassociation has particular impact as it applies to women, given the traditional relationship between domesticity and femininity. This may explain the tendency for homeless women in the shelters to define homelessness in the narrowest sense, as "lacking a roof over my head," in an effort to maintain connection to some notion of "home" when in the shelter.

Although the majority of homeless women in the Phoenix interviews were part of supportive networks, most friends and family lacked the resources to take them in for long periods. This means that many members of a woman's social network were low-income and had themselves experienced significant and ongoing relationships with social service agencies and received public assistance. This suggests another explanation for Bassuk's contention that some homeless people can name few, if any, other adult supports. In general, shelter residents are suspicious about how recorded information will be used and who will have access to it. Some women may claim they cannot think of anyone to list in agency paperwork as an emergency contact or reference simply because they do not want to expose their friends to social service agencies. They are concerned that their friends will be angry that possibly hostile social service representatives will have their names, addresses, and phone numbers. For example, if housing authorities find that those living in subsidized public housing have taken in individuals not on the lease, they could be evicted. Others may simply want to maintain a modicum of privacy for themselves.[47] My contact with shelter residents, both in the role of caseworker and as participant-observer, indicates that casual conversations about friends and resource networks usually result in more information being shared than do requests for names and phone numbers that will be recorded in agency files.

CONCLUSION

Women's stories paint a complex picture of homelessness. An attempt to cite the single circumstance that led to homelessness for each woman would be difficult and even impossible for most of the women in this study. Their multilayered and convoluted histories cannot be whittled down to one overwhelming incident or lifestyle choice. Something of a pattern emerges, though, in the economic marginalization consistently experienced by most women well before they sought shelter. Within a context of poverty, women described varied events and problems that contributed to their loss of housing. In juxtaposing multiple stories, this chapter provides evidence for both the striking similarities and the heterogeneity of the women living in family shelters and transitional housing programs.

Although homeless women are a heterogeneous group, some of the public discourse on homelessness is nevertheless borne out by women's own descriptions of their histories. María and Betsy, for example, attribute their homelessness in large part to their husbands' refusal to work and addiction to drugs. Ann engaged in theft to support her drug habit. Frances has trouble distinguishing her dreams from reality, and Sharon's mental illness requires that she be constantly supervised. On the other hand, the experiences of Ella and Gloria refute arguments that people become homeless because they do not wish to work, are mentally ill, or are addicted to drugs. Ella cites domestic violence and poverty and Gloria specifies divorce as reasons for their homelessness; both show admirable personal fortitude in succeeding at work and in school despite formidable obstacles. Perhaps more important, focusing exclusively on Ann's criminality or María's drug use ignores other problems that contributed centrally to their becoming homeless. The point is, both the position that women are responsible for their own homelessness and the argument that women become homeless through no fault of their own miss the most intriguing facets of these stories. Both approaches fail to capture the multiple events and life choices each woman recounts. Women's reasons for homelessness are complex and ambiguous, and the search for either a pure victim or an unmitigated villain results in little more than the erasure of important pieces of their stories.

Finally, the role of domestic violence is central and much more complicated than the public discourse concerning "battered wives" might suggest.[48] Although the labels *battered woman* and *homeless woman* assume distinct experiences associated with the two groups, women's stories show that significant overlap exists between the two categories. In fact, both those in homeless shelters and those in domestic violence shelters emphasize the intertwining of abuse, poverty, and low-income housing shortages to explain their need for shelter. As Chapter 5 will explain, however, shelters tend to downplay such similarities between women defined as homeless and those classified as battered. In fact, battered women's shelters struggle to distinguish "real" battered women from those who are merely homeless, arguing that homeless women have different needs than battered women and therefore belong in a homeless shelter. Likewise, many homeless shelters refuse to accept women who emphasize the importance of battering to their homelessness, contending that battered women's shelters are the appropriate place for them.

GEOGRAPHY OF
THE HOMELESS SHELTER

Most homeless women express a mixture of gratitude to homeless shelters for providing a roof over their heads and distaste for some aspects of the communal living arrangements, staff interference, and shelter rules. Although the architecture and rules of the shelters featured in this study vary somewhat, they share basic regulations that serve as surveillance and control mechanisms. Each has a curfew, ranging from seven o'clock to midnight. Each has mandatory meetings with caseworkers, where clients are expected to reveal to the staff their personal histories, current goals, and daily activities. Finally, shared living space and caseworker surveillance make it difficult for homeless residents to find time to themselves and to keep many aspects of their lives private.[1] Indeed because of shelter rules and invasive staff practices, many homeless women exhaust other options before turning to a shelter as their last resort. Yet because so many people do have to choose between the street and a shelter and because there are too few shelters for the number of homeless people, the shelters in this study are almost always full; they constantly have to turn people away for lack of space.

By examining the physical environments of the shelters and relationships between the staff and residents, I hope to demonstrate that spaces where homeless shelter residents interact with one another and with the staff are as important as the stories women tell about how they became homeless. Shelter environments, philosophies, and programs both reflect and help to create understandings and beliefs about homelessness. By analyzing each shelter in depth, I attempt to integrate homeless people's life stories with an understanding of the institutional spaces where sheltered homeless people reside and to answer Jennifer Wolch's question: "How does the homeless 'industry' intersect with the biographies or life paths and daily routines of individuals to affect their ability to cope with the institutional context of homelessness, particularly to resist domination by helping institutions?"[2] Institutional spaces impact homeless people in multiple ways. The physical environments of the shelters provide the context for staff surveillance and attempts to control the daily lives of homeless shelter residents. Moreover, they shape the ways homeless women resist caseworkers' surveillance and control.

Michel Foucault has written of the advance of "disciplinary technologies," utilized by the state in a variety of institutional settings to control bodies, to create docility, to "transform" and "improve" those who are the targets of discipline.[3] The homeless shelter as institution relies on constant observation and recording of resident actions, as well as their social and sexual histories, as techniques of power that allow the staff both to "know" homeless shelter residents and to measure and judge them against a "homogeneous social body"[4]—conceived as the productive, sane, and moral norm.

Foucault notes that the development of "hierarchized surveillance" as a tool to both objectify and control those in prisons, schools, and hospitals creates

> An architecture that is no longer built simply to be seen . . . but to permit an internal, articulated and detailed control—to render visible those who are inside it; in more general terms, an architecture that would operate to transform individuals: to act on those it shelters, to provide a hold on their conduct, to carry the effects of power right to them, to make it possible to know them, to alter them.[5]

The physical environments of People in Transition, the Family Shelter, the Lighthouse, Rose's House, and La Casa differ significantly. Yet each fits Foucault's description in the sense that each is to some extent organized to watch and monitor homeless women's daily routines, conversations, and goals.

The physical environments of the shelters are only meaningful, however, in the context of specific rules and program organization. Resident files are a case in point. As a key staff tool within the shelters, the creation of a file on each resident—including a case plan (a list of goals the resident is to work on while in the program)—combines the techniques of observation and normalization to transform "the economy of visibility into the exercise of power."[6] As the central means by which residents are known, objectified, and controlled, professional social workers in Phoenix shelters detail each resident's past personal history and current goals and record the resident's progress by following her activities on a daily basis. As Foucault argues, "The case is no longer . . . a set of circumstances defining an act . . . it is the individual as he may be described, judged, measured, compared with others . . . trained and corrected."[7] Through the case plan and case file in which the staff records client progress, the homeless person himself or herself—rather than homelessness as a political and social issue, or the events and issues that cause someone to lose housing—becomes the object of inquiry, control, and correction.

The focus on individual behavior provides another case in point. Shelters do not ignore low-income housing shortages or the value of the minimum wage as reasons for homelessness, but many of the most important facets of their programs address the perceived *behaviors* of the homeless. Dysfunctional behaviors are believed to have been instrumental in the process of becoming homeless. In addition to constructing the case plan, then, emergency shelters provide ninety days of shelter and a plethora of mandatory classes on budgeting, parenting, and other "life skills"; mandatory meetings with a caseworker; and often deadlines by which a person must find employment. Although clearly too little time to make a difference in the training one has or in the type of employment for which most shelter residents can apply, ninety days *is* sufficient time to restructure a person's perceived work ethic or value system through coercion.

The cultural construction of the homeless as a socially, mentally, and emotionally stunted "underclass" leads to social control as a primary solution to homelessness. Such an underclass needs access to long-term low-income housing or jobs that pay a living wage but will not make use of these commodities without staff enforcement of cultural standards of work and social interaction. Therefore social workers focus on control of residents' employment decisions, as well as on oversight of social interactions within the shelter. As Constance Nathanson argued,

> There is in the United States a powerful strain toward locating the sources of social conflict and social change in the failings of individuals rather than in the inadequacies of social institutions. Social dislocations that result from large-scale social and economic change are framed as personal problems and their solutions couched in terms of alterations in individual behavior.[8]

The construction of homelessness as a problem of mental illness, drug and alcohol addiction, and a "street person" or "underclass" mentality reflects the understanding of poverty as an individual failing. Homelessness is seen, at least in part, as the result of personal problems and faulty life choices on the part of the individual.

Despite a general reliance on regulating homeless people through the case plan and daily surveillance, shelter programs differ from one another in sometimes significant ways. The descriptions of each shelter's environment and mission in the next sections of this chapter will indicate that variances in shelter philosophies can affect a resident's opportunities to find housing, pursue higher-paid employment, and access counseling or drug treatment. Although battered women's shelters closely observe residents and use controlling measures similar to those of homeless shelters, they also tend to condemn residents for their current predicaments less than homeless shelters do. Homeless shelters also differ from one another, however, suggesting that multiple, sometimes conflicting beliefs exist about why people become homeless and how best to solve the problem. Besides variance from shelter to shelter, a single shelter usually operates with several definitions and diagnoses of homelessness at play simultaneously.

Further, a certain contradiction is inherent in shelters' reliance on coercive and controlling rules to reach their ultimate goal: self-sufficiency.[9] As a Lighthouse staff person put it: "We want to run a highly structured shelter. We want to be in control of helping them to help themselves." In the context of the shelter system, self-sufficiency is defined as financial support of oneself and one's family, the ability to pay for housing, budget one's money, and in general provide a stable lifestyle for one's children. Yet the goal of independence is pursued through a program that allows homeless people little input in decisions regarding their own money and employment, what clothes to wear, whom to socialize with, and how to care for their children. The idea that social control—achieved at the expense of resident independence—will lead to self-sufficiency is deeply problematic.[10] The discussion in the next sections will indicate the many consequences of such a paradoxical mission for both staff and residents at homeless and battered women's shelters.

HOMELESS SHELTERS

The Family Shelter

The Family Shelter provides housing for homeless adults with children. A renovated, one-story motor lodge, the shelter sits on a street lined with similar motels, most in varying states of disrepair and offering week-to-week rentals. Although the street has the reputation as a site for drug dealing and sex work, it is flanked by low- to middle-income, tree-lined residential communities. During the day the streets are filled with people walking and bicycling to and from work and school.

The Family Shelter has twenty-six units; each houses one family. Shaped in a "U" around a grassy field, the units have separate outside entrances and thus resemble small apartments. The smaller units consist of a bedroom and small kitchen; and the larger units contain a family room, bedroom, and kitchen. The rooms tend to be small and dark, the carpet and linoleum old but not in disrepair. Most residents try to make the rooms more homey by throwing colorful blankets over dingy couches and occasionally taping a child's drawing to the wall.

Several other buildings on the site accommodate a child care center and offices for the caseworkers and the "job developer," the staff member assigned to help residents find work. The well-lit, colorful child care center has a room for infants filled with toys, cribs, and high chairs; a toddler room; and a room for children age five and older that contains computers, books, and games. All the rooms display children's drawings and paintings, and the fenced playground outside is scattered with toys and bikes. In addition to the child care area, several other grassy or sand-filled areas contain swings and other toys for children. Available from 7:00 A.M. to 6:00 P.M. to residents who are working or have appointments, the on-site child care center is a luxury most shelters cannot afford. Children are fed breakfast, lunch, and a snack; they work on art projects and play on the computer or outside in the yard, overseen by a full-time staff and volunteers.

When families first enter the shelter, a caseworker meets with the parent to draw up an individualized case plan for securing housing and employment, facilitating entrance into general equivalency diploma (GED) or job training classes, or mandating attendance at drug rehabilitation counseling. The caseworker continues to meet weekly with the resident to update her progress and offer intervention and advocacy when needed. These meetings are fraught with staff demands for information about a homeless woman's activities, feelings, and motivations[11]—providing the basis for the exercise of "disciplinary technologies" to "transform" the homeless resident.[12] Such requests for information begin even before admittance to the shelter, since each person must respond to a series of personal questions regarding his or her current circumstances to be considered for the shelter. Once accepted, the homeless person is subject to even more demands for information, including those about current personal relationships and social history. Those unwilling to answer personal questions or to keep the staff constantly apprised of their whereabouts and daily activities may be considered uncooperative or suspected of having something to hide. Residents who appear to provide the staff with relatively easy access to their personal lives—those who bend to the surveillance and control that are key to disciplinary technologies—are more likely to be defined as "good" clients. The good client, in turn, has a better chance than others to stay at the shelter for a full ninety days.

Residents, however, attempt to avoid sharing information with the staff. Most perceive caseworkers not as friends but as professionals with the power to allow or deny homeless women the roof over their heads. Some homeless women balk at being asked to reveal personal details to a relative stranger. Others are uncertain whether the staff will approve of how they have spent their time and fear eviction should a caseworker believe they have squandered their days. Still others want to avoid incriminating themselves or another family member by giving personal information to a social service agency that will record it permanently. In writing about her work in a shelter for single homeless women, Lisa Ferrill makes a similar point. She describes helping a homeless woman who had lived at the shelter for some time settle into a permanent placement in a nursing home: "Nancy had given us all firm orders not to keep in touch with her. She wanted to 'forget about that place.' Mary and I wished her well and said good-bye, knowing we would miss her endearing personality, knowing she would not miss the invasion we represented to her. We had become uninvited participants in Nancy's life; she would have it back now."[13]

Echoing Ferrill's argument, Erin, a homeless woman, expressed anger at the constant requests for personal information she experiences in her interactions with social service workers. Arguing that homeless people are not "sick or diseased" but rather "could be anyone," she despairs of keeping any part of her life from being entered in agency files: "I have to answer to AFDC [Aid to Families with Dependent Children], Vocational Rehab, [and the shelter]. I have to tell all these people what I'm doing. . . . I didn't tell them about my relationship with my new boyfriend because I wanted one part of my personal life to myself." She believes the requests for information stem from staff members' distrust of homeless women and complains that the distrust social service workers show her has sometimes made hers and other homeless people's lives more complicated. For example, her welfare caseworker wanted Erin to look for work, but she was excused from doing so because she was taking classes through Vocational Rehabilitation. The welfare caseworker demanded that Erin come into the office to do her homework to prove she was too busy with it to search for employment. She would have had to do so, but Vocational Rehabilitation stepped in on Erin's behalf, and the welfare worker withdrew her request.

The expectations that residents should share their private lives with the staff, combined with staff monitoring and regulation of both community and private space, mean the Family Shelter staff can keep residents under constant observation. Residents may not entertain people from outside the shelter in their rooms and must leave the doors and windows of their units open whenever another shelter resident visits. The shelter staff thus has access to residents' personal space through almost uninterrupted supervision; such scrutiny is an essential aspect of Foucault's notion of "hierarchized surveillance."[14] Moreover, Leslie Kanes Weisman posits that rules prohibiting visitors and the lack of private space in which to entertain them should they be permitted on site "suggests that homeless people do not need privacy, self-expression, friendships, and sexual relations, or at least that these needs should not be taken seriously."[15] Indeed the Family Shelter regulations regarding private space and the overseeing of public space by caseworkers seem designed to discourage the formation of friendships or sexual relationships among residents, as well as between residents and those not staying at the shelter.

A more detailed exploration of the monitoring of public space at the shelter illustrates caseworkers' attempts to control residents' interactions with one another. The Family Shelter has two community areas for adults, a large room attached to the staff offices and an outside covered patio. The room next to the staff offices contains couches, a phone, and a desk residents can use to make calls for housing or jobs. Because an open door leads from this room to the main shelter reception area, the staff member on duty at the reception desk can easily overhear conversations. As a result, socializing generally takes place on the patio. It is surrounded on one side by a fenced children's playground and on the others by a small parking lot, so any approaching person can be seen well before he or she comes within earshot. The fact that women prefer the patio over the air-conditioned community room on a Phoenix summer day—which can be as warm as 110 degrees—suggests a powerful desire to be relatively free from staff members' management and control. Indeed residents assume they are under surveillance; conversations stop or lower to a whisper when a staff member walks by, no matter how commonplace or innocuous the topic.

Such regulation of private and community space works against community building among residents. As Charles Hoch and Robert Slayton have argued, shelters, including longer-term transitional programs, often define their goal as "prepar[ing] the clients to reenter both the labor and housing markets without the aid of other social ties."[16] Thus shelter staff members' visions regarding how best to prepare their clients for economic stability are supported by rules that discourage the building of community. In fact, staff members routinely inhibit friendships between residents. Betsy and Ruby's experience exemplifies the clash that results between staff and residents.

Betsy and Ruby were very close friends. Having met at the shelter, they immediately became a support system for one another, sharing job and housing tips and babysitting for each other. Ruby helped Betsy when she had an urge to use drugs again, and Betsy stood up for Ruby—the only out lesbian at the shelter—when other residents ridiculed her. One night Ruby stayed out past curfew, breaking two rules by missing curfew and leaving her children with Betsy. Betsy did not consider reporting Ruby; her loyalties lay with Ruby, not with the shelter staff. In fact, Betsy, like most other residents, saw the staff as a sometimes helpful yet condescending and overly controlling presence to be worked around as much as possible. Betsy's caseworker did not understand this feeling. When he found out about Ruby he was angry at both Ruby and Betsy, telling Betsy she was on his "shit list" and threatening eviction. Mark, the caseworker, was angry because they had broken rules and because Betsy's allegiance to Ruby undercut his authority. He asserted that Betsy should by loyal to the staff—who were there to help her—rather than to Ruby, whose homelessness proves she will only bring Betsy down.

Mark believes friendships between homeless people can only lead to a continuation of the dysfunctional lifestyle that originally led to homelessness. Thus homelessness is explained in part by one's participation in a milieu where drugs, alcohol, domestic violence, and dependence on welfare thrive. Worse, parents caught in such a lifestyle teach their children dysfunctional behaviors that make it more likely that homelessness will be passed down. The Family Shelter staff's focus on dysfunctional families of origin as an explanation for homelessness helps to account for their mix of kindness, respect, and condescension toward residents. If a person now homeless grew up in a home where violence and drug use were the norm, this way of thinking goes, then that person can be forgiven—at least in part—if she married an alcoholic and neither of them can find permanent work. The belief is that she witnessed certain behaviors as a child and so is likely to participate in a similar family structure as an adult. The same explanation accounts for Mark's inclination to treat homeless people as if they were less than adults, as he believes they lack fundamental life skills that will allow them to be successful and happy—life skills, he argues, are his responsibility to ensure they learn. He espouses a theory akin to the "culture of poverty" thesis, arguing that low-income people from dysfunctional families—including those dependent on welfare—pass such dependency and deviancy on to their children. According to Mark, mandatory parenting classes for low-income people provide a key to breaking the "cycle of dysfunction," as such classes teach different ways of parenting that avoid passing down dysfunctional behavior.

Like Mark, culture of poverty advocates claim low-income families are poor as a result of behavioral deficiencies (such as laziness, inability to delay gratification, and irresponsible sexuality) that they will teach their children. This tends to create one generation after another that, "lacking family organization and reared without consistent and close relations with adults, . . . are passive, have difficulty with abstract thinking and communication, seek escape from problems through relatively uninhibited expressions of sex or aggression, lack ego strength and are unable to plan for the future."[17] Where the culture of poverty is used as an explanation for poverty or homelessness, those trying to "help" the homeless will—like Mark—insist on compulsory parenting classes and mandatory meetings with the job developer at the shelter. In general, residents deeply appreciate the job developer's assistance with job searches and interview skills. Resentment results from the fact that these aspects of the program are mandatory, suggesting that unless they are forced, residents will not make use of classes or the job developer's services. Making key aspects of the program compulsory suggests that shelter residents will avoid work if they can and would rather not change their current circumstances if they have to expend any effort to do so. As Michael Katz has argued, reliance on the culture of poverty precludes a focus on the patterns of "inclusion and exclusion in American life" and on "unemployment and structural dislocation" to understand why people are poor.[18]

Mark tempers his reliance on the culture of poverty with other explanations for homelessness, most of which focus on work. Only about 5 percent of homeless shelter residents' irregular work histories can be attributed to laziness, Mark asserts. Most do want to work but are depressed or afraid to look for work or to participate in interviews. Others, despite their best efforts, cannot find permanent, full-time employment; and still others have a mental illness that interferes with employment. In addition to these difficulties, he argues, many homeless people lack family support, and others have problems with drugs and alcohol.

In keeping with the culture of poverty thesis, however, the Family Shelter has a very detailed list of rules addressing child rearing, work, drug and alcohol consumption, and a host of other items. Acceptance into the shelter program is contingent upon homeless women agreeing with and signing the list. Many of the regulations are basic to a comfortable and safe living environment, such as those disallowing weapons or fighting at the shelter. Other regulations include a curfew of ten o'clock during the week and midnight on weekends, significantly later times than those at most shelters. Residents are also asked to sign out when they leave the shelter, indicating their destination, departure time, and return time. When on the shelter grounds, clients are to keep their children under age ten constantly in sight. Other important rules include obligatory attendance at meetings with a caseworker, meetings with the job developer, and a parenting seminar within two days of arrival at the shelter, as well as at weekly "resident meetings" run by the staff.

The compulsory resident meetings provide a glimpse into shelter life and suggest how little homeless women's opinions are taken into account. A resident meeting might be an opportunity to air grievances, to discuss homeless women's ideas about running the shelter, or to give residents the opportunity to interact with one another. Instead the meetings signal the residents' almost complete lack of voice in the shelter setting. The meetings consist primarily of staff members announcing upcoming activities or classes at the shelter and passing around completed room evaluations. Staff members inspect residents' rooms weekly, entering whether the resident is at home or not. They note whether floors or appliances are dirty, and the homeless women are expected to clean them. The staff decorates the doors of units with perfect "cleanliness" records each week, and those women are rewarded by being allowed to take a gift out of the prize box, which is filled with lotions, free movie tickets, and the like. As the staff member talks, residents roll their eyes and snicker at the idea that they—as adults—should be told how and when to clean their rooms and then be rewarded like children with prizes.

Notwithstanding the patronizing attitudes toward homeless women, the Family Shelter staff also emphasizes that residents have rights the staff must respect. The list of resident rights includes fair treatment, personal liberty that should be restricted only when "necessary to comply with case management needs," and the right to an individualized treatment plan and to participate in the formulation and revision of such a plan. The shelter staff also promises confidentiality and a "humane living environment that affords reasonable protection from harm, appropriate privacy, and freedom from verbal and physical abuse." Finally, homeless women have the right to file grievances and have access to their own case management records.

The Lighthouse

In contrast to the occasional warm or bright touches and a somewhat supportive environment at the Family Shelter, the Lighthouse family shelter is stark and depressing. It too is housed in a former motel. Here the small rooms, bare linoleum floors, and fluorescent lights create an uninviting atmosphere. Moreover, because the rooms open onto a narrow, shared hallway, homeless families have even less privacy than those at the Family Shelter. For most families the accommodations consist of a bedroom and a bathroom. Those with several children have two connecting rooms. The two-story building that houses families is one of several similar structures within a large complex. Other buildings in the complex contain an alcohol rehabilitation center and a large cafeteria, and they are arrayed around a courtyard with a pool. The complex is in a dilapidated, high-crime area of the city, surrounded by boarded-up buildings, junkyards, and the occasional rundown diner or auto shop.

Community areas are in short supply at the Lighthouse, limited to a playroom for children, a small sandy area next to the parking lot with a swing set and several picnic tables, and a small library that remains locked except during specified hours when a volunteer reads aloud to the children. Although the cafeteria and several meeting rooms in the complex might serve as alternative community areas, residents cannot use the meeting rooms and can enter the cafeteria only during specified mealtimes. During the hours when breakfast and dinner are served at the cafeteria, clients must exit from the shelter, and the doors to the building are locked. Families cannot eat in their rooms. Thus numerous regulations direct and restrict homeless women's movements; such rules seem designed to ensure that the staff retains the power to observe and monitor residents as much as possible.

The Lighthouse describes its family shelter as a "work program." Homeless women who do not find a job within two weeks, working regularly at least thirty-two hours a week, will be asked to leave the program. Alternatively, if caseworkers allow it, a resident can participate in a combination of job training and part-time work totaling at least thirty-two hours a week. Even with the assistance of the job developer, work opportunities are limited. Many male residents have experience only in construction or other jobs typically offering work on a project-by-project, seasonal, or part-time basis. Female residents may have worked for housekeeping services, in fast-food or other restaurants, or as cashiers in retail stores. Juggling child care needs can preclude accepting certain jobs, since most day care facilities (secured for residents with the help of state funding) do not care for children in the evenings. Transportation is also a problem. Buses in Phoenix do not run after 10:00 P.M., and in some parts of the city the last buses come at 7:00 P.M. and do not run on weekends. A number of residents take jobs in fast-food restaurants at minimum wage to ensure that they can stay in the shelter, and the few with better-paying jobs typically make no more than two dollars to three dollars above minimum wage. Yet poverty is a primary reason people end up at the shelter, traceable largely to low-paying or irregular jobs.

The Lighthouse has many of the same rules as the Family Shelter, including prohibition of alcohol and drugs, weapons, and verbal and physical abuse on or off the shelter grounds. Such rules minimize chaos and ensure that life at the shelter feels as nonthreatening as possible.[19] Moreover, in theory, a formalized set of rules provides a modicum of assurance that residents will be treated fairly, without some receiving privileges others do not.[20] In addition to rules basic to safe and comfortable communal living, however, the Lighthouse imposes others that seem invasive and condescending.

The dress code at the shelter provides an example of the way shelter rules are designed to give staff power and control over the minutiae of homeless women's lives. Detailed regulations describe acceptable clothing for the shelter. Everyone must wear shoes at all times when outside their rooms, although men may wear sandals whereas women and children may not. Women are instructed to dress "modestly," which includes "loose fitting blouses and regular T-shirts . . . short shorts and tank tops are not permissible. Brassieres are required." Although no written mandate insists that men dress "modestly," they must always wear shirts, and the rules forbid "open shirts showing [the] chest." In the cafeteria, neither women nor men may wear shorts: women are told to wear jeans, dresses, or skirts; and men must wear jeans or other slacks.

The Lighthouse sick policy is also spelled out in some detail. Unless a client complains of illness, the staff expects everyone to leave the shelter from 8:30 A.M. to 2:30 P.M. while undertaking their mandated daily job search or participating in training or employment. Shelter group and individual meetings are also mandatory. If a shelter resident becomes ill, regardless of symptoms the rules state that the resident must have his or her temperature taken by a caseworker. If the resident has a fever, she is deemed ill, even if her original complaint was unrelated to fever. If she has no fever, she must participate in the daily activities. Should a resident continue to feel sick, she may return to the shelter and rest for twenty-four hours, but she must stay in her room during that time.

Taken together, the sick policy and dress code suggest that shelter residents conform to the lazy, sexually irresponsible, and immodestly uninhibited "underclass" of the culture of poverty thesis. Thus Lighthouse staff members assume that residents cannot be trusted to look for jobs based on their motivation to work. In fact, they believe homeless people will feign sickness to avoid work. Further, they cannot control themselves sexually, especially when faced with people of the opposite sex dressed "immodestly." Lest their libidos or laziness infringe upon their abilities to pursue employment or care for their children, Lighthouse rules are designed to guide residents toward "acceptable" behavior.

The Lighthouse staff also tends to enforce rules to the letter, regardless of residents' special circumstances. Angelo, Lori, and Melissa—all residents of the Lighthouse—were expelled from the shelter on separate occasions when the staff refused to bend the rules to compensate for complicated situations each person faced. Angelo, an African American man with two children, had traveled to Phoenix from South Carolina in search of better-paying work. He had never been outside of his hometown but received information from a friend in Arizona that better job prospects were available in Phoenix. Shortly after being accepted into the shelter, he found a job in electronics—his area of expertise—and enrolled his children in school. Thereafter he discovered that the rental agency from which he had rented a car to transport his family to Phoenix would charge him a significant fee for returning the car in Phoenix. He asked to be allowed to leave the shelter for four days to return the car and hitchhike back to resume the program. The Lighthouse staff denied his request, and Angelo had to leave the program. Likewise Lori, an African American woman who entered the Lighthouse with her husband and two children, requested an overnight stay away from the shelter to care for her sick mother. Again the request was denied, and the family left the program.

Relatedly, the experience of Melissa and her husband, Chris, a white couple with two young children, demonstrates the disparity in power between staff and residents. Prior to applying to the Lighthouse program, the couple had been evicted from their apartment and, like many in their situation, had stored their furniture and other belongings in a storage facility. On a visit to pick up extra clothing, they discovered that someone had broken into their storage facility, and they spent the day moving their belongings to another place. The staff issued a written "noncompliance warning" (two such warnings result in termination from the program) because the couple did not complete the mandated five job searches that day. When the couple discovered that the caseworker had written them up, Chris became angry and swore at the caseworker. Although Chris wrote a letter of apology, the staff evicted the family for verbal abuse.

Coupled with blanket policies that ignore individual circumstances are rules that allow caseworkers to supervise and monitor homeless women's movements and activities. First, residents must sign out at the staff office whenever they leave the shelter and sign in when they return. According to the director of the shelter, residents sign in and out so the staff can monitor them after residents have been away for the day. Urinalysis or breathalyzer tests may be given whenever a client is suspected of drug or alcohol use, and anyone refusing to take such a test will be evicted from the shelter automatically. Second, to further ensure that close supervision can be maintained, staff members keep resident room keys. Whenever a homeless woman wants to enter her room, she must get a staff member to let her in.

The Lighthouse accepts people for two weeks when they initially arrive at the shelter, with a longer stay contingent upon satisfactory performance in the program. Caseworkers send a mixed message, however, when they also state in the rules that residents must secure their rooms on a night-by-night basis, creating fear in a resident that she will return to the shelter after 6:00 P.M. to find that her room has been given to another family. Residents must complete five job interviews or applications each day and pick up their children after school or day care before returning to the shelter. Particularly for the majority of residents who have no cars and must walk to appointments or ride often unreliable buses, it may be difficult to time their arrival at the shelter precisely. Lighthouse staff members are prone to suspect that residents who arrive late in the evening as a result of special circumstances have actually been using drugs or are lying about their whereabouts, and those who need to return regularly after curfew because of a job must usually undergo a test for drug or alcohol consumption. Thus homeless women at the Lighthouse constantly fear eviction.

Staff members' authority to admit or discharge any homeless family weighs heavily on the minds of most residents.[21] Women repeatedly approach caseworkers about their status at the shelter. A woman might ask whether, for example, she has been blamed for an argument among several residents or whether a caseworker thinks she is working hard enough to resolve her situation. Others turn in to the staff each week a record of every job application they have filed or employment prospect they have investigated to ensure that the staff knows they have not squandered their time. To the homeless people living at the shelters, this is not a petty detail; their ability to remain housed depends on it.

With its emphasis on close supervision and monitoring of residents, the Lighthouse program seems to be organized on the principle that people are homeless through their own fault, because they do not want to work, or because they are using drugs and alcohol. More obviously than in other shelters, some staff members seem predisposed to distrust homeless people. One staff member, Tom, a white man in his late twenties, described shelter residents this way:

> Ninety percent of homeless people don't want to work. Most shelters don't force people to work—they're like three-month vacations for people. You get your rent, your food paid for—it's great! Why wouldn't anyone want to live for free? I know people who go to Alaska, then come here for three months and stay in a shelter for that time.
>
> I know there are a lot of people who go from shelter to shelter—they'd rather do drugs and drink than have to work. For some of them, they make more money from benefits than they do at work; why would they want to work?
>
> All shelters should be work programs like the Lighthouse. You can't just provide free shelter to these people and not force them to work. It's like giving a fat person who's on a diet lots of food—cake and candy bars—it's too tempting for them. These [homeless] people have to be taught responsibility.

Tom saw no irony when, during the same conversation, he described his own job search that had culminated in a position at the shelter. Some months ago Tom had finished college and secured employment in another state but had to move to Phoenix to care for a sick parent. His job search in Phoenix proved much more difficult: "I looked and looked for a job, applying, applying, applying for months. It was very discouraging. I was really depressed because I didn't get one offer."

Even though his own search took months, Tom argued that it was easy for residents of the shelter to conduct five job searches a day and have employment within two weeks. In his own quest for employment, Tom never even considered applying at a fast-food restaurant, and some might argue that since he obviously had the resources to forgo that kind of job and continue to look in his field, his story is not comparable to homeless people's situations. Yet the point is that for someone like Tom, with more skills and education than the great majority of the homeless, not being able to find a job is somehow excusable. No one accuses him of laziness. Instead his perseverance in the face of such a "discouraging" few months is congratulated. Homeless people tell similar stories of moving to Phoenix in the hope of finding higher-paying jobs and using up their savings before they can find employment in fields such as construction or factory work. But they are assumed not to have tried hard enough, perhaps to have been extravagant with their savings and, simply put, to deserve the position in which they currently find themselves.

Work Requirements

When family homeless shelters operate on the belief that the culture of poverty influences residents' motivation to work, mandatory work requirements will usually become part of the program. Such programs may vary significantly, with the Family Shelter and Lighthouse providing examples of two approaches to incorporating work requirements into shelter programs. Perhaps the most important difference between the two is that the Lighthouse forces people to find work immediately, at the risk of being asked to leave the program. The Family Shelter, on the other hand, encourages residents to pursue jobs that have opportunities for advancement rather than dead-end jobs and to consider whether the salary will provide enough money to live on. The Family Shelter also supports resident participation in education and training programs more than the Lighthouse does. Both, however, are circumscribed by their three-month limits on assistance for each resident. Education usually demands more time. Three-month emergency shelters restrict employment opportunities for the homeless, regardless of the intentions or philosophy of the job developer. Homeless adults will leave shelters without a real change in their skill levels or in the probability of finding employment that pays enough to keep them stably housed in the future.

Fifty case files randomly selected from the Lighthouse indicate that many residents had not attained a high school diploma and had work experience in historically relatively low-paying, low-skill fields. Of the sixty-seven adults represented in the fifty files (the statistics given here count each adult in two-parent families separately), 40 percent of the adults had not finished high school, and three of that group had not gone beyond eighth grade. Another 42 percent had graduated from high school or obtained their GED, and only two people (3 percent) had college degrees. The remaining 15 percent had completed high school and attended trade or vocational school or completed some years of community college or university classes but had not obtained college degrees. Work histories included unskilled physical labor such as warehouse loading and factory work, skilled labor such as construction and clerical employment, positions in retail such as a cashier, working in fast-food restaurants, and domestic work.

Even though the short-term nature of emergency shelters limits the possibilities for real change in resident employment opportunities, differences can be observed in the approaches of the Family Shelter and Lighthouse job developers. The Lighthouse job developer, Sam, meets with residents shortly after their acceptance into the shelter to assess their work experience, skills, and employment stability. With just two weeks to find employment or be terminated from the program, Sam stresses an immediate job search. He teaches the "basic philosophy of job search," including skills residents can use in future attempts to find employment. Even for residents who lack a high school diploma, Sam encourages them to work rather than attend basic education classes.

According to Sam, the Lighthouse consistently boasts a 90 percent employment rate. Of that number, however, a large percentage is underemployed, defined by Sam as a resident working for one dollar to two dollars an hour less than she has in past jobs. Many residents, male and female, work in fast-food restaurants at minimum wage: "We have women who get into fast food, who under a different set of circumstances can get into a real company, with benefits and a salary above minimum wage. They need to do an extended job search later, after they get out of the shelter. There are a lot of restrictions on what we can do in three months." Rather than assist people to undertake an "extended job search," Sam pushes people to accept any job, regardless of whether the salary can support a family. Sam argues that programs that do otherwise "are designed to be enablers rather than getting people employed. They're keeping a client a client rather than getting them working. We don't have the luxury of working with people on long-term goals. I see problems with some of the GED programs looking too much at long-term goals when people are in a crisis situation." Sam admits, however, that most Lighthouse residents cannot reach financial stability without a year or two in a transitional housing program after they leave the Lighthouse, where they remain a "client."

The Family Shelter job developer, Carlos, has goals similar to Sam's: assisting residents to "get on their feet," build cash reserves, and find housing. He spends more time initially with each resident, however, talking about her employment history and running interest and personality tests to determine her "ideal job." Carlos also helps each resident write a résumé and practice job search techniques, including how to contact potential employers via telephone and how to present herself during an interview. Moreover, he maintains a computer file of employers with whom he has created relationships to facilitate new resident job searches. Although Carlos, like Sam, prefers that people find employment as quickly as possible, he remains more flexible, and the Family Shelter does not place a firm deadline on finding employment.

Like Sam, Carlos considers education and training programs too long term and expensive for most residents. He suggests that they apply only when a program is short term or part-time or the resident has fashioned some way to support herself until she has finished the program. Even so, Carlos strives to place people in jobs that offer upward mobility and lead to a career, as opposed to fast-food jobs:

> I'm a firm believer that if we look now at a job that people will stay in, that it's worth the extra time it takes to find them. Just putting people into a fast-food job and telling them to look for something later is very frustrating. People can do more than that. . . . A lot of times my job involves building people's sense of security about what they're doing. I try to show them how to get into full-time work from a part-time position or better positions within a company. Most people don't know how to look into a career path at a company. I teach them not to be passive about reaching their goals.

In contrast to Sam's assertion that resident underemployment is an insuperable fact of his job, Carlos contends that almost all Family Shelter residents make above minimum wage—for example, as receptionists or doing technical assistance work. He boasts a number of people accepting jobs paying significantly more than minimum wage—doing data entry, bookkeeping, and the like.

It is difficult to assess whether these differing attitudes affect the incomes or career paths of residents, since the shelters do not collect detailed data on incomes upon arrival versus incomes upon exit and over the next years. Each has a "success rate" based on the percentages of their clients who find housing and leave the program for an affordable apartment or to live with relatives or friends in a situation that appears viable for the long term. The Lighthouse shelter director claims a success rate of 35 percent for people who remain in the program the full ninety days, but even for that group, housing stability is often contingent upon receiving government housing assistance or entering a transitional housing program.[22] The Family Shelter asserts a higher success rate of 60 to 70 percent but maintains that an unknown subset of that number "cycle back into homelessness."[23] It is instructive that the Family Shelter allows residents more flexibility in their job searches, eschewing a hard-and-fast employment deadline in favor of encouraging homeless residents to find a career path that will allow upward mobility. The Lighthouse, on the other hand, maintains that "any job is a good job" and urges residents to accept work at fast-food restaurants or in other dead-end jobs at the risk of being forced to leave the program. According to the data gained from interviews with job developers at each site, the Family Shelter strategy pays off in higher salaries and jobs that are the first step in a career path.

The Family Shelter overall has a more individualized approach to residents. Rather than apply the same strict regulations and deadlines to everyone's job search as the Lighthouse does, the Family Shelter allows residents to make their own decisions about how to proceed. Support services, such as résumé writing and Carlos's job bank, are more intensive than those at the Lighthouse. The Lighthouse is generally more authoritarian than the Family Shelter, and their differing philosophies are reflected in the job developers' approaches. These differences, in turn, are apparent in resident salaries— minimum wage and underemployment at the Lighthouse versus above minimum wage at the Family Shelter.

People in Transition

If the Family Shelter tends to treat homeless residents with a mixture of warmth, support, and paternalism and the Lighthouse regards them with suspicion and blame, People in Transition caseworkers often treat residents with neglect or indifference. Just a few blocks from the Lighthouse, People in Transition uses three buildings within a city public housing project. Whereas the Family Shelter and the Lighthouse are homeless shelters serving adults with children, People in Transition describes itself as a transitional living program and assists single, elderly men and women and those over eighteen who are physically or mentally disabled. I refer to it as a "shelter" because in many ways it more closely resembles an emergency shelter than a transitional housing program. Indeed although both the Endowment for Phoenix Families (EPF) and People in Transition refer to themselves as transitional housing programs and differ from shelters in that they provide service to their clients for two years rather than three months, they vary even more significantly when compared with one another. EPF, which is mentioned occasionally in this study but will not be profiled in detail, is a more conventional transitional housing program. It offers an array of services and houses homeless families in apartments or single-family homes throughout the city; families pay one-third of their incomes to EPF for rent.[24]

The physical environment of People in Transition, on the other hand, in some ways looks much like an armory-style shelter. Clients live together in a complex made up of several large sleeping rooms. Three rooms are reserved for men and two for women, and each houses up to nine people who share a bathroom. These "dorms," as the shelter refers to them, have nine beds placed around the room at different angles in an attempt to provide a bit of privacy. Each bed has a nightstand beside it and a padlocked trunk at its foot, the only space for residents' personal belongings besides several shared dressers. On top of the dressers are stacked piles of women's clothing, bedding, and personal belongings; and women also use the space under their beds for belongings that will not fit into the trunks. The People in Transition complex also includes a large kitchen, a community dining area, and a recreation room with couches, several bookcases holding tattered novels, and a television. The rooms, including the dorms, are uniformly bare and drab; neither the staff nor the residents attempt to provide wall hangings, rugs, or other domestic touches. When, for instance, a woman moves out of the shelter and another has not moved in to take her place, the bed she used remains stripped of sheets, blankets, and comforter—with the bare, stained mattress and institutional brown metal bed frame serving as ugly and depressing reminders that this is not "home."

The area of town and the housing project itself are dangerous places for the largely elderly clientele. Some residents are in wheelchairs, use walkers, or move around slowly and painfully; others have hearing or vision problems. Afraid to walk around the surrounding area, which is known for muggings, robbery, and sex work, many residents stay within the small yard directly in front of the buildings that house them. They are frustrated and depressed by their isolation, and even within the housing project they do not always feel safe, as theft, vandalism, and assault have also occurred within the yard. While I interviewed Sharon, for example, two other residents witnessed several young men beating another person on the project grounds and immediately called the police. As the police hauled the youths away, the young men pointed to the elderly shelter residents and threatened that they would return and that they "knew who they were."

The staff offices at People in Transition are in a separate building across the small yard from the dorms. The office has a phone for resident use, and messages and mail can be picked up as well. The two caseworkers and director of the shelter stay in their offices and rarely speak at length with those who live there, except during the hour-a-week meeting each resident has with one of the caseworkers. At this meeting the caseworker is to monitor and offer aid in a resident's search for housing, employment, benefits, or health care and is supposed to check on his or her mental and physical health. One caseworker routinely spends five to fifteen minutes with residents rather than the hour set aside for the weekly meetings. Moreover, this caseworker generally emerges from his office only once during the day, and as a result, residents most often deal with Beth, the administrative assistant.

Beth speaks to residents in a rude and condescending way, and they appear reticent and apologetic around her. One day I lunched with Beth and two female residents, Pat and Cathy, and Beth spoke as if Pat and Cathy were not present. She suggested that it would be "good for" the homeless people at the shelter to dress up in costumes on Halloween and participate in a talent show because it might "increase their self-esteem." Beth also monitors residents' mail, which they must agree to receive at People in Transition to be admitted into the program. When disability checks, food stamps, or paychecks arrive, the office records the date; and the residents (who every month pay the greater of one-third of their income or $100) must sign for their checks and are asked to pay their fees. The system relies on the expectation that those living at the shelter will not pay in a timely manner; Beth has access to their personal mail before the residents do.

In a typical month, People in Transition houses thirty-one men and twenty women. Eighty percent are white; 12 percent are African American; and Native Americans, Latinos, and Asian Americans make up the remainder of the group. Sixteen of the residents, only three of them women, are designated as having "substance abuse" problems. Anyone with a history of heavy alcohol or drug use is not accepted into the shelter without having had a three-month period of abstinence or having completed a one-month treatment program prior to applying to the shelter. Caseworkers may allow someone into the shelter who had a shorter abstinence period, but such a decision is rare. Moreover, "substance abusers" have to submit to random breathalyzer or urinalysis tests and attend Alcoholics Anonymous or Narcotics Anonymous meetings, and they cannot drink on or off the shelter premises. Although no one can use drugs in their free time away from the shelter, caseworkers allow moderate alcohol use. If someone drinks and acts in a threatening or "uncontrolled" manner, however, he or she will be placed in the substance abuse program and will be unable to drink alcohol again. When they initially arrive at the shelter, staff members warn residents that they will conduct unannounced, random searches of the dorms; such searches occur when the staff suspects a resident has been using drugs.

Allowing residents to consume alcohol off the shelter premises is one of several ways regulation is more limited than that at the Family Shelter or the Lighthouse. Many rules are similar at all three programs: keeping weapons at the shelter, stealing from the shelter or other residents, engaging in violent or threatening behavior, and missing the 10:00 P.M. curfew can result in eviction from People in Transition. On the other hand, caseworkers permit residents to stay off the shelter grounds overnight as long as they submit a request in advance, a "privilege" other shelters do not offer. And although residents are not supposed to visit in others' dorms, staff members do not monitor resident movement closely or regularly, except for a nightly bed check.

BATTERED WOMEN'S SHELTERS

Rose's House

Unlike People in Transition, the Family Shelter, and the Lighthouse, which primarily serve homeless people, Rose's House and La Casa are battered women's shelters. Upon entering Rose's House one immediately notices the homelike atmosphere, which differs significantly from the more institutionalized environments of the homeless shelters. Rose's House is a converted two-story, five-bedroom house in which each family or single woman has her own bedroom; in addition it contains a caseworker's office, children's playroom, kitchen, and a dining room. Only the caseworker's office, the first room one enters when coming into the house, suggests that this is not simply a large home like any other on the lower-middle-class residential block where it is located. Each bedroom contains a set of bunk beds and a trundle bed, two with cribs for women who have infants with them. The bedrooms are plain but clean, with freshly painted walls and new carpeting. The ground-floor bathroom and two bedrooms are designed for disabled women, one currently occupied by a woman who has undergone open heart surgery after her husband stabbed her repeatedly in the chest. Three families reside upstairs—one in each of the three spacious bedrooms—and they share one upstairs bathroom.

Although the shelter provides food and linens, the residents of Rose's House share among themselves the tasks of preparing food, cleaning, and keeping the shelter running smoothly. One of the women serves a communal dinner in the large dining room at six o'clock each evening. Three tables, all old and some in slight disrepair, are arranged around the room and accommodate four to six women and at least one high chair apiece. The residents talk and eat together, then quickly clean up the remains of the meal to prepare for group counseling, which is mandatory and occurs three nights a week. During the women's group session the children play outside in the yard—climbing on playground equipment or riding old bicycles—or occupy themselves with games, puzzles, and toys in the playroom. Rose's House employs a children's caseworker who meets regularly with the mothers to assist with learning or discipline questions or problems and who conducts group sessions with the children.

Like the other shelters that accept state funding, women may stay at Rose's House for up to ninety days, but caseworkers accept them initially for thirty days only, subject to review of their progress on the case plan at the end of that period. Developed jointly by a caseworker and the woman resident, the case plan lists the goals a woman would like to reach while in the shelter, such as obtaining housing or employment, and staff members provide referrals and advocacy in support of her goals. In addition to keeping the staff apprised of her progress, each woman is encouraged to meet with a caseworker individually to discuss her emotional reactions to the abuse she has experienced and to leaving her partner. Once the case plan has been drawn up, a woman can be fairly sure she will not be asked to leave before the end of thirty days, even if she does not work on her goals consistently. Women who have exerted little effort to find housing or a job, however, will probably not be allowed to remain at the shelter longer than thirty days.

Although each woman's case plan is reviewed and updated weekly by her and a caseworker and the caseworkers supply as much feedback and as many referrals as they can, Rose's House believes the onus is on the residents to pursue their objectives at their own pace. The staff members see themselves as a support system for the women, helping them to get access to social services and other resources and to provide advice when women ask for it. They argue that when staff members in a domestic violence shelter do too much, it takes power away from women rather than helping them take responsibility for their own lives and decide what they want to do for themselves.

Rose's House staff also believes it is each woman's decision whether to return to the partner she left. Although caseworkers try to explore a woman's options with her to find what serves her best, repeatedly saying that it is a woman's own decision whether to return to a relationship, some women who decide to return to their partners pretend they are leaving to live elsewhere. Perhaps because so much of the group and individual counseling focuses on domestic violence and its effects, many women feel ashamed to admit they are returning to their relationships, notwithstanding the staff's insistence that they will not be judged whatever their decision.

The rules at Rose's House echo those of most of the other shelters, including prohibition of drugs and alcohol on or off the shelter grounds and a seven o'clock nightly curfew. Women are asked to check out with a caseworker before leaving the shelter during the day or to sign out on a sheet tacked to the office wall indicating their destinations and times exited and to check back in when they return. Caseworkers submit that this encourages interaction among the staff and residents and facilitates the staff's job of recording a woman's progress on her case plan goals each day. In addition, the rules request that women who spank or yell at their children to discipline them work with the children's caseworker to develop alternatives to such methods, as the shelter believes such disciplinary techniques constitute a form of violence.

As evidenced by the foregoing discussion, Rose's House, like most battered women's shelters, focuses more on emotional support and healing than on the nuts and bolts of finding work that pays a living wage and supports affordable housing. Many battered women criticize the shelter's lack of assistance in these areas, and indeed most find it difficult to locate housing and, if need be, a job within a month. A number of them leave the shelter without stable housing arrangements in place.

La Casa

La Casa has its roots in an effort begun in the 1980s by a local Chicano/a advocacy group to provide "safe houses" for monolingual Spanish-speaking women who often could not find a battered women's shelter with a Spanish-speaking staff person. These safe houses were simply homes of families in the community who would allow a woman in need of shelter to stay with them. Although reliable quantitative data showing how many Latinos seeking shelter speak Spanish exclusively are not available for the Phoenix metropolitan area, other studies in Southwest regions have confirmed as many as 75 percent are monolingual.[25] In a city with a large Spanish-speaking community, most Phoenix shelters lack even one Spanish-speaking staff person and do not offer programs for women who are in the country illegally. Often, shelters will not accept monolingual Spanish-speaking women or those who lack proficiency in English.

Several years after the beginning of the safe house movement, organizers founded La Casa—with a fully bilingual and bicultural staff—designed to cater particularly to the needs of Latinas but serving other women of color as well. La Casa's emergency shelter program currently houses up to fourteen women and children, offering them a maximum of ninety days in the shelter. In addition, the La Casa complex contains several apartments that house women in its transitional living program. Those who apply and are accepted from the emergency shelter program—there is room for sixteen people—may live in transitional housing for up to eighteen months. Most families stay less than a year while they wait for government housing subsidies or a low-rent apartment to become available.

Housed in a quiet, lower-middle-income residential neighborhood, La Casa is composed of a group of white buildings arranged in a square around a yard. Screened from the street by buildings on all sides, the yard contains a large sandbox, a swing set, and many toys. The doors to the women's rooms open onto the yard and are painted with curlicues of brightly colored flowers. Although clean, cheerful, and freshly painted, the rooms are spare, each with a dresser and two bunk beds, with one bathroom shared by every two families. Across the courtyard are the buildings that house women in the transitional living program. Each family's quarters in this area contain two bedrooms, a kitchen, and a living room. Like the emergency shelter rooms, they are bright and clean, with vivid red and blue Mexican blankets serving as curtains and potted plants clustered near each door.

Another building serves as a dining room. Six tables are arrayed around the room, each with a centerpiece of homemade paper flowers in a vase and set for four people, with a ribbon tying a napkin around sets of silverware. In the adjoining kitchen pots of rice, vegetables, and chicken simmer on the stove during the lunch and dinner hours. Families come in at their leisure, serve themselves, and sit at one of the tables while tape-recorded guitar music plays.

In the converted house at the front of the complex are the staff offices, private counseling rooms, a conference room for nightly group meetings, and a children's room with books, toys, and a blackboard. Amid a relaxed and informal atmosphere, residents move freely in and out of these offices as well as the dining and courtyard areas. The staff appears to be continually available to the women, who stop by to chat with the receptionist or counselors; when a woman comes in crying in the middle of the day, clutching her baby, a staff member quickly hugs and speaks soothingly to her before ushering the pair into her office.

La Casa's philosophy on battering, including why it occurs and how it affects women, is similar to that of Rose's House and other domestic violence shelters. They cite the stress, frustration, and low self-esteem that can result from battering. Like Rose's House, La Casa addresses physical, emotional, mental, and sexual abuse but additionally argues that the most damaging is spiritual abuse. Sylvia, a caseworker, explained: "When you kill the spirit you have nothing left. We're the only shelter that addresses that issue. We developed our own circle, based on indigenous thought, to take the place of the circle of abuse usually used." In the "circle" to which she refers, developed by the Domestic Abuse Intervention Project in Minnesota and generally utilized by battered women's advocates to educate people about domestic violence, battering is equated with gaining "power and control" through emotional, physical, and economic abuse—including the use of intimidation, isolation, and threats. La Casa adds "spiritual abuse" in the sense that the abuser attempts to convince his partner that he is her "higher power," that she does not matter.

As a way to heal spiritual abuse and in addition to the individual and group counseling most shelters rely on, La Casa incorporates a sweat lodge ceremony as one of its most important methods for working with shelter residents. According to La Casa's literature on the sweat lodge, this indigenous ceremony is used as a "purification and healing ritual [that] . . . facilitates the cleansing and healing of exterior as well as 'interior' wounds." The women come together with the staff and a facilitator in a domelike structure made from willow bark and sit around a fire pit. Water is poured over heated lava stones to create deep steam. The women are encouraged to share their experiences behind cover of the blinding steam of the sweat lodge, to support one another, and to sing and pray together. Sylvia believes the sweat lodge ceremony works so well in healing women spiritually because "in the sweat lodge we're equal. You can't see race, age, or gender, and it frees the women, it empowers them to trust themselves."

Moreover, La Casa's staff emphasizes the role of women's poverty more than other shelters of its kind. Sylvia argues that battered women who must flee to shelters are in essence homeless once they arrive at such shelters: "For a long time homeless advocates in this area didn't want to include domestic violence victims [within a definition of homelessness] because, they would say, 'they have a home.' But it's not a home they can live in; they are fleeing for their lives." And in addition, Sylvia points out, some women go to domestic violence shelters because they wish to end a relationship but lack the resources to support themselves and their children: "The issue that surfaced again and again [in Spanish-language battered women's support groups] was economics. The reason women go back to the batterer is they don't have enough money to support themselves and their kids. Even if she's on AFDC and food stamps, the money runs out by the end of the month." Although La Casa does have a curfew and rules disallowing violence, drugs, and alcohol, the shelter focuses on mutual respect between the staff and residents, on "spiritual recovery," and on women's economic constraints rather than primarily on physical violence. In addressing the needs of women of color, who are disproportionately low-income, the shelter has altered the traditional understanding of domestic violence that emphasizes a woman's need to escape and hide from a physically violent mate who threatens her life. Rather, La Casa considers factors associated with race and class to be most important in understanding and interpreting women's experiences.

Like other shelters, La Casa constantly turns women away because of lack of space. But the stakes are higher for women trying to get into La Casa; they have few other options when La Casa is full. If monolingual Spanish-speaking women enter another shelter, they may not receive the same level of assistance from the staff that other women receive, and they are often isolated.[26] Ana, one of the clients at La Casa who speaks limited English, had previously lived in a different domestic violence shelter where staff members asked her to watch the children while the other women participated in group counseling. Thus she was not treated as a full member of the shelter community. In fact, it appears that the staff, unable to speak Spanish, simply gave up on attempting to assist Ana and did not include her in what purportedly were mandatory aspects of the shelter program, including counseling. Ana left the shelter and returned to her abuser until she found La Casa.

Sylvia, the La Casa caseworker, argues that such isolation affects both shelter residents and women who look for assistance after completing a shelter program:

If you're white, blue-eyed, and battered, you have a better chance of recovery—there are more resources for you. If you're poor, brown, monolingual, [have] no skills—you have all those things against you. . . . For an English-speaking client, once she gets situated out of the shelter her need for support is met by Codependents Anonymous, Alcoholics Anonymous, and other groups. For a Spanish-speaking client, there aren't any resources or support groups.

The issues Sylvia points to are clear, particular examples of the "structural intersectionality" Kimberlé Williams Crenshaw discusses in terms of battered women of color.[27] Most battered women's shelters are organized around the image of a white, middle-class woman, and the many women seeking assistance who do not fit this image appear to be misfits—somehow not quite "real" battered women—and are treated as outsiders.

Many white shelter directors contend that Latinos "take care of their own" by doubling up, taking in family members, and the like. Thus, they claim, because of a cultural emphasis on family, fewer Latinas are looking for shelter than the Latino poverty rate would suggest. But this claim operates as an excuse, in a sense, for the lack of shelters or other support systems for monolingual Spanish-speaking women. If shelters do not provide a Spanish-speaking caseworker on the crisis line or to field intake calls, if all staff members are Anglo, then Latinas are less likely to seek help from the shelter system. Interviews suggest that often the organization of the shelter system causes Latinas to have to look to other sources of support—or even to return to their abusers.

The idea that Latinas will not be on the street because they are more likely than Anglos to double up in overcrowded conditions also ignores the importance of battering as a reason for homelessness. Even if they have family members in the area, Latinas—like other women who leave abusive relationships—may be unable to stay with extended family because of safety concerns, or they simply may not be welcome. A study in El Paso, Texas, found that "a majority of Hispanic females cite relationship problems as the cause of homelessness," and thus they were unlikely to be doubled up even when they had family members living in the area.[28]

HOMELESS CAMPS

One alternative to shelters that still provides a semblance of community and mutual support exists in the organized campsites that dot the desert and fruit orchards around Phoenix. One such homeless campsite is on state-owned property that abuts a freeway overpass. Just a half mile off a busy thoroughfare, rusty vans and campers sit in a small ravine completely obscured from the road by desert brush and trees. Approached by a dirt road that ends at a chain-link fence, the camp can be reached only by foot through a break in the fence. A whistle hangs on the fence with a hand-lettered sign reading "Beware! Blow whistle before entering!" The sound of the whistle will summon one of the camp residents, usually surrounded by a pack of mangy dogs known to bite people who venture unaccompanied into the camp. Residents have arranged several camper shells, an abandoned bus, and some rusty vans that serve as living quarters into a rough circle. Scattered about the edges of this circle are a variety of old cars, trucks, and bicycles that Bruce—one of the residents—is either attempting to repair or using for parts to fix other cars. One camper serves as the community food pantry, to which people staying at the camp for longer than a week are expected to contribute according to their means.

Although some people come to the camp in search of an alternative to the shelters with their regulations, curfews, and requests for personal information, the camp has its own set of rules. Very sick people—mentally or physically—are not welcome; neither are heavy drug users or those who become violent when drunk. Such people disturb the quality of life, which at least during the day seems peaceful and somewhat solitary. Moreover, severely ill people require care the other residents cannot or do not wish to provide, and they might call undue attention to the camp, attracting visitors from social service agencies or city authorities demanding that the camp be vacated. Most residents are childless single men or male/female couples. If families are present here or in similar alternatives to shelters, they tend to be two-parent families rather than female-headed, single-parent families.[29]

The camp has existed for five years, with a changing population, although Bruce—a thirty-five-year-old white man—has lived here nearly that entire time. At six o'clock on a Thursday morning in September, Bruce is already awake and working on his latest mechanical project, a 1973 Chevy with chipped green paint and missing front fenders, muttering to himself and the dogs that range around him while he works. He sports a scraggly beard and wears only loose-fitting jeans held up by a piece of rope. Bruce's reputation as a gifted mechanic often attracts people with automotive problems and limited resources to the camp. Some remain only until Bruce completes the repairs, whereas others stay on for months and even years.

My visits to the camp occur in the company of Leon, a thirty-year-old African American social worker from a city organization that sporadically sends someone to the camps to offer the residents aid and housing options. Bruce is not friendly toward us, as he might be toward people who hear about the camp through word of mouth and seek it out as a place to stay or for Bruce's automotive expertise. Bruce, not happy about being disturbed, chats for a few minutes about his attempts to gain ownership of the Chevy, then turns back to his work. He responds to Leon's offer of blankets and sleeping bags with a gruff refusal.

Bruce particularly resents Leon's intrusion, complaining that social service representatives have no right to meddle in his life by coming to the camp uninvited. To accept blankets, clothing, or other assistance would imply a relationship with Leon and would carry an unstated quid pro quo: if Bruce accepts the help, he has to allow Leon into his life. Given the regulations at most shelters that demand personal information from "clients," eventual requests that Bruce reveal his life history or listen to Leon's counsel about the benefits of living in conventional housing rather than the camp would not be unexpected. A relationship with Leon might also be the first step in what Bruce suspects is a campaign to break up the camp and place residents in shelters or halfway houses. Yet Bruce is not openly hostile. He must remain civil because of what Bruce perceives is Leon's (or his agency's) power over the camp residents. Leon's agency could complain about the camp to the city, and since it is on public property, the police could be brought in to close the camp down.

Another camp resident, Nancy, is a forty-year-old white woman. On the day we visit the camp, Nancy, her boyfriend, and another woman staying at the camp are preparing for day labor at a construction site. The man who located the job and has arrived to drive them to the site is a former camp resident who now has his own apartment and occasionally drives out to the camp to visit current residents. He has driven Nancy and the others to the construction job all week, and although Nancy admits that the work is physically very difficult, she and the others have been ready each morning at 6:30. Her boyfriend's wrist is swollen from an injury incurred the day before, but he plans to work anyway.

In contrast to Bruce's barely concealed annoyance, Nancy is articulate, funny, and warm. With her hair brushed back in a ponytail, freshly polished nails, and clean shorts and T-shirt, it is difficult to tell that she lives in the desert without running water. Leon believes she would leave the camp if he could help her enter a shelter or find subsidized housing, but her boyfriend is "a drinker" and does not wish to work with social service agencies, and Nancy wants to live with him. According to Leon, most people at the camp have at one time or another looked to social services to help them find housing or receive benefits. Many became discouraged, though, when their benefits were cut without an explanation, or they became disgusted with the array of caseworkers assigned to them—some working at odds with one another and others overlapping. Bruce's antipathy to social workers' requests for personal information or the attempts to "change" homeless people that accompany most offers for assistance probably echoes the complaints of many who live in such camps. By contrast, social service workers tend to display grudging admiration for the campers. Leon described them as "sometimes more determined than people doubled up or on welfare, since [those on welfare] may tend to be hopeless."

Nancy is in the process of "winterizing" her trailer, adding another layer to the outside walls of scrap wood, metal, and corkboard and filling in cracks and holes from the inside. Complaining that she has been cold during the increasingly cool evenings because she only has shorts to wear, she asks Leon for blankets and jeans. When we return to the camp another day, Leon brings sweatshirts and blankets only for Nancy and her boyfriend, believing the rest of the residents would refuse them.

HOMELESS WOMEN'S RESISTANCE

Completely eschewing social service assistance and choosing to camp in the desert represents a fairly extreme response to homeless women's dislike of shelters and social service agencies. Nevertheless, most homeless women in short-term emergency shelters share Bruce's and Nancy's antipathy toward onerous shelter rules, invasive staff practices, suspicious staff attitudes, and demands for personal information. A clear and forceful message comes from homeless women's perspectives on the shelter system and the staff: shelters do not work on behalf of homeless women's best interests and do not supply what homeless residents want from "helping" institutions. But given homeless women's dependence on shelters and staff to meet their basic needs, they are often at a loss as to whether and how to communicate their objections. As a result, they often use methods such as uncooperativeness and other "isolated acts and gestures" that do not require direct dissent.[30] Moreover, women want to do more than simply share their beliefs; they also want to undercut the discipline of the shelter and representations of homeless people— for example, as drug addicts and lazy—that portray them as undeserving.

I have defined homeless women's arguments and actions against shelters as *resistance*, as activities that are political in the sense that they are intentional and reasoned. That is, homeless women's complaints, secrecy, and uncooperativeness, their flouting of shelter rules or decisions to live in camps, signify not deviance but a form of political protest. Recognizing resistance among homeless women demands acknowledging actions other than organized demonstrations. Although mass actions may attract a short-lived flurry of attention, they rarely represent the resistance of homeless women—especially residents of small, tightly controlled short-term shelters. Many large-scale demonstrations are coordinated by nonhomeless advocates or service providers or are dominated by male homeless leaders. When the term *political* is limited to mass demonstrations, homeless women—who rarely participate in such demonstrations—are more likely to be perceived as passive, apolitical, and unwilling or unable to understand and resist the workings of power inside and outside the shelters.

By focusing on what James Scott has called "everyday forms of . . . resistance,"[31] this study brings a different kind of analysis to questions about how power and resistance work in the lives of homeless women. Following Scott, I define *everyday resistance* as the "prosaic but constant struggle"[32] by shelter residents to avoid staff control and surveillance, to be seen as deserving assistance, and to define homelessness based on the circumstances of their lives. These are the activities that best represent women's ongoing participation in creating cultural meaning—and that most affect their lived experiences, the relationships they develop, and the solutions they devise to their situations.

Frances Fox Piven and Richard Cloward suggest that political acts like the ones homeless women engage in will likely be defined as *deviance* when definitions of *resistance* or *protest* are limited. The authors point to the inadequacy inherent in identifying political protest as only those actions characterized by mass demonstrations or by organizations associated with "middle-class" values:

> The effect of equating movements with movement organizations—and thus requiring that protests have a leader, a constitution, a legislative program, or at least a banner before they are recognized as such—is to divert attention from many forms of political unrest and to consign them by definition to the more shadowy realms of social problems and deviant behavior. As a result such events as massive school truancy or rising worker absenteeism or mounting applications for public welfare . . . rarely attract the attention of political analysts. Having decided by definitional fiat that nothing political has occurred, nothing has to be explained, at least not in the terms of political protest.[33]

Such is the case with shelter residents' resistance to social worker control, manifested by breaking shelter rules or living in camps. They are defined as deviants who have not yet decided to "help themselves," who have not achieved the emotional and mental growth necessary to admit that they are living "dysfunctional" lifestyles. Such homeless women are accused of being unable or unwilling to live with the discipline demanded by the shelter, a discipline put in place "for their own good."

To reject the representation of shelter residents as deviants is to understand their resistance in the context of homeless women's reliance on the shelter system. Women rely on shelters for basic survival—for food, housing, clothing, and referrals to jobs and other social service agencies. The "choice" to apply to and stay in a shelter is circumscribed by homeless women's lack of resources. For most women a shelter is a last resort after she has used up her other options, such as staying with friends or family members, living in a motel, or—for some—living on the street. With few other options, homeless women avoid open defiance of rules they find onerous or unfair and rarely confront the staff verbally. Either kind of challenge puts women at risk of being kicked out of the shelter. "Evasion," "false compliance," and "deception"[34] are some of the few tools available to them, and homeless women's use of these tools may be read as resistance to staff oversight and unjustifiable rules.

Although resistance is pervasive, it is also scattered and sometimes feeble. Noting the limitations inherent in homeless women's resistance does not suggest their actions and demands are inconsequential. By undercutting the play of power in the shelters, homeless women refuse to be labeled "passive and dependent."[35] They are agents rather than a socially, culturally, and economically impoverished class that can only be helped by social service agencies and only be defined as objects in relationship to the caseworker as subject. Michael Gismondi has argued: "Recovering the human agency of dominated people requires consideration of how their social experiences inform the subjective initiatives they take in the face of objective determinants—i.e., the sense in which dominated classes make history, even if they do not always make history to their choosing."[36] Thus resistance must also be understood in the context of the organization and philosophies of small, family homeless shelters. Resistance is shaped by shelters' reliance on "disciplinary technologies" to alter homeless people: the tendency of the shelter system to offer the homeless primarily short-term housing, the emphasis on mandatory programs and the suspicious attitudes of caseworkers, and the control wrought by the rules and physical environments of the shelters. A significant amount of control over shelter residents' lives is institutionalized, existing as a seemingly "natural" and unquestioned part of the rules and everyday running of the shelters.

Constraints of Professionalism

The professional ethics of the social work occupation, as played out in homeless shelters, significantly affect the kinds of resistance homeless women engage in. Caseworkers utilize emotional distance,[37] objective and rational review of homeless women's "presenting problems," invasive demands for personal information, and reliance on a case plan to resolve a woman's homelessness. Each of these tools has been institutionalized as part of a professional standard, claimed to be necessary if homeless or low-income people are to be helped.[38] The professional relationship between social worker and client sets up the homeless as "passive and dependent subjects of care."[39] The shelter caseworker, on the other hand, is the expert, operating according to the values of professional distance, objectivity, and rationality.

Professional standards provide a set of codes that dictate how homeless women should be approached and treated; they specifically emphasize limiting personal interaction with residents and eschewing individualized treatment. In particular, staff members should not allow their personal feelings to enter into relationships with clients. Rather, they must maintain emotional and physical distance from all residents. Additionally, all homeless women should be dealt with in the same way, with a case plan drawn up to address work, housing, drug use, and life skills. Individual needs that deviate from the subscribed goals are generally ignored, or the staff discourages residents from focusing on them.

On the positive side, adhering to professionalized rules regarding contact with homeless women can discourage disparate treatment of residents.[40] Professional social work standards may provide relatively untrained caseworkers with a gauge regarding how to respond to homeless women in specific situations. It might be argued that some of shelter residents' complaints about social workers result from a lack of professionalism, in the sense that professional safeguards ostensibly should keep employees from abusing their power. Caseworkers at Rose's House and La Casa battered women's shelters in particular treat residents with compassion, and La Casa seems less interested in keeping residents under constant surveillance than is the case at the homeless shelters. Although many shelter staff members are sincerely interested in helping their clients, then, their relationships with clients are circumscribed by their professional identities and occupational goals.[41] Moreover, individual caseworkers' perspectives on why people became homeless, particularly at places like the Lighthouse, are not always conducive to respectful or kind treatment of clients.

Most homeless women assert that staff distance and the lack of specialized treatment for individual residents undermine the likelihood that they will become housed. Michelle, a white mother of two, complained that the shelter staff does not approach each resident in an individualized way, attempting to ascertain the specific reasons for her homelessness and making exceptions to rules when needed:

> The only thing I don't like about this program is that I've seen them throw out five families with no place to go. Marta had bad credit, so she couldn't get an apartment. Now she's living in her car. . . . They're no better off than when they came in here. The thing is, she has the money for a place, but no one would rent to her. It wasn't like she didn't try. I'd see her on the phone all the time.

If the Family Shelter staff provided the individualized treatment Michelle argues should routinely govern the staff's work with clients, Marta may have been allowed to stay at the shelter rather than having to leave to live in her car. Every indication suggests that Marta was a "good" client, part of the deserving poor in the sense that she became homeless after leaving an abusive spouse and could not support herself and her children on welfare benefits or the meager wages paid for unskilled service-sector work.

Relatedly, Michelle objects to caseworkers' assumption that every woman's poverty can be addressed through counseling and life skills classes. She does not believe she is learning from the mandatory classes at the shelter: "It gripes me that I have to go to parenting classes, since I've been twice already. And in Life Skills class we were given an exercise to budget for a man who made $60,000 a year. If any of us made that much, we wouldn't be here. I told the lady that, that she should give us an exercise to budget with $1,000 a month." Michelle argues that most women's homelessness cannot be attributed to budgeting problems and be fixed with a class on such skills. It is difficult to support a family of three on $1,000 a month, and learning how to divide up a $60,000 income, to add and subtract figures in columns of expenses and equity, will not help most homeless women.

Abuse of Power

Beyond professional ethics, many caseworkers use their power to control residents in ways that seem to have little to do with professional distance and objectivity or enforcement of the written rules. The majority of homeless women argue that caseworkers often abuse their power. Freda, a twenty-eight-year-old African American resident of the Lighthouse, contends: "This place is great if they didn't have assholes who felt really powerful. . . . The [case managers] have the key to your room and we don't. I'd be crazy to leave my TV in my room. They make you wait and wait to get your key, even if your kid has to go to the bathroom. They unlock the door for you, and the same key unlocks all the doors." Freda goes on to describe an incident with the staff that succinctly captures the relationship between staff and "client":

> What I don't like about this place are the rules and regulations and the abuse of authority by case managers. The other night at 8:30 I was doing laundry, and I laughed loud with a woman I was talking to, and the case manager told me to be quiet, that he had made another parent go to bed at eight o'clock and he could make me go, too. . . . They don't respect our privacy. They talk and laugh about you, make fun of you. . . . They bring their personal lives into this place. If they have a bad day, you feel it.

After the incident in the laundry room, Freda asked to see her file and found that the staff had been keeping track of the checks that arrived for her. She conjectured that caseworkers were able to see the amount of the check through the envelope and record it.

> I was hesitant about getting my file. If you try to enforce your rights, they give you the message not to rock the boat. Technically, they could kick me out on the street. I'd have to stay in a motel, but the motels around here really suck. The one we were staying in [prior to coming to the shelter] had two rats. A lot of people would complain if they felt safe that they wouldn't be put out. You can get put out for talking back to a case manager.

Although she was upset that her privacy had been violated, Freda had little recourse. Most women share Freda's criticisms of the shelter, but most do not openly defy the staff or complain too strongly about unfair or even unethical treatment. This is the case because most women are much like Freda in other ways: she has been poor all her life and has little education, a history of low-paying jobs, and therefore few options besides the shelter.

Who Is the Expert?

Homeless women criticize the notion that social workers are experts with little to learn from shelter residents.[42] Ella, a white homeless woman, contends that caseworkers need to "see things from homeless people's perspective" to better assist them. She believes homeless people and domestic violence survivors "need to be led by the hand more . . . to have things explained better." This position somewhat conflicts with the philosophy at Rose's House and other shelters, which purports that women will be "empowered" by being forced to find a job and housing by themselves. Many staff members do not understand, Ella suggests, that homeless people enter the shelter after months of barely scraping by, when all their funds went to fulfill immediate needs. Knowing they have only three months in emergency shelter and often promised only two weeks to a month at the outset, they remain focused on immediate needs rather than on saving money. They may also require assistance finding a job that pays a living wage and may favor that option over entering school or training programs. Such beliefs and actions, Ella argues, are rational responses to the circumstances of homeless women's lives.

Similarly, Dee Dee maintains that she has valuable ideas and advice the shelter staff should heed. In fact, she was asked to leave the Ministry for Families Shelter after she wrote a letter of complaint about an employee who "used to whisper in the women's ears who couldn't speak English, saying they need to go back to their own countries." After the Ministry evicted her, the Lighthouse accepted Dee Dee and her daughter: "This is like a country club compared to the Ministry . . . they have 400 people [at the Ministry] and not enough staff. The kids ran around like animals and were treated like animals."

Although she is happier at the Lighthouse than she was at the Ministry, Dee Dee still calls it a "circus on all ends," actively critiquing the program and caseworker decisions. And although the Ministry evicted her for asserting her belief that a staff member should change his behavior, she remains outspoken at the Lighthouse: "I was told to put my seventeen-year-old daughter on the city bus [to go to school] on [a very dangerous street in front of the shelter] at 5:30 in the morning. I had to call some of the caseworkers on their advice to me. I think I can give them some unbiased advice." By asserting that she has a perspective from which Lighthouse caseworkers can learn and in particular that her criticisms are unbiased, Dee Dee places herself in the same league with the staff, undercutting their claims to "expert" status. As argued earlier, the position of social worker as professional relies on the ability to remain fairly detached from people's lives while offering specialized advocacy and "objective" advice. Dee Dee argues that she is as capable of enlightening the staff as they are of imparting knowledge and advice to her.

Like Dee Dee, Gloria believes shelter regulations can work to the detriment of residents:

> All of these programs lack the ability to be comprehensive. All of them rely on other organizations to fill in for things they don't provide. EPF provides housing and sponsors, but they don't provide health care.
>
> At the Ministry shelter they don't serve breakfast, and kids go to school without breakfast. And you're not supposed to have food in your room, and it forces people to be dishonest. So if that's the little lie you're telling, then what other lie will you tell just to stay in the program? I was lucky enough to have a car, and I kept a cooler in it with ice. I'd take [the kids] to school, and we'd sit at the picnic table and have cereal with milk.
>
> At the Ministry, any child over age sixteen has to stay in the single people's section. My sister-in-law stayed there after a domestic dispute with her husband, and she had to lie about the age of her son [who was sixteen]. Otherwise he would have had to stay with another single man.

Gloria maintains that shelter rules create situations for homeless women that force them to be dishonest. Just as other women point out the ways they shape their histories to fit into existing categories of need so they can get into a shelter—categories that may have little resemblance to homeless women's lives—Gloria asserts that shelter programs also often ignore crucial aspects of homeless women's realities. Specifically, shelter rules separate parents (usually mothers) and sons and disallow some activities (like feeding one's children breakfast) a "good mother" must perform. Gloria's critique stems from direct experience in the shelter system, noting that her own and others' attempts to follow certain rules make their lives considerably more difficult. Arguably, if the staff listened to Gloria, the shelter would be more humane and able to diminish stress in the residents' lives.

Residents sometimes unite in their disapprobation of a certain staff member or shelter regulation, as in the example of George—a People in Transition caseworker who basically ignored homeless residents, rarely emerging from his office to speak with them. Homeless people at the shelter refused to carry out the charade that George as a "professional" was helping them once they learned that he did not take an active interest in their lives or work with other agencies on their behalf. Residents held an ongoing contest to see who could spend the least amount of time in his office for their weekly appointments (supposed to last an hour); the record was three minutes. The residents were disgusted with the caseworker's approach to them, particularly in light of the privileges George continued to enjoy as a respected professional. They could not complain outright or refuse to meet with George, so they showed their resentment the only way they could.

Just as shelter residents rarely take their complaints and demands directly to the staff for fear of eviction, however, this practice puts People in Transition residents—who have very few resources to begin with—in an extremely tenuous position. Without the advocacy of a caseworker, even an inactive one, shelter residents have little chance to receive low-income housing or other assistance. When Sharon, a mentally ill resident of the shelter, decided to switch from George to another caseworker, her only choice was a staff member whose constant sexual talk "stressed her out." Sharon continues to meet with the second caseworker, despite his sexual innuendos, because she perceives him as more willing than George to help her secure housing and other benefits. For a homeless woman who wants to get out of the shelter more than anything else, the sexually harassing caseworker's behavior might be more bearable than someone who does nothing to help her. After all, if Sharon cannot find housing and begin to receive disability payments by the end of her allotted time at the shelter, her severe memory lapses and other mental problems probably mean she will be living on the street.

Resisting Representations

Women also resist representations of the homeless as "dysfunctional," lazy, addicted, or mentally ill. Shelter residents demand to be treated as human beings with particular histories and issues.[43] They refuse to be identified as a mass of "the homeless," all of whom are to blame for losing housing and who must follow shelter rules and bend to staff discipline to reject their old dysfunctional lifestyles. Others resist the notion that the shelter is helping them to fit back into the mainstream by learning middle-class values and a work ethic. They reason that they should be treated with dignity and humanity and not simply as a "case."

Homeless women resent it when caseworkers assume it is the shelter resident herself, rather than the structural reasons why she became homeless, that warrants investigation and correction. Tracy, a Family Shelter resident, protests a perception of homeless people as not "equal" to others:

> [People] don't look at us as the same as them. The case managers don't even think of us as the same as them. [Mark, the caseworker at the shelter,] got mad at me for worrying about Julie when she was sick. He said I should just worry about myself because I have enough to do. We shouldn't have to be any

different than other people . . . it's human nature [to care about a friend]. I don't
have to care so much that I'd let people stay with me, but I care about friends.

Also complaining that the child care workers "look down on her," Tracy
asserts: "If we had jobs and those other people became homeless, we wouldn't
look down on them 'cause we've been there, we know what it's like." She
distinguishes between herself and the child care workers, making a claim to
moral superiority and greater life experience, and at the same time maintains
their equality. By arguing that "anyone can become homeless," Tracy suggests that it is plausible that someday she and the child care workers could
exchange places.

Marta, another Family Shelter resident, routinely feels disrespected by
staff members. She states that the caseworkers "gossip about people's private
lives" and that the facilitators of the parenting and budgeting classes "act
snobby." Moreover, the two maintenance workers have "no compassion" for
the people at the shelter, acting as if people became homeless because they
were lazy rather than because they had "run into crises." In addition to
criticizing individual staff members' philosophies and treatment of residents,
Marta is disturbed by the staff's constant surveillance of residents. For example, homeless people at the Family Shelter must request and sign for clothing from the donations room, as well as for even the most mundane or
personal toiletries and hygiene items. Marta expresses uneasiness about having to ask staff members for personal items, fearing the staff will think she is
"using too much" or is "greedy." She goes so far as to borrow laundry soap
from her husband, who does not live at the shelter and from whom she
separated because of his physical abuse, so the staff will not think she has
used too much of the shelter soap.

When Resistance Isn't Necessary: The Deserving Middle Class

The majority of women engage in resistance because they dislike shelter
rules pertaining to curfew, signing in and out of the shelter, and staff control
of public and private space in the shelter. But, importantly, exceptions exist.
For example, Lisa agrees with the shelter staff that many of the regulations
and controlling measures at the shelters are necessary. She and a few other
women support the notion that social control provides crucial structure that
will lead to their eventual independence. Lisa states that the Family Shelter's
rules make her feel safe and provide a structure that is helping her get back
on her feet. She understands the detailed regulations and even surveillance
of residents as important components of a program geared to self-sufficiency.
Much in the way caseworkers explain their roles at the shelter, Lisa and a few
other residents see the staff as guides who will lead them, stage by stage,
through a specific process they must complete to become financially stable.

Unlike most homeless women, Lisa comes from a middle-class background. She is one of the few in the shelter with a college education, and she is articulate and forceful about her opinions. For those reasons, perhaps, she maintains a different relationship to many of the shelter staff that leads her to an alternative conception of the rationale behind some of the regulations and also means she receives better treatment. In looking back at her experience in the Family Shelter, after she had been accepted into a transitional housing program, Lisa admits that many people took a special interest in her and her children and even bent the rules for her: "There were lots of human factors involved in why I made it to this point . . . if people hadn't seen that I deserved a chance and would make good use of it, they wouldn't have gone to bat for me." Specifically, a high-profile, selective job training program deviated from its usual practice of requiring that applicants be in permanent housing before they apply and accepted Lisa while she was still living at the Family Shelter. Through her participation in that program, Lisa met a college professor who helped her enroll in a computer class at the community college without paying a fee. Moreover, the fact that she had been accepted into the job training program helped her to get into the transitional housing program, a program that accepts people based largely on their ability to show motivation. She used both the job training program and her college degree to demonstrate her ability to work hard and complete tasks she sets out to do.

Sharon's experience provides another example of how class status may help residents appear exceptional to caseworkers, ensuring different treatment than most other homeless women receive. Sharon is a well-spoken, middle-class, college-educated homeless woman. She confides that she has not experienced the same problems other clients have with the state-run agency for the indigent mentally ill. Although the agency schedules appointments for most people only once a month and they see different therapists (whomever is working that day) every time they go, Sharon sees the same therapist each week. She argues that this is a result of the perception that she is not "safe" (in her case, suicidal), asserting that if the agency staff has the impression that one is safe—although not necessarily well—they are less likely to make time to counsel people. But it also has something to do with Sharon's ability to advocate for herself. This same agency accepted Sharon into its housing program with a package including subsidized rent, counseling, and assistance with personal expenses.

Both Lisa and Sharon possess recognizably "middle-class" credentials—such as education, use of language, and work experience—that not only facilitate access to the best services but also provide proof of the "motivation" these programs so often demand. Both women possess personal and work credentials that easily translate into probable success stories. The staff might be less likely to question Lisa or Sharon about their willingness to work hard than they would be a person with a high school education (or less) and a work history dominated by short-term jobs at fast-food restaurants and in domestic service.

It is interesting to note that Sharon is African American and Lisa is white. Evidence shows that emphasizing one's whiteness may be an expedient means to appear deserving of assistance, particularly when it suggests one is approaching middle-class status as opposed to being part of the "underclass." Yet in limited instances class may override race. Specifically, a college-educated homeless woman is so rare that she immediately stands out. For agencies anxious to show results, college-educated women—regardless of race or ethnicity—may be easiest to place in above–minimum wage jobs. They are singled out for the best job and housing placements and often receive more respectful treatment than those with less education. Sharon and Lisa may also appear to caseworkers to be similar to them, so the usual staff/client relationship—with its unequal power and inherent distrust of homeless women—does not apply in the same way.

CONCLUSION

Even as shelters focus on poverty and the lack of low-income housing, they do so within the context of utilizing a range of "disciplinary technologies" to control and mold homeless women. Shelters do not simply house homeless people; they also regulate and dominate them. Disciplinary techniques go beyond monitoring shelter residents' activities, although certainly the staff wants to supervise daily activities by mandating job and housing searches, overseeing parenting choices, and managing residents' personal relationships. Significantly, however, controlling homeless women's daily activities occurs within the framework of changing "underclass" behaviors and values. Ideally, the various methods of surveillance allow staff to "know" homeless women, to see their motivations and values, which must be modified if homeless women are ever to become stably housed and part of the mainstream.

An important aspect of changing shelter residents' values and lifestyles is to separate homeless women from the culture of poverty and underclass circles perceived to have contributed to their homelessness. Thus observation and regulation of personal relationships becomes an important focus for shelter staff. Caseworkers discourage friendships and intimate relationships among homeless people, going so far as to define those who maintain friendships with other homeless people as "bad clients," as women who do not wish to change their dysfunctional lifestyles by rejecting others enmeshed in the culture of poverty.

When homeless women break shelter rules and complain about the staff, they not only criticize specific regulations but also resist representations of homelessness that blame homeless people for their circumstances.

Their resistance is shaped by the organization of shelters, by the focus on homeless deviance and individual explanations for poverty and homelessness. When surveillance and control are emphasized, homeless women's resistance will likely focus on avoiding revealing their actual activities and true motivations to caseworkers, appearing to comply when they are not, and deceiving caseworkers. Their resistance is also shaped by their dependence on the shelter system. Thus women in Phoenix shelters sometimes "play the part" of the deserving homeless or battered woman, fitting themselves into existing categories of need and appearing to bend to shelter rules and requirements.[44]

MEANINGS AND MYTHS
OF HOMELESSNESS
Housed People Speak

On the surface, people who are not homeless—ordinary, everyday housed people—appear to have little relationship to homelessness. They do not make policy. They cannot decide how and whether homelessness will be addressed, and they lack the resources to solve the problem of homelessness on their own. They may have little personal experience or interaction with homeless people. Yet housed people play an important role in generating understandings of homelessness. When pressed to discuss what homelessness means and why people become homeless, several common threads emerge in housed people's beliefs. These common threads represent—and help to further create—cultural constructions of homelessness; in other words, housed people reveal the shared, recognizable perceptions of homelessness that often go unspoken and unexplained. For this reason it is imperative to explore housed people's ideas in concert with homeless women's narratives and an investigation of the shelter system. These three elements together tell the story of homelessness in the United States.

Interviews with housed people suggest how thorny and difficult homelessness is as a cultural and political issue. As they talk, housed people shift back and forth between blame and pity, anger and guilt. They may empathize with homeless people while arguing that homelessness is a chosen lifestyle, sometimes reflecting incongruous views about the relationship between homelessness and poverty. Many housed people are compassionate toward the homeless, giving assistance to individuals or to charities. But they also question their charitable impulses. Articulating deep distrust of most homeless people, housed people fear the homeless pretend to be in need so they can get assistance they do not deserve. A further paradox exists when housed people base deservingness on a homeless person's perceived ambition or drive but at the same time use the very fact of homelessness as proof that the homeless lack motivation. Finally, housed people tend to define women and children as less able to care for themselves and, as a result, as more deserving of assistance than men. But women are also assumed to be primarily responsible for children and so are reviled for not properly caring for their offspring.

These contradictions and complexities become evident in the sections in this chapter where housed people's comments appear. Because their beliefs are complicated by inconsistencies and they are responding to multifaceted aspects of homelessness, most housed people's observations do not easily fit in any one section. In this sense the sections are inadequate, used more for organizational purposes than to definitively categorize a housed person's beliefs. Housed people's descriptions and analyses of homeless people create a complex, even tangled portrait of poverty and homelessness.

Interview responses attest to the resonance of homelessness as an issue for many nonhomeless people. The depth of emotion homelessness produces in housed people indicates that it is anything but an esoteric policy issue distant from most housed people's lives. Although housed people react to homelessness in diverse ways, relating a battery of emotions from pity and guilt to anger and fear, such reactions are in general surprisingly intense. Their reactions and beliefs often stem from personal experiences with homeless people, most frequently arising from interactions with people on the street begging for money or food or selling the local homeless newspaper, the *Grapevine*. Sometimes a housed person has been exposed to stories about homelessness through television news programs, and that combined with passing panhandlers on the street corner is enough to produce certain beliefs about homelessness. Other people come to their views through employment at a social service agency, volunteer work at a shelter or food line, or their own personal experiences with homelessness or near homelessness.

Just as shelter caseworkers rely on single-issue explanations for homelessness, many housed people also tend to separate homeless people into distinct categories. Even though they comment on the myriad reasons for homelessness, nonhomeless people generally believe one person is homeless strictly because of behavior, attitude, or mental illness while another is homeless only because of job loss, low-income housing shortages, or low wages. Few assume that many low-income people become homeless for a combination of reasons that include both low wages and individual choices or lifestyle. Even fewer ground their comments in a discussion of poverty or note the effects of longtime poverty on housing status. In many ways housed people's responses reflect the adherence to specialism they see in the organization of homelessness policy on both national and local levels.

In addition to single-issue explanations for homelessness, housed people fundamentally mistrust the homeless. Housed people wonder whether panhandlers who claim to be homeless may actually be housed and whether those who claim to need shelter for circumstances beyond their control are actually homeless by choice. If homeless people do misrepresent themselves, housed people surmise, it is because they do not truly deserve assistance. Those who are worthy of help—the hardworking, situationally homeless— are believed to be few in number. The majority distort their reasons for needing shelter precisely because they do not intend to change. This undeserving majority tries to get assistance with as little effort as possible, an orientation many housed people believe is indicative of the lifestyle and value system that caused their homelessness.

THE DESERVING POOR: WOMEN AS VICTIMS

Housed people struggle to distinguish the deserving homeless from the undeserving in part because they do not want to overlook the few homeless people who are worthy of assistance. Those few deserving people—mostly women—are often seen as "victims." Charles Hoch and Robert Slayton have written of advocates' and researchers' efforts in the 1980s to define the current homeless population as victims of crises and economic downturns beyond their control, to characterize the "new" homeless in a way that distinguishes them from the wino and skid row identities of old. The authors argue that such a construction was advanced as part of a "politics of compassion" that would reinvent the "new" homeless as victims of Reaganite cuts in the social safety net.[1] Disentangling the homeless from a conservative stigma of undeserving poor led to some increases in funding and support for shelters and other programs. At the same time, however, it "casts [the homeless] as passive and dependent subjects of care."[2] As David Wagner contends, that characterization "has obscured the strengths of the homeless and the very poor."[3] And I suggest that it has contributed to the perception that those who cannot be interpreted as weak and helpless—the prerequisites for victimhood—are wholly personally responsible for their homelessness.

Housed people's interview responses indicate that in attempting to get sympathy, homeless people must first be defined as "passive and dependent" victims—much in the manner Hoch and Slayton and Wagner proposed. But most housed people use the idea of passivity in complex ways. The perception that some homeless people are victimized by circumstances beyond their control is tempered by the simultaneous belief that both the deserving *and* the undeserving homeless are dependent and passive. Indeed many housed people imply that low-income people as a group can be defined by their passivity. They simply float through life without having goals and a work ethic that encourage them to push forward in the face of adversity. This belief makes it difficult for housed people to distinguish between deserving and undeserving homeless people based on the passive, helpless persona. Somewhat paradoxically, the perceived general passivity or lethargy that taints the homeless is assumed to result from a conscious, active choice to eschew "mainstream" values of productivity and vigor.

Understood to be weak, dependent, and appreciative of "our" help, white women with children are most likely to be thought of as victims in the sense Hoch and Slayton discussed.[4] Such a demarcation of the deserving homeless relies on an intersection of paternalistic definitions of the dependent poor—as inferior to the mainstream because they need assistance and are humble enough to accept it—and of women—as less able to take care of themselves than men. Robert Coates, in his book on homelessness, provides an example of such convictions in his discussion of homeless women and children:

> Women—women whom we men in the chivalrous world have been taught to revere, and to tenderly care for, to protect and fight wars for. Women who are vulnerable, who ought not to be abandoned. Women who may be very sick, in the agony of depression and madness, in cold and in want. Women being robbed, beaten, raped with impunity. Women living in barbarism. If men love not women, whom will they love?[5]

According to Coates, women must be "saved" from homelessness because they are, in essence, the "weaker sex." Thus it is more barbarous for women to be homeless than it is for men and easier to pity rather than blame them. Although the increasingly acerbic response to welfare recipients indicates a diminishing tolerance for women who rely on the state for support, men have in general been held to a higher expectation of economic self-reliance than women have.[6] Women—particularly white women with children—could depend financially on a man or even, in some historical periods, the state and retain their full humanity. This is clearly racialized: black, Latina, or Native American women are rarely held up in public discourse as the icons "men in the chivalrous world have been taught to revere."[7]

Housed people's inclination to sympathize more with homeless women than with homeless men exists uncomfortably alongside their tendency to conflate women who receive welfare benefits with homeless women. In fact, many housed people slip back and forth between a discussion of homeless women and (housed) women on welfare as if the two were equivalent. Phoenix housed people, reflecting a general trend among the U.S. public, show less support for welfare in the form of cash aid than for other antipoverty programs such as Head Start or Job Corps and thus in general express little compassion for welfare recipients.[8]

Lars Eighner, a formerly homeless man who wrote a book about his fight for daily survival while precariously housed and living on the streets, gives voice to the welfare queen stereotype. As his comments indicate, the welfare queen image is not strictly limited to black women. Although he rarely mentions women (indeed they are conspicuously absent from gatherings of the homeless in several different cities), Eighner does use them as a foil to underscore his own relative deservingness as an honest and hardworking homeless person. He describes his attempts to secure assistance from various agencies:

> Wherever I went I noticed an enormously fat blond woman, at least twice my size, with two screaming, undernourished brats. She fared better than I at the public and private agencies; they could hardly do enough for her. The waifs were about three and five years of age. The peculiar thing is that they were never the same children. She had a different pair with her every day. So I must assume she had at least sixteen children under the age of six, and I can hardly begrudge her all the assistance she received.[9]

Eighner calls up the stereotype of the woman who, by cheating the system, grows literally and figuratively fat on welfare largesse while the children (whether hers or someone else's) go hungry. And Eighner himself, to the extent that he cannot garner benefits to keep himself adequately fed and sheltered, loses as a result of the woman's gains.

This slippage between welfare recipients and homeless women also brings race to the fore. Interestingly, Eighner uses a white woman for his example, but historically African American women have been most vilified as the symbolic freeloading welfare queen—reflecting the idea that black women should not be dependent on the state. This idea has its basis in "nineteenth-century culture in the United States, [which] stereotyped White women as too frail and dainty to undertake physical labor, [but] Black women were viewed as beasts of burden and subjected to the same demeaning labor and hardships as Black men."[10] Fifty or more years later, in the 1930s, many black women were excluded from the Aid to Dependent Children program. Mimi Abramovitz quotes a "southern public assistance field supervisor":

> The number of Negro cases is few due to the unanimous feeling on the part of the staff and board that there are more work opportunities for Negro women and to their intense desire not to interfere with local labor conditions. The attitude that they have always gotten along, and that "all they'll do is have more

children" is definite. . . . There is hesitancy on the part of the lay boards to advance too rapidly over the thinking of their own communities, which see no reason why the employable Negro mother should not continue her usually sketchy seasonal labor or indefinite domestic service rather than receive a public assistance grant.[11]

The legacy of their exclusion from the nineteenth-century "cult of true womanhood" has been the expectation—continuing in the present day—that African American women will be self-reliant and autonomous.[12] Housed people are therefore less likely to use African American women as the embodiment of the helpless victim generally associated with deserving homeless women.

The slippage between welfare recipients and homeless women also points to the invisibility of the latter. More pronounced than housed people's tendency to sympathize with or blame homeless women, then, is their general ignorance of the presence of women within the homeless ranks. When asked to picture a homeless person, the overwhelming majority of housed people describe a tattered, bearded, dirty man pushing a shopping cart. To the extent that housed people appear to lack immediate referents and symbols when considering women's homelessness, homeless women are characterized as not representative of the "real" homeless population.

Like the association of women with welfare, in the public mind women are also identified with children. This connection sometimes increases housed people's sympathy for homeless women, but it can also undercut that sympathy. The presence of children is more likely to affect the conceptions people have of homeless women rather than those of men, in part because the nonhomeless correctly assume that women are more likely to have children with them. Cultural attitudes that perceive women as primarily responsible for raising children also sustain the association.

When housed people do argue that homeless women deserve compassion, it is usually in the context of their being identified with a "family," in particular with children. Lucy, a white housed woman, asserted that she responds to homeless people in significantly different ways depending on who they are: "If they are single men, I feel like they don't want to work for a living like the rest of America. If it is a family, I feel like all they need is a helping hand and they will be off the streets shortly." Lance, a white man in his late forties, supported the idea that families are categorically different than other homeless people. When asked who he thinks makes up the homeless population, Lance responded: "Predominantly single people. The ones with families usually aren't chronically homeless because they have a priority to take care of their family. Usually for them it's because they lost their job or fell on hard times. They don't stay homeless because they're usually looking for work." For Lance and Lucy, the presence of women and children indicates that homelessness resulted from crises that could not be controlled, whereas a single man in particular is expected to be able to take care of himself no matter what crises occur.

Notwithstanding the greater support for families some housed people expressed, other people's reactions call into question whether any group of homeless people is seen as a vulnerable population worthy of assistance. In fact, the notion that mothers are considered more deserving of help is undermined by a belief that homeless women are not responsible just for themselves but are also hurting their children when they become homeless. Housed people sometimes single out homeless mothers for especially harsh condemnation. Linda, a thirty-five-year-old white graphic designer, vilified homeless mothers: "I feel abject disgust for the women who use their kids to try to get money on the street corners. . . . If it were me, I would do everything possible to protect my children and keep them off the street. It seems like I never see those women without a cigarette, or they're more adequately protected clothingwise than their children. The children aren't protected from the filth or the cold or the heat." Karen, a white receptionist in her early twenties, concurs with Linda, basing her personal animosity toward homeless families primarily on her sympathy for their children. When asked about her emotional responses to homeless people, Karen stated: "Nothing. Only if it's a family I get angry! If the adults want to live a life of homelessness, don't drag your children into it. The children need a safe place to live and [to] have food and warm clothes."

Although Karen's comments are not gender-specific, most of the other housed people who singled out family homelessness made it clear that they consider homeless families to consist primarily of women and children. Christine, a white editorial assistant in her mid-forties, vacillated among censuring women for failing to support their children, comparing her own superior work ethic to theirs, and stating that she understands how difficult it would be for her to support children without her husband's second income:

> I work very hard to support my family, and I would do anything [to remain housed]; I'd sling hamburgers if I had to . . . but I guess there might be reasons I can't even comprehend why people don't work.
>
> I've been approached by women asking for money for milk for their babies, and they have a full pack of cigarettes. There are people that don't know any better who have lived generation after generation on welfare. If they work, they lose health care. If I was on my own I'd be below the poverty line, so I understand why some don't work because they'd lose their benefits.

Christine's contradictory statements shift back and forth between criticism and empathy. Underlying her inability to decide whether homeless women deserve reproach beyond others or whether they warrant more understanding, however, is the fact that she identifies with homeless mothers more than she does with other homeless people. This kind of comparison and connection, albeit beneath the surface of many women's comments, may explain in part their strong feelings about mothers. Seeing homeless women may remind housed women of their own vulnerabilities.

"I JUST THINK, 'AM I A SUCKER?'"

As the arguments over perceptions of homeless women and families indicate, housed people hold varying views of the homeless. Many individual housed people advance inconsistent explanations for the existence of homelessness and justifications for their behavior toward panhandlers and others perceived to be without housing. For example, the comments of Marielena, a seventeen-year-old Latina waitress, reveal the contradictory nature of her understandings of homelessness, forged through regular contact with homeless men in her neighborhood:

> I feel sorry for them. It's the kind of sorry that I want to help them. I want to go to my house, find blankets, give them food, and even take them clothing. I sometimes give change, but there's times they make me angry. You do it once or twice, and they expect it all the time. I would do it if I knew it wasn't going for alcohol. . . .
> I don't think anyone wants to be homeless. What I think happens a lot is that people lose their jobs. Also, a big one is depression, giving up on life. . . . Everyone fucks up, but it doesn't mean I'm going to go and throw my life away. Some people just take things different. They don't want to be homeless.

In referring to her interactions with a group of homeless people, Marielena described the compassion, charitable impulses, distrust, and anger repeated by many respondents in this study. One of her comments in particular stands out as a commonly recurring one. Marielena expressed frustration at her inability to ensure that her assistance is not misdirected, that it is not going to undeserving alcoholics rather than truly needy people who are not "throwing their lives away."

A number of other housed people from varied backgrounds and income levels also asserted their suspicions that homeless people are misrepresenting themselves. Herb, a forty-five-year-old white realtor and owner of a construction company, argued that most people claiming to be homeless may simply be trying to cull money from unsuspecting "suckers":

> When I see a homeless person, or one that purports to be homeless, asking for money on the corner, I suspect that there's a four-to-one chance that I'm going to get screwed when I give them money. I just think, "Am I a sucker?" When you

see a guy who purports to be homeless and has better shoes than I do or a nice watch, you start wondering. And yet you know that there are some who are legitimate, but I suspect that those are the people you don't see on the corner.

Herb traces his beliefs about homeless people to his interactions with precariously housed men with whom he works:

I deal with a lot of people who are right on the border of homelessness. A large proportion of the people employed by my company are those who live in the hotels where you pay on a weekly basis; it's the last stop before homelessness and the first step out of it to live at the hotels. . . . A number of my men have drifted in and out of their situations. These are the kind of people who come in with a disaster story every week about why they need an advance. Most of them are drug addicts or alcoholics, which is frustrating because there's a labor shortage. They don't even realize that they're telling the same story over and over again.

Herb's personal experiences with a certain population of near-homeless men—those who do day labor or are sporadically employed—predispose him to suspect homeless people in general. The men he employs, according to Herb, do not "have any problem putting their hands out" and try to get by doing as little work as possible. He interprets this as proof that homeless people lack a work ethic or values similar to his own. Herb's assertions are reiterated by others in the Phoenix housed population: people feign homelessness to make money without effort, they stay in shelters because it represents a better alternative than work, and a "homeless lifestyle" provides an attractive option.

Given housed people's frustration with what they believe is constant dishonesty on the part of homeless people, the homeless who appear to be telling the truth may be rewarded. As Jill's comments indicate, even homeless people who would otherwise be defined as undeserving grow in some housed people's estimation if they are honest about wanting money for alcohol: "I've given money to one homeless man who said he was 'shaking like a whore in church' and asked if I had any spare change at the time. His honesty appealed to me. I used to buy cigarettes for a homeless woman who would sit outside the 7-11 by my house. She would give me the money, and I would go into the store and buy them, Carltons. She wasn't allowed in the store because they said she stank." Thus the desire to feel that one has not been "suckered" can extend to giving money for or assisting homeless people in the very habits or lifestyles that would generally taint the homeless as undeserving of help. Jill's actions are somewhat rare, however, in the sense that her admiration for honesty translated to monetary handouts. More usual is the reaction of guarded support or amusement that a homeless person would be willing to admit that he or she wanted money for alcohol, but a handout follows infrequently.

"REWARDING UNDESIRABLE ATTITUDES"

Themes of work, productivity, and personal responsibility weave through many housed people's discussions of homelessness. The housed public tends to blame homeless people themselves for their failure to remain housed, perceiving that they have failed "just as a business person might who has invested wrongly."[13] In other words, often little distinction is made between the low-income person who cannot make ends meet on her salary at a low-paying job or on her welfare benefits and the wealthy person who loses his or her money as a result of an unwise investment or profligate spending. Both lend credence, in the minds of housed people, to the presumed disintegration of the work ethic, and both provide opportunities to demand that "personal responsibility" be reworked into the country's moral fabric. In both cases personal choices are thought to have brought each unfortunate to his or her current predicament.

Linda pointed to the refusal to take "personal responsibility" as the key reason people become homeless:

> I see a lot of this as lack of personal forethought and responsibility in terms of education, drug and alcohol abuse, and a lack of desire, that someone will pick up the pieces for you. Primarily it's a lack of educational drive. I see these college students I work with lacking morality—they take food stamps and don't have any problem with going on total welfare! I don't see them making a total effort to do anything! If they ever graduate I can't imagine what kind of adults they'll be.

Linda answers a general question about the causes of homelessness with commentary about college students who "lack morality" and "sponge off the system." Although she indicates awareness of homeless people who clearly are not college students, mentioning those who panhandle on street corners, her primary analysis of homelessness centers on those who squander their considerable resources. Homeless people, then, are those who simply choose to waste their talents, resources, or chances in life because they are too lazy or dissolute to work for their rewards. A forty-five-year-old white attorney, Georgia, also underscores the importance of attitudes and values, implying that homeless people lose housing because they do not want to work and do not value productivity:

> If I gave money to a homeless person, I feel that I would be contributing to the problem and encouraging them to become a beggar and rewarding undesirable attitudes and a lack of long-term values and goals. I have contributed to charities

because I feel they will make better use of the money and hopefully help these people change their attitudes.

We all experience financial ups and downs in our lives. I have been very close to bankruptcy and had periods where debt far exceeded my assets. It would have been easy to bury my problems in abuses (i.e., drinking . . .) instead of changing course and addressing the problems.

A homeless person's predicament is again compared to the situation of a well-off person who has invested unwisely or squandered her money on superfluous items or leisure activities. Both are equally responsible for their financial status. Both need to rectify the situation by facing their problems, addressing them rationally, and finding solutions.

Sheila, another white housed woman, also emphasized the lack of "motivation, drive, [and] ambition" that differentiates financially stable housed people from the homeless. For Sheila, this perceived lack of drive permeates everything about the homeless:

It is frustrating to observe the growing numbers of these people with no programs on-line to help them. But they must also show a genuine desire to improve their conditions. It bothers me that so many of them refuse to keep clean. Even in Third World countries where the poorest conditions exist, one sees more attempts (and successes) at cleanliness—Haiti being a perfect example. Where is the pride in these people? There are public facilities with indoor plumbing, and still they choose to be as they are.

If homeless people cannot even generate enough concern for their personal hygiene to make efforts to wash, clearly they have little desire to change their personal circumstances. Similarly, Sam, a white professional in his early fifties, associates the lack of drive with a different value system:

I've dealt with [homeless people] in the construction industry. Out of desperation some have joined labor pools—they're living in their cars or at camps. . . . Their set of values are intriguing. They have the feeling that somebody owes them, the bitterness. They'll not try to present themselves in a way—they're concerned on the job [with] how little they have to do. One guy looked pretty dirty, and we were pouring concrete; this guy didn't want to get his sneakers dirty. They were going out that night, probably to get drunk. That's the morals and values problem. They think they're too good and everyone owes them. I get in there myself, and I'm the owner of the company.

I spent a year in Vietnam in a worse position than most of these guys. There's no excuse for the noncleanliness level, that's the values issue I was talking about. In Vietnam I'd find a mud puddle so I could wash my hair and get my teeth clean. They [homeless people] don't seem to have the hygiene.

Like Sheila, Sam also uses the dirty and unkempt appearance of the men in the day labor pool as visible proof that they are too lazy or immature to apply themselves. Further, they do not look beyond immediate pleasures (like getting drunk) to work for future financial stability.

"REJECTION OF THE AMERICAN LIFESTYLE"

Demands for personal responsibility often reflect discourses about the individualist, self-reliant "American character" and the necessity of productivity to maintain one's status as full citizen. Thus the theme of personal responsibility is often interwoven with a reverence for productivity as a central component of "Americanness." One of the few housed people to stress the general poverty of the homeless, Joyce, a twenty-year-old data processor, also emphasized homeless people's disassociation from the "American lifestyle": "I would think that the majority of the homeless population comes from a lower economic background. Their resources—financial—are limited, and this contributes to their inability to deal with everyday life. Perhaps the presence of many stresses leads to their loss of hope and ambition, which will eventually lead to their rejection of the 'American lifestyle.'" To lose one's "ambition," then, is a key development in becoming homeless. Where the "American lifestyle" is contingent upon ambition, productivity, and some degree of wealth or at least the desire to accumulate it, homeless people lack a primary marker of "Americanness."

The notion of "Americanness" is often racialized; many white housed people use "American" interchangeably with "Anglo" or, more specifically, to refer to nonimmigrant Anglos, in addition to identifying Americanness with productivity. Some white housed people perceive Latinos—in particular Chicanos—as too "different" to be considered American, regardless of their citizenship status. Further, these housed people claim that poor or homeless Chicanos are to blame for their own circumstances because they do not want to work to climb the social or economic ladder. In fact in Phoenix, where racism against Chicanos runs high, whites often refer to Latinos—homeless or not—as if all of them are poor and receiving welfare benefits.[14] Thus Chicanos are doubly distant from the "American lifestyle": stereotyped as lazy foreigners, they are categorized as the undeserving poor because of their ethnic background and their presumed related lack of productivity.

Helen, a forty-six-year-old white housed woman, associates class status with different ethnicities, where poverty implies an aversion to work and to the "American dream":

> You have all these ladies, they're ready to pop, they walk across the border to San Diego and they have their babies, so their babies are automatically citizens. So they get all our free medical, they get all this help. Wait a minute: you're not here working, you're not contributing to the system. . . . For some reason you know the Oriental—the boat people that came—they didn't become the

siphons as much as the people from south of the border. And the Asians, the Cubans, they believe in the American dream; for some reason, I don't know if it's the culture or the people or the background, but for some reason these guys are more like the Europeans who saw that this is a country of opportunity: if you're willing to work hard, you'll do well, where the other people are like, "you guys are filthy rich, just give us your money."

In Helen's view, by definition Chicanas are unproductive and therefore un-American, selfishly using the generosity and wealth of the United States to their own benefit. Yet Chicanos are highly visible laborers in Phoenix; many are engaged in service work and difficult manual labor.

Helen's own near miss with homelessness may explain in part why she stereotypes Chicanas; she wants to ensure that she is not mistaken for one of the mass of undeserving poor or homeless people. In attempting to call upon whiteness as a marker of deservingness, Helen must emphasize her ethnicity and distinguish her experiences, work ethic, and status from those of non-Anglos. If race or ethnicity provides a convenient marker of deservingness, Helen's comments suggest that it may not be automatic; nonwhites must be sufficiently marked as different and undeserving for whites to be perceived as deserving.

Helen and her five children nearly became homeless when she and her husband divorced and she discovered that her $31,000 annual salary did not cover the house and car payments and food and clothing expenses for herself and her children. Several months after their separation Helen's husband claimed he had lost his job, child support payments stopped, and he cut off contact with the family. Helen's economic situation rapidly fell apart:

We had a five bedroom, two bath in a nice neighborhood, nice lifestyle; it's probably a lower-middle-class neighborhood, but it was comfortable. . . . [After the divorce] I lost my house, I lost our reliable transportation. . . . I made three dollars a week too much, I couldn't get help from welfare. So there's that group of people like me, you know, you just make a little too much. You don't make enough to live, you know the kids have one pair of shoes where the soles are flopping apart, they have no coats, we have no money to buy anything.

Everyone thought, "Oh, here's this happy Mormon family," five kids, you know, they have the stereotype. They didn't know there was no man and I was going through the divorce and foreclosure. . . . They have no idea! You're living paycheck to paycheck, and all you can pay is the food and to keep going. I couldn't make mortgage payments. I was just barely meeting the electricity to keep the service on.

From December through April I made hundreds and hundreds of calls, looking for a house [to rent], and the lower-income homes, they're snapped up just like that. So I'm at work, and I'd call at lunchtime and go to look at it after work and it's already gone. In all my phone calls that I made—and it was ten to fifty a day—it was either the rent was too high, I had too many kids, or the house was gone. Everything in my price range was always gone, or they'd want first and last month's rent plus deposit, you're looking at $2,000, $2,500, where am I going to get that? So we were facing going on the street. The judge told me I needed to be out of there in three days, and I had nowhere to go.

Finally, the leadership of Helen's church agreed to help. They wrote a check for the first and last month's rent for a house and signed a statement agreeing to pay the rent if Helen did not.

In contrast to the undeserving Chicanos Helen derides, she defines herself as a hardworking victim of circumstances beyond her control. She emphasizes her job, the symbols of middle-class status of her former life—a house, furniture, and cars—and the intense effort she put into finding housing to separate herself from the undeserving homeless. And she uses her whiteness as a sign of her status as an "American," a productive person with a strong work ethic.

Yet Helen's use of race to distance herself from other impoverished people, in particular from the category of undeserving poor, does not fully explain the way she racializes poverty and "Americanness." This becomes clear when considering similar comments made by Anglos who were never precariously housed. For example, Christine, another white housed woman, argues that Latinos—in particular recent Mexican immigrants—represent the undeserving poor:

> I think there are a lot of people who come here and just take and don't give back, like the fathers who don't work except for minimum wage jobs. These men can have several families and float [from family to family], live off Aid to Dependent Children that the women receive, and the women don't work. . . . I only had two kids because that's all I can take care of. The rest of these people have five or six kids, and unfortunately most of their kids will live the same way, that's all they know.

Christine resents such men's apparent ability to elude the strictures she contends circumscribe her life choices. Her comments suggest that they work at minimum wage jobs because they are lazy, not because they do not have the skills to get other jobs or because they lack documentation and must settle for the most difficult or demeaning work. The evidence Christine cites for Latino laziness—the acceptance of minimum wage jobs—suggests that those who work, even *as* they work, are constructed as lazy. This turns on its head stereotypes of low-income African Americans as lazy and undeserving of assistance where the evidence is in their supposed outright rejection of work and acceptance of living on welfare. The simultaneous arguments that Latinos are "coming over the border to take our jobs" and that they are lazy and just want benefits suggest that conceptions of homelessness and poverty must be understood within their specific local bounds. Cultural conceptions of deservingness may be circumscribed by national policy and institutional pressures, but reconfiguration and reinvention occur constantly on a local scale.

Other interviews reflect similar attempts to base deservingness on race or ethnicity. Rhonda, a nineteen-year-old white student, has come close to living on the street herself, and she has relied on friends to keep her from becoming homeless when she lacked her own apartment. Although she believes "there's a percentage [of homeless people] that are from my neighborhood or have similar values," Rhonda generally does not extend her understanding of homelessness to include her own experiences. Unlike Christine's and Helen's remarks, Rhonda concentrates on blacks as the categorical undeserving poor: "I think the blacks do have a different set of values, and I'm not saying they're not as good as mine, but . . . they have different standards. Among the homeless, the ones that want to be or are career homeless people, they do have their own thoughts about acceptable standards of living that are different from mine. . . . Also, it's the Malthusian or Darwin idea that some people have to live like that and some people don't." Rhonda reflects the arguments of other middle-class housed people who experienced near misses with homelessness. Although some assume that most homeless people have resources similar to their own, including friends and family members to turn to for financial assistance, others separate their own circumstances from their definitions of "the homeless." Rhonda does this by implying that the homeless are a different race and class than she is.

"ANYONE CAN BECOME HOMELESS"

On the other hand, some middle-class, currently housed people who were threatened with or actually experienced homelessness made connections between their own histories and those of other homeless people. David, a twenty-five-year-old white man, and Sandra, a nineteen-year-old Latina, formerly struggled with homelessness. Sandra, who works at a community agency to assist the elderly, had been homeless for several months a year before the interview took place. Sandra believes "anyone can become homeless," and although she has little disposable income herself, she gives money when she can to people she encounters on the street and spends time speaking with them. Likewise, David's two years of homelessness have increased his empathy and understanding of those living on the street or in shelters. He described his history: "I was asked to leave the house by the folks after getting arrested. I didn't have money for the first month, last month, and security deposit. It took two years for me to be able to get that kind of money together and get an apartment. I had a job. I was pulling my hair out—my self-esteem was for shit. I was paranoid I'd be arrested for sleeping in parking lots in my van." David, who currently works as a carpenter for $15,000 a year, continues to have financial problems because of his low wages but has been stably housed for five years. Drawing on his own story, David suggests that many people are working when they become homeless, but since wages have not kept pace with the cost of living, they remain precariously housed and financially insecure: "In the economy we must survive in, sometimes we have to make financial choices (do I pay this or this), which may cause us to get behind in another area, which soon snowballs until the rent is late, later, and then you get evicted."

Like David, some housed people look beyond a supposed laziness in the homeless to emphasize the impact of the economy and job opportunities. Those housed people who have some connection to social service work are more articulate in identifying the structural reasons for people's homelessness. This suggests that even though interviews with homeless and battered women's shelter staffs reveal sometimes suspicious and blaming attitudes toward the homeless, overall they and other caseworkers in poverty agencies tend to have a more comprehensive understanding of the effect of national economic forces on homeless people than the general public does. Pam, a white employment counselor, stated that people become homeless as a result of "changes in life situations, circumstances—loss of job, health problems, lack of financial resources." She argued that these issues—along with "lack of support from family" and mental, physical, or emotional problems that "make them incapable of functioning adequately"—comprise the most pertinent reasons for homelessness: "I'm sure there are a few people who beg for money or handouts because that is easier than having a regular job. However, I believe the vast majority of homeless are in that situation because they cannot afford permanent housing or keep a job or have physical/mental problems and that we need to create more ways to get them off the streets." Although Pam, like most housed people, maintained that some homeless people are undeserving of assistance, she inverted the more prevalent belief that most are irresponsible, lazy, or homeless by choice, arguing that they represent a small fraction of the homeless population. She cited job assistance, low-interest housing loans, and more temporary housing as key programs needed to assist the homeless.

Larissa, a seventy-year-old retired teacher, concurred with Pam's assessment of why people become homeless, providing a more consistently structural explanation for homelessness than most other housed people did. She pointed to the roles of economic restructuring and government policies in increasing the risk of homelessness:

> The economics of our country are forcing people into homelessness. There's just no jobs; many [homeless people] aren't physically or mentally able to hold a job, and there's no safety net for them.

Most of the people in the shelters are Anglos. The Hispanics have the same problems with homelessness, but it doesn't show. They're living in the orchards under tarps. The Hispanic families tend to help each other more to live with relatives and friends. They'll crowd four families into one apartment rather than let someone live on the streets. But that's a form of homelessness too.

Larissa empathizes with homeless people, believing most are people like her who have simply "hit on bad times." She argues that prospects for economic advancement are circumscribed by dwindling employment opportunities at which low-income and working-class people without a college education can make a living wage. Larissa believes her currently more stable financial circumstances are largely a result of different opportunities available in the 1950s and 1960s: "I grew up very poor, and in my decade of growing up, education was the way to get out of poverty. Now you need so much education to get a step up. It's harder to climb out of poverty."

Regarding which policies will best respond to homelessness, Larissa's ideas sound much like the arguments of many homeless women. Many women in family shelters suggest that more individualized treatment by shelter staff would make the shelters more humane and improve residents' chances for future financial stability. Likewise, Larissa posited:

We need to look at each individual person and develop a plan for each based on their needs. The people who are emotionally ill, retarded, or whose minds have been dulled by years of alcoholism need housing and treatment programs, and that's about half the homeless. The other half are people who've had tough breaks, who need to be retrained, get help with jobs. Of course, in our society there aren't enough jobs to go around, and no matter how much job training there is, we need more jobs or people will stay unemployed.

Like Pam and Larissa, Jim initially also focused on job opportunities— among other issues—when he talked about homelessness. In answer to the first question put to him about the reasons for homelessness, Jim, a white accountant who works for the state, blamed shortcomings in federal government programs: "The system has failed. I think the government system fails. It starts with schools at an early age, their parents get failed along the way, so they can't bring them up well. If they lose their jobs we don't have enough retraining. I don't go along with this business that people need to pull themselves up by their bootstraps. The government is not there to help them and should be. It hinders them." Although Jim argued that homelessness results from job loss and the lack of retraining programs, at the same time he indicated that homeless people as a group suffer from flawed value systems. In fact, as the interview progressed Jim increasingly ascribed to homeless people a lack of motivation and questionable attachment to work: "I think the backgrounds [of homeless people] are quite different [from mine]. I grew up in a pretty work-oriented family and society; education was valued. We were a strong family. I don't think a lot of people had that privilege." His suggestions about jobs and job training were countered by an emphasis on homeless people's disregard for the value of work. When asked whether any programs should be addressed to homelessness, however, and whether the government should be involved at any level, Jim slipped back into a discussion of jobs:

> There are programs that try to get these people jobs, so that needs to be explored and expanded. Somehow we need to provide education for the children that are involved in this mess. It gets a lot tougher with chronic homeless types, and I'm not blind to that. I know these people exist. I think you start working with those people you have the most probability for success with. You're not going to solve everyone's problem, and that's when charity comes in. You just keep feeding these people out of love and don't expect anything in return.

Jim's comments indicate that even among housed individuals more likely to favor federal government responsibility for addressing homelessness, a perceived lack of personal responsibility on the part of the homeless usually remains central. A housed person rarely feels as empathetic as Larissa; more often homeless people are accused of neglecting or even disdaining the values of hard work, thrift, and education, becoming homeless at least in part as a result of their indifference toward applying themselves at both the workplace and in school.

"ONE COMMON FACTOR—LOW SELF-ESTEEM"

Existing alongside the argument that homeless people lack motivation and could become stably housed by showing initiative and applying themselves is a therapeutic model that psychologizes the reasons for homelessness.[15] If low self-esteem, personality disorders, or mental illness cause homelessness, personal rehabilitation and counseling become the solutions. Housed people may see motivation and self-esteem as intertwining reasons for homelessness, as does Cami, an engineer who argues that although the homeless represent a variety of genders, races, and ethnicities:

> All backgrounds had to have one common factor—low self-esteem. They had no motivation to overcome hardship and survive catastrophe. What do I see? A huge population that never had the nurturing of a family or the consistent expectation of a good education. . . . Homelessness [and] juvenile delinquency are the result of *nonfamily* in our society. If family were paramount in our society, we would have far more educational support and as a result minimal delinquency and homelessness.

As opposed to linking motivation to a healthy work ethic, motivation here is connected to a person's self-perception, and self-perception is an outgrowth of family support and nurturance. Likewise, Nicole, a financial analyst, argues that the best programs for assisting the homeless would not involve government-sponsored job training, education, or long-term care. Rather, programs that stress self-esteem are the key to decreasing the number of homeless: "We need to assist the homeless in ways we're real comfortable with—to provide a shelter for them, have a place where they can work, and increase their self-esteem."

Louise similarly attributes homelessness to a "lack of self-esteem" and links becoming housed primarily to personal fortitude:

> I realize that some people lose their jobs, lose their possessions even. Women get taken advantage of a lot, but there are lots of opportunities people don't take advantage of. If your mind is at a poverty mentality, you won't take advantage of opportunities, you won't even see that they're there. Because something costs money, people will think that they can't do it. . . .
>
> I'm sure a lot of homeless are getting negative feedback, come from dysfunctional families that lower their self-esteem. Empowerment is an important key for people in shelters—anyone can get out poverty if they believe they can do it. . . . I think a lot of people could get out of it. I think affordable housing would help, but people have to learn that they can't live like pigs if they're going to live in a neighborhood where people don't live like that.

Louise implies that homelessness is little more than a "state of mind" to be overcome with positive thinking. Her perspective is particularly noteworthy because Louise herself nearly became homeless.

A well-paid professional, Louise explains that some years ago an associate "embezzled" all her money. Unable to pay for housing yet with most of her possessions and her job intact, Louise turned to friends and associates for help: "A realtor friend of mine let me live and sleep in houses [he was trying to sell or rent]. I didn't have to pay rent, and I never used the utilities unless someone was coming over." Other friends offered to lend her money, but Louise refused, not knowing when she could pay them back since she had to work herself out of her "six-figure debt."

Louise held two jobs, eventually paid off her debt, and achieved financial stability. A professional with a degree and many years' experience in the medical field, she has resources and salable skills. Undoubtedly, Louise's wealthy social network and secure job enabled her to pay off her debt and move to her own apartment more quickly than is possible for those living at a shelter, in an apartment with another family, or in their cars. Yet she gives no credence to the social networks or structural conditions that enabled her to avoid some of the challenges and humiliations associated with living in a shelter or on the street. Instead she focuses on self-esteem and personality traits to explain the difference between the homeless and the housed. Louise's comments make apparent the importance of the notion of "low self-esteem" to the public discourse on homelessness. The association of homelessness with self-esteem is derived from—and helps to produce—an individualized critique of poverty and the loss of housing.

Interestingly, when a conception of homelessness is linked to psychological problems, shelter residents are more likely to be seen as the deserving homeless than those on the street. They are deemed superior to those living in camps or on the street, since their residence at a shelter proves they want to do something to "help themselves." Their entrance into a program provides evidence that they are willing to admit they need help and achieves the first step in remaking themselves. Likewise, they are placed in opposition to people living on the street who have supposedly chosen homelessness. Maryann described those who apply to a shelter as "ready to change their lives" and as "people who want to get their life in order." In Maryann's understanding of homelessness, the truly homeless people live on the street, and those who are in a shelter are on the way to becoming stably housed: "I think there's a certain amount of people who once they see what it's like on the street want to turn their life around. There's a lot of homeless people who will never be ready to take that step." Robin concurred: "For those who are in shelters trying to get a job and maintain some income at all, I feel sorry for them. As far as the ones that stand on the street corners, most of them don't want to work."

In their article on network news coverage of homelessness, Richard Campbell and Jimmie Reeves illuminate a central aspect of the connection between self-esteem and homelessness and the more positive critique of those in shelters as opposed to the homeless on the street. Part of a therapeutic explanation for homelessness is the expectation that homeless people *should* feel ashamed of their lives, as would be expected of any "normal" person. Campbell and Reeves discuss representations of homeless people on the street by unpacking several news vignettes: "Most of the homeless people portrayed in these packages . . . lack the *common sense* to dig themselves out of their under-class hole. They even lack the 'sense' to hide from the scrutiny of the television camera, as would many 'invisible' homeless who feel that burden of shame and failure that goes with living on the margins."[16] When housed people argue that those in shelters are "taking the first step" by admitting they need help, then, the housed are referring to help with a person's self-esteem or work ethic, not with finding a job that pays a living wage or locating affordable housing. Homeless people's "rightful" position is one of shame; and rather than criticize the invasiveness, rules, and staff control in shelters, most housed people support such measures. The poor show they are worthy by indicating gratitude to social service agencies and deference to their authority,[17] and they prove they are one of "us" or at least are redeemable by feeling ashamed of their lives.

"I MOSTLY THINK OF THEM AS SCUM"

Distrust of the homeless sometimes feeds vehement anger toward them. Those who expressed such anger often spoke bitterly and even became enraged. When asked about her perceptions of the homeless, one housed woman retorted, "I guess I mostly think of them as scum." Donna, a white journalist in her twenties, argued angrily that people become homeless because they lack motivation: "I think we need to solve this problem, but I believe that many people feel that survival is possible on charity alone! If the signs and begging were banned, couldn't we instill a sense of integrity? Also, as long as we welcome teen pregnancy as an alternative, many neglected and unwanted children will grow up to be irresponsible, dependent, and unmotivated adults."

Not surprisingly, Donna's ideas about how to address homelessness are based on punitive and controlling devices. She wants any homeless program to be short term and "under contract with the government"; recipients would be forced to be "law-abiding and drug free, place their children in foster care," and agree not to get pregnant again. Any funds the program spent for a particular family would operate as a loan: "The money shall be repaid, with interest, to the government within a specified time frame, or those people shall be prosecuted and dealt with severely. This would ensure that those participants take the program seriously and feel compelled to take responsibility for themselves." Her reliance on contracts and prosecution speak to the extent to which Donna believes individual failings and a dissolute lifestyle explain homelessness. For her, homeless people, by virtue of being homeless, are not fit parents and should have their children taken from them—at least for the short term—and "contract with the government" not to become pregnant again.

Herb, whose comments appeared earlier, spoke scornfully about the homeless, his voice rising in anger several times during the interview. He described homeless women as childlike and unmotivated to change their situations: "If you reward something you get more of it. Our very substantial welfare state can be a large proportion of the population if you're looking at certain areas. If you're trained to be like a Pavlovian dog—push the button, get the money— you don't understand that you don't have the foresight or planning to get ahead in the world." Anger may sometimes grow out of a feeling of frustration that the problem seems insurmountable and that individuals can do little to solve it. But many housed people also indicate true disgust with and suspicion of the homeless. In fact, Donna and Herb, like many others, expressed a feeling of efficacy and believe homelessness would be significantly diminished if the homeless would adhere to the same work ethic they do. Both donate time and money to charities where, as Herb maintained, "I know the people who are handling the money have proper judgment, and the money will get to the people who need it." Homelessness is depicted less as an insurmountable social problem than as an indication of massive individual failing and a government system that refuses to punish people for their shortcomings; rather, it makes the problem worse by turning lazy people into "Pavlovian dogs." Dwayne, a forty-five-year-old white police officer, supported this analysis: "Comparing me, a mainstream person, with a homeless person, it's not incumbent upon me to provide for them. If I decide to do that, that's wonderful. But I don't think the government should force me."

Anger may also arise from fear of the homeless, in particular of homeless men. Those who spoke of fearing the homeless implied that they were part of a criminal element that included illegal drug users and the mentally ill. Andrea, a fifty-year-old teacher, admitted that she "avoids or ignores" homeless people whenever possible because she is convinced they pose a threat to her personal safety. Her fear that they will rob or assault her is only part of Andrea's anxiety. She suggested that homeless people might target her as a result of jealousy because she is more affluent than they are: "I have so much in comparison, and what's to keep them from taking it or wrecking it for me."

Elsa, a sixty-five-year-old retired Latina nurse, admitted to fearing for her personal safety around homeless men but also maintained that the fear of becoming homeless herself affects her interactions with the homeless, both men and women. A number of other housed women also mentioned a fear of becoming homeless, regardless of their financial situations or backgrounds. Elsa stated: "If I go to the grocery store, there's often a young man with a sign saying 'Will work for food.' I'd be afraid to pick someone up like that because I fear for my personal safety. I think we're all a little afraid to become personally involved with homeless people, and that makes me very sad. . . . [When I see homeless people I have] a feeling of fear that but for the grace of—whatever—there go I. It could happen to anyone at any time." Although Elsa began by defining her fears as situated within anxiety about personal safety, she switched suddenly to concerns that she herself could become homeless. Her words were repeated by Dolores, a white woman in her late thirties who works part-time at home while raising her child: "I feel compassion for [homeless people], like it easily could be me. . . . I'm lucky enough to have health insurance and a husband who has a job." Although she and Elsa relate similar emotions, Dolores's words suggest that the fear of becoming homeless can engender compassion for and some identification with homeless people rather than simply avoidance or disdain.

Like Elsa and Dolores, Patty, a twenty-five-year-old white woman, also pointed to her fear of becoming homeless as the prism through which she thinks about homeless people. Although she comes from an upper-middle-class background, she currently earns less than $12,000 a year as an intern at a city agency (although her father supplements her wages). She maintained: "Despite my education and privilege and even despite the fact that my family keeps their home open to me indefinitely, still I do not feel completely immune to becoming homeless." Likewise Laura, a social worker in her forties, reiterated many of the conflicted feelings others mentioned in regard to homelessness and maintained that they are connected to her own fear of being on the street: "[Homeless people make me] feel hopeless, helpless, sad, frustrated, angry—and afraid because I could become homeless too under the right (or wrong) circumstances. I always feel very grateful for what I do have."

Although all of these women are financially stable, Dolores and Patty rely on other (male) family members for their primary support—Dolores on her husband and Patty on her father. Elsa is retired and living on Social Security benefits, supplemented by her retirement pension. Their fears speak to women's general financial insecurity and lower incomes than those of their male counterparts during both work and retirement, as well as to their awareness of the feminization of poverty. Yet none has been precariously housed or shared many class-based similarities with homeless women. None lives on earnings or benefits significantly below the poverty line, as do women who are most likely to become homeless.

By contrast, Marielena's socioeconomic and educational status corresponds more closely to that of many homeless women. Having recently dropped out of high school, she nominally supports herself as a waitress and lives with her family. Marielena felt "insulted" by the interview questions, perhaps because she experiences herself as realistically at risk of becoming homeless. Indeed one of her relatives had recently experienced a bout of homelessness. She maintained that discussing homelessness is akin to "criticizing" homeless people: "I'm not homeless, and I feel insulted—embarrassed—by these questions, I don't know. But think of this. How do you think a homeless person feels; we don't know what goes through their heads. Imagine not knowing where you're going to sleep, when is the next time they're going to eat."

The common response of anger or pity sometimes gives way to real empathy on the part of the housed, as with Yolanda, a Latina high school student. Contact with homeless people makes her feel "sad and confused because I don't know what he's been through and why." Similarly, Alisa, a Latina teacher, stated: "When I see a homeless person, I feel sad and wish that things could be different for them. I wonder how they found themselves homeless and am amazed that in such a rich country as ours that such a thing as homelessness exists." Both Alisa and Yolanda try to put themselves in the homeless person's place, expressing concern for the person and curiosity about his or her life experiences. Alisa pointed out the dissonance between the existence of poverty and the wealth in the United States, opening the discussion to the systemic aspects of homelessness. Pete, a white engineer, takes up these issues in communicating his feelings about the homeless: "I feel sad that anyone has to live that way. I'm upset that our legislators and governor have such misplaced priorities—social and education programs keep getting cut while taxes on businesses are also cut."

It is relatively rare to hear housed people discuss homelessness in the context of critiquing political decisions or pointing to systemic issues that impact low-income people in general.[18] In fact, when most housed people express sadness regarding homeless people, it tends toward pity—which implies a status difference—rather than empathy—which rests on the housed person's ability to share in the pain of the homeless. In addition, when housed people like Sheila exhibit pity and guilt, they often grow out of the same convictions about homelessness from which anger and fear of the homeless develop.

"PEOPLE WHO FEEL FREEDOM WITHOUT A WHOLE LOT OF POSSESSIONS"

The conventional explanation for housed people's disassociation from the homeless—that they maintain distance to calm their fear of becoming homeless themselves—helps to account for some housed people's conflicted emotions about homeless people. It cannot explain, however, the combination of "hatred and longing" some housed people exhibit toward the homeless. In his analysis of nineteenth-century blackface minstrelsy and working-class whites' celebration, exploitation, and derision of black culture, Eric Lott points to the complex reaction toward the "other" that encompasses both disdain and envy of the lifestyle the other is perceived to embody.[19] Through his analysis, Lott insists that envy and repulsion can exist simultaneously in the appropriation and caricature of the culture and identity of the other.

Although his analysis is attuned to very different concerns than those inherent in late-twentieth-century homelessness, Lott may help to provide an explanatory framework for housed people's argument that homelessness is a chosen lifestyle—a perception that resounds throughout cultural understandings of homelessness. Even for those homeless not explicitly placed by housed people into the category of homeless by choice—in particular, families are usually excluded—the perception remains that all homelessness results at least in part from personal choice.

A number of housed men expressed both disdain and a certain admiration for the perceived "choice" of some homeless men to "leave their troubles behind" and live a "carefree" lifestyle. Although Sam declared disgust with many homeless people, in particular for their lack of motivation and concomitant demand for assistance, he took a different tack when he discussed those he insists choose homelessness. He displayed a grudging admiration for those

> Who've gotten tired of the system and have tried to get ahead, but they say the heck with it, I want an easy way out and want to live in lala land. . . . There are those who want to live the way they do—the hobo. Hey, they're taking responsibility for themselves, and then it's their right as long as they're not infringing on anyone else. They have a place to sleep, scrounge for food. They're saying, hey, leave me alone, let me live my life.

Lance, who like Sam is a middle-class white professional in his early fifties, supports the concept of the homeless man as self-reliant wayfarer: "I've met people who like being homeless. They like to wander. They're like the old-fashioned hobo. They're not always homeless, though; they work to get by, going from city to city." Zachary, in a similar demographic group as Lance and Sam, argued that "40 percent" of the homeless choose their lifestyles: "A third major category would be choice, people who feel freedom without a whole lot of possessions." Still others suggested that a number of the homeless are involved in a journey of self-discovery, putting aside the more mundane responsibilities of day-to-day life to pursue "freedom" and ruminate on larger philosophical questions.

The wandering hobo concept, used almost exclusively by housed men to describe homeless men, speaks to gender roles and the construction of masculinity in multiple ways. Men, of course, have traditionally had greater cultural and material responsibility for financially supporting a family. In their simultaneous disgust for and admiration of some homeless people, housed men display a rejection of the traditional male provider role, if only metaphorically. All the men in this study who suggested that homelessness is associated with the romance of the road were in their late forties or early fifties, having grown up during the 1950s when expectations that they would fulfill the male provider role shaped them significantly. Zachary described homeless men as having had many of the same influences he did while growing up: "Broadly speaking, many [homeless men] will be my age and have grown up with comparable influences: by the feel of the culture, by the 1950s. . . . There was a certain comfort, a range of expectations that are shared: typical family roles, that the business of life was to raise a family and provide for their success in life in some level of comfort."

As Ruth Rosen has argued, a 1950s "oppositional culture," represented by Jack Kerouac's On the Road, responded to these social pressures directing men to conform to the responsible patriarch model of manhood: "On the road, cut loose from crabgrass and family responsibilities, a man took what he needed, indulged his appetite, and freed himself from the responsibilities of conventional marriage and fatherhood. . . . Male freedom, then, meant cutting loose from women and children."[20] Images of male freedom that contain the imprimatur of escape from familial obligations seem to speak in particular to men of Zachary's generation who envision homeless men as wanderers, managing to evade the duties they themselves accepted.

Although the 1950s offered a story of male freedom as escape from home and family, Rosen contends, women who were attracted to such promises of freedom on the road or who tried to identify themselves with such a culture were faced with narratives that lacked female protagonists.[21] It was difficult for women to affiliate themselves with an oppositional culture that figured them as part of the package men wanted to escape. Not surprisingly, housed men who participated in the Phoenix interviews contended that it is men who choose homelessness so they can live as the wandering hobo.[22]

The hobo concept offers a clearer representation of homeless person as active agent than most other portrayals of the homeless, ensuring that the "strengths" of homeless women remain less visible and that women are more likely to be represented as the "passive and dependent subjects of care," when they are referred to at all. Stephanie Golden has argued that exclusion from the hobo tradition also makes homeless women more marginal than men:

> The acute discomfort [a homeless woman] creates in many people arises from a violation of another, perhaps more fundamental norm: the idea that an essential attribute of humanness—a basic distinction between the human and the animal—involves living under shelter, and further that because she is a woman, her violation of it is more disturbing than it would be were she a man. . . . Not only is there no tradition of vagrancy to which she can be assimilated as the male vagrant can, but the very idea of female humanness depends on being part of a family. The homeless woman is far more anomalous than the homeless man, for since there is no category to which she can be said to belong, she is indefinable; she has no recognized status. If one thinks of society as a pattern of social forms that create categories into which its members fit, her lack of category makes her marginal, in the sense that because she fits into the pattern nowhere she has to exist at its edge.[23]

Such an anomalous status—or lack of status—is centrally connected to gender constructions that associate women with home, family, and domesticity.

Perhaps not surprisingly, then, housed people in Phoenix did not romanticize homeless women as independent or on a spiritual trek. In her interviews and interactions with housed people, however, Golden found some identification of homeless women with a version of the romanticized wayfarer. For example, one housed woman in Golden's study regularly observed a homeless woman on the street whom she characterized as autonomous and self-reliant, throwing off society's constraints more bravely than the housed woman ever could: "When she pees on Madison Avenue, she's saying 'Fuck you.' . . . I couldn't do anything so far out even if it made me happy. There's a reason that I'm so conventional looking."[24] Another housed woman described homeless women as "the wholly liberated female," suggesting that female liberation—like male liberation—may depend on the rejection of conventional standards of respectability.

Even though few housed people represent homelessness as linked to the "romance of the road," most argue that homelessness is a choice, a concept dependent at least in part upon the construction of the homeless as hobos and tramps of yesteryear. And although it does not clearly speak to housed people's perceptions of homeless *women*, the construction of homeless men as less constrained by daily obligations may help to explain the vociferous reactions some housed people have toward the homeless in general. Although the homeless wanderer may receive guarded admiration from some housed men, he remains quintessentially unable—or perhaps more to the point, unwilling—to move beyond the adolescent yearning for freedom. Thus the man who somehow "gets away" with rejecting the nine-to-five drag engenders both envy from those who perceive such a luxury as distant from their own lives and disgust because they also perceive the acceptance of familial responsibility as the mark of maturity.

In the face of repeated accusations from housed people that the homeless choose their lifestyles, homeless people attempt to disassociate themselves from the homeless label. They do not interpret their experiences as providing them with a time for spiritual awakening and certainly not as an escape, since life becomes more stressful and overwhelming without a stable base. Further, they do not appear to rely on the hobo construction to create a more empowering homeless identity. Indeed they desperately want to be perceived as having lived middle-class, conventional lifestyles before becoming homeless.

Harold, for example, a homeless man in his mid-fifties who lives at People in Transition, visually fits the stereotype of the unencumbered man on a spiritual trek. A husky, tattooed white man, Harold presents a tough, hardened demeanor. Since becoming homeless, however, his energies have gone primarily into finding a shelter that provided a safer environment than the camp and armory-style shelter where he previously lived. Both were rough and relatively unstructured with a mostly male population. Harold stated that the shelter had few rules and even fewer staff members to monitor other residents' behavior; as a result, during the two weeks he lived there he witnessed several fights each evening, a robbery, and a stabbing. Not interested in a place where he constantly had to be on guard and live by his wits, Harold searched for a safer shelter with more rules and structure.

Likewise, many of the women attempted to depict themselves as conventional members of the middle class, often relying on physical markers of "normalcy" like furniture, pets, or cars. Betsy and Denise, for instance, individually described in detail their bedroom suites and Betsy her "real wood" living room furniture she had placed in storage. Julie and Janet both referred to the cars or houses they had owned during earlier, more financially stable periods of their lives. And Kelly stated repeatedly that she had "grown up with a lot of nice things," that her father is wealthy, and that she had "grown up with money"—all to support her argument that she conforms to middle-class standards and status.

Nobody, then, advanced a romanticized "life on the road" story of homelessness. Indeed to do so would have suggested the "street person" persona, the mythic homeless person who does not mind being homeless—who, in fact, prefers it to the rigors of work. This image is one from which homeless people regularly disassociate themselves. In addition, no homeless person argued that anyone chooses to be homeless because they like the "lifestyle" it affords them, that it is a journey of self-discovery, that it is comfortable, or that they sought it out as a "vacation." Although some homeless people argued that other homeless move from shelter to shelter because they are lazy or want to see how much they can get from the system, they did not intimate that such people enjoy shelter life or find living on the streets somehow enlightening.

"GIVE THAT MONEY BACK": THE CHARITABLE RELATIONSHIP

Reactions to homeless people almost always play on the question, to give or not to give? Decisions about whether and how to donate money, time, clothes, or food to homeless people relate directly to conceptualizations of the deserving and undeserving poor.[25] Whether and how to give is tied up further with notions about charity and the charitable relationship. For most housed people charity represents unilateral, unreciprocated giving to someone of lesser status. Indeed charitable giving is ensconced in maintenance of hierarchy and status, providing verification that the giver is not only noble but also clearly more prestigious than the recipient. Because charity has a "status-maintaining" function, in giving charity the giver confirms her or "his benevolence and the legitimacy of his position, while the poor [are] expected to understand their inferiority, the stigma attached to their position, and the docility and appreciation they should feel toward the giver."[26]

When housed individuals donate clothing, household items, time, or money to a shelter or to an individual on the street, it is often with the understanding that the housed giver is better able to decide how donated resources (particularly money) should be used than are homeless people themselves. True to the representation of the deserving poor as docile and appreciative of help, housed people assume that the deserving homeless will respond positively to their direction. Many housed respondents expect their giving to be met with gratitude and deference.

Not surprisingly, many housed people refuse to give money to people on the streets, preferring to buy them food or to donate to a third party assumed to be more responsible and accountable for how the funds are spent. For example, in response to a question about whether she gives money to homeless people on the street or to a shelter, Dolores described a relationship she had with a former coworker, Emily. Emily was employed at minimum wage, attended school full-time, and lived in a shelter because her job paid too little to allow her to support herself and pay for school. Although Dolores knew her coworker fairly well, respected her work, and knew she did indeed attend school and live at the shelter, she remained leery of offering Emily cash assistance: "I bought her lunch so I knew the money went for food. I think it's better to provide a service for people, and the personal contact is important so you're treating them like they're a real person. I don't think she was on drugs or alcohol, but I wanted to be there to make sure she used the money for food." Emily may have been able to bring a bag lunch from the shelter (a service some institutions provide) and to put a cash donation to better use as a supplement to her wages. Or she may have wished to save toward moving into her own housing. Dolores, however, appears not to have considered such possibilities. Assuming that her presence would be uplifting to Emily, Dolores portrayed Emily as dependent upon a guiding hand to ensure her funds were well spent.

Zachary and Elsa both echoed Dolores in their belief that they have better judgment regarding homeless people's finances than the homeless themselves do. Zachary usually avoids giving money to the homeless: "I have some reservations about the effect of the money I might contribute. I don't know what it's likely to go for. I suppose that's the effect of our larger, impersonal society. It used to be that you'd know people in your community, know what the money would go for, and perhaps be able to direct it in some positive way." Likewise, Elsa stated that she does not give money to homeless people: "I don't wish to encourage purchasing drugs or alcohol for a person who really needs a good meal. I buy food for them because I think many face a crisis regarding getting enough nourishment. I think food is one of their primary needs." Elsa assumes she is capable of naming homeless people's "primary needs," although she admits to having had little personal contact with any homeless person. The status differential automatically gives her superior judgment, and her belief that homeless people are drug addicts and alcoholics undergirds her argument that they cannot be trusted to make wise financial decisions.

The homeless person as the recipient of charity, then, is stigmatized; and an important aspect of such a stigma is the accompanying expectation that the recipient will be appreciative and docile.[27] This attitude was clearly expressed by Linda, who noted that she used to give to people on the street but no longer does after two experiences in which she did not receive the response she expected:

> I was still a housewife at the time, and there was a woman at the gas station with her child. I gave her money to get her child some food and said, "buy that kid a hamburger!" The mother said, "I have more important needs," so I said, "give that money back." She said, "but you gave it to me." I took it and went to the McDonalds and bought that kid a burger and fries!
>
> [Another time] I gave a Mexican child who was begging at the supermarket—with his mother and other children—macaroni and cheese out of my basket. He was about twelve. The derisive look I received from that twelve-year-old just froze me. I thought, well this is a fine how do you do. My experiences have made me not want to give and not really care because of the attitude I've had exhibited toward me.

Because she was unable to mandate how "her" money was spent in one case and did not receive the kind of gratitude she wanted in the other case, Linda refuses to give to people on the streets. She indicates that it was the recipients who broke the contract implied in charity: they rejected the part of grateful underling.

Although less bitter toward the homeless, Mike, a twenty-year-old white college student, displayed a similar inclination regarding the charitable relationship. In answer to a question about whether he gives money to the homeless on the street, Mike stated: "Yes sometimes, and on occasion no. It depends on the amount of money in my pocket. The situation and location have played a part in it. I'll have more tendency to give to a passive person rather than an aggressive [one]. If a family is using the children to approach hopeful donors I'll be reluctant to give money." Mike rewards certain behavior, in particular passivity, and punishes aggressive panhandling by refusing to give. His actions suggest the assumption that the charitable relationship demands a level of quiescence, if not submissiveness, on the part of the recipient.

"PLAYING THE PART": HOMELESS PERSPECTIVES ON CHARITY

The homeless are conscious of the distinctions drawn between the deserving and undeserving poor, which they show through their awareness of the charitable relationship and of housed people's expectations that they keep their place. Some work openly to fit into a constructed "category of need"—that of homeless person—even while indicating awareness that such categories do not necessarily correspond to the realities of their lives.[28] For example, Janet panhandled every day for several weeks prior to entering a shelter, spending the money she and her husband garnered from begging on food and motel lodging. During the interview she referred with pride to her wedding ring, a small diamond ring she treasures as one of the few symbols of her life before becoming homeless. In talking about her ring Janet reveals her understanding of the meaning of charity and the expectations housed people hold for her: "I would never sell this no matter how bad things got. It's my wedding ring. Of course, I wouldn't wear it when we were panhandling. We always dressed nice, looked like regular people, but you have to kind of play the part."

"Playing the part" when they panhandled meant looking respectable but not too well-off. Janet had to conform to housed people's desire to give money to "regular people"—in other words, people who would not spend the money on drugs and alcohol, who were temporarily down on their luck but not chronically homeless. Janet and her family, then, had to become objects for housed people to pity enough to part with their money, and in that sense they had to be recognizably human but not close enough to the giver's financial status that they risked robbing the giver of the sense of donating to someone beneath him or her. Janet's own experience tells her that people may become homeless or require income support without being completely bereft of all symbols of working-class or middle-class status, such as furniture, clothing, or jewelry. She realizes, however, that being a homeless person who elicits sympathy requires that she appear destitute but not disreputable. Janet aspires to the category of "situationally homeless," signifying a person who requires only a "helping hand" to become permanently self-sufficient. In other words, the person does not necessarily have long-term needs that are essential to remaining housed but requires relatively simple assistance, such as help with finding a job or a new home, and he or she will no longer be homeless.

In another example of homeless women's awareness of the demands of the charitable relationship, Freda also attempted to fit herself into existing categories of need. Freda made herself look the part of the helpless female victim by telling the Lighthouse shelter staff that she was homeless because her husband had abandoned her and her children. In reality, she remained happily married to a delivery driver who was working and living in his truck. Freda made use of a construction of women as less able to support themselves than men, hoping that as a single woman she would receive more assistance than she and her husband would have been given as a couple. Freda knew that the Lighthouse, which describes itself as a "work program," did not allow unemployed residents to remain at the shelter, so she did not tell her story as a ploy to receive welfare benefits. Instead she was convinced that homeless programs, like much of the public discourse around homelessness, would sympathize less with a two-parent homeless family than with a single mother. Freda applied to the shelter without her husband because she knew the staff would be more likely to believe a mother with three children could become homeless than they would that two adults could not support a family. She was afraid the shelter staff would think she and her husband were not trying hard enough to remain housed or were using drugs and alcohol and therefore would not accept her. Freda argued that she was using the caseworkers' stereotypes against them to house her family while still maintaining her dignity.

Because the Lighthouse staff generally suspects shelter residents of being untrustworthy, Freda's fear that they would not accept her if she could not fit into a recognizable category of need may have some basis in fact. Even if it is true, her story does not seem credible given the widespread belief that homelessness can be avoided with hard work and perseverance. That version of homelessness, of course, ignores the numbers of homeless people employed full-time or part-time, which the U.S. Conference of Mayors reports is about 26 percent of the homeless population[29]—a figure higher for those accepted into family shelter programs. Indeed Freda and her husband were a two-parent family in which at least one adult worked full-time, but they remained precariously housed. Once at the Lighthouse, Freda found a full-time job as a receptionist at slightly above minimum wage, and her husband continues to work for similar pay.

Although Freda's fears that the shelter might refuse to assist her have some basis in fact, so do housed people's beliefs that homeless people misrepresent themselves. Janet's and Freda's stories prove this point. Homeless women, however, are laboring to fit into the public's conception of the "acceptable" homeless. Rather than recognize the extent to which homeless people tell partial truths about their lives to fit the stereotype of deserving homeless, housed people tend to believe most homeless people perpetually misrepresent everything about themselves to get assistance they do not deserve.

"THE SEASON FOR GIVING"

The increase in charitable donations during the holiday season suggests another angle of the charitable relationship.[30] Housed people's requests to give parties for residents and to donate canned goods and presents usually overwhelm the capacity of shelters during November and December. In some cases staff members have to turn people away because there are more groups of volunteers offering to throw parties, especially for the children, than there are empty evenings on the calendar. Homeless shelter residents conjecture that it must be particularly important for housed people to remind themselves of their virtue and willingness to sacrifice during this season; donations of time, presents, or money can symbolize the giver's morality.

Angela, a white resident of the Lighthouse, stated that since arriving at the shelter in mid-December she has become acutely aware of how charity is configured. The amount and kind of charitable giving during the holiday season has allowed Angela to develop a clearer picture of why people give and what they expect in return: "Charity and giving should be a year-round thing. People only think about it at Christmas—they look at homeless children, feel sorry for them, and throw a party. I'm angry 'cause we need services and don't get them the other 364 days a year. People just think about it now 'cause it's the 'season for giving,' but a family can come into the shelter at Christmastime, but then they're here for another two months—what about their needs then?" As Angela implies, most of the giving is in the form of parties and other one-time interactive events—mostly for children—that do not respond to homeless people's material needs in any systematic way. Jerry, another Lighthouse resident, agrees: "The only time people give is at Thanksgiving and Christmas. People feel sorry for kids that don't got nothing. They think they can put themselves at ease, like they did something righteous and almighty."

Ella, another homeless woman, made a similar argument about the tendency for charitable giving to reflect the needs of the housed rather than of the homeless: "The shelters are bombarded at Christmas with help. Nobody helps during July when the kids really need it. People feel in the giving spirit; they feel guilty because of all they have." Ella also suggested that housed people donate items they no longer want, which sometimes are unusable. Indeed shelters often receive clothing that is worn out or ten years out of style, which residents cannot wear for interviews or to work. And Ella pointed out that people give "canned green beans, pork and beans, creamed corn—no one wants these things. We have enough to last us a year. . . . People who give think poor people would rather have used underwear than no underwear, but they give things that aren't usable, that are broken or full of holes." Housed people rarely give cash or gift certificates because "people don't get a warm fuzzy from gift certificates, [and] people don't want to give cash because they're afraid people will use it for alcohol, drugs, or frivolous stuff, whatever their definition of frivolous is."

Instead some programs have a system in which housed people can "adopt" a homeless family and purchase items from a list that family made up. Alternatively, housed people can buy single gifts from a general list containing both the shelter's and individual residents' needs. Even recipients in these programs, however, may find they cannot use the "gifts." Ella commented that she has received new items, particularly clothing and shoes, that are inappropriate for her needs or that her children refuse to wear, even when she specified the size. These problems arise because the housed want to be charitable in a way, as Ella put it, that will give them a "warm fuzzy" while still feeling reasonably assured that they can dictate how their money is spent. Receiving a list of requests and purchasing the gifts, then, enables the giver to feel a personal connection to the recipient while having the power to decide what the homeless person will receive.

Mark J. Stern has argued that if charitable gift giving is to maintain or underscore the status of the giver, it demands a personal relationship: "If it is depersonalized, the gift loses its defining features: the elements of voluntary sacrifice, prestige, subordination, and obligation."[31] Housed people often favor throwing parties as opposed to less personalized forms of giving because they perceive personal contact with homeless people to be an important aspect of the charitable relationship. Carli, a Family Shelter employee, described calls from people who want to come and "see" the homeless "like at a zoo," as if they will be confronted with an exotic species of animal. Others come to the shelter with donations and ask to hand their contributions directly to a resident. Housed people wish to come face-to-face with and experience the homeless in a context in which giver and receiver are clearly identified and in which the giver sets the terms of the relationship. In most cities in the United States, of course, housed people can see and talk to homeless people on the streets any day of the week, but such interaction might not include the personal connection implied in the charitable relationship. Perhaps more important, the housed person can significantly control the interaction at the shelter, whereas one on the street might appear more dangerous.

"TO GIVE WITHOUT ULTERIOR MOTIVE"

Despite the widespread adherence among the housed to a conception of charity based on maintaining hierarchy and status, several housed people appeared aware of homeless people's perspectives on giving and receiving. The alternative senses of charity these housed people proposed coincide with homeless women's views. Anita, a twenty-year-old Latina cashier, defines charity as "to help. Not to give handouts in a forceful, trying-to-save-the-world type of way but to give with good spirits without holding resentments." Anita recognizes the extent to which the giving of charity may be fraught with power differentials and struggles between giver and recipient to define the terms of the relationship. Similarly, Patty stated: "To me, charity means to give without ulterior motive, without feelings of pity or the desire to 'save,' when 'save' is condescending and patronizing. To be charitable is to help someone in his or her time of need, to share your wealth as purely as possible." Both Anita and Patty implicitly critique a sense of charity in which the act of giving in and of itself characterizes the giver as socially, morally, or financially superior and the act of receiving stigmatizes the recipient. They also identify the extent to which charitable giving rests on the assumption that the giver can "save" the world or at least one homeless person and the often patronizing behavior that results from such an assumption.

Joyce provides another example of charitable behavior that avoids the status-maintenance sense of charity: "My boyfriend and I just opened up a savings account together. We'll start out by putting in ten dollars each. We'll then put in five dollars from each of our paychecks. Once we have accumulated enough money, I was going to find a family that was having hard times and give it to them anonymously." By donating money anonymously, Joyce refuses to demand a personal connection to the recipient or to receive any visible thanks for her charity. Moreover, she allows the recipient to avoid feeling uncomfortable or inferior in the act of receiving. In giving cash, Joyce also suggests that a family experiencing "hard times" has not necessarily created their situation through bad financial planning, laziness, or irresponsibility and that the family itself can best decide how to spend the money.

Not surprisingly, perhaps, the housed people who offered alternatives to the dominant model of charity tended to be more empathetic toward homeless people. For example, when asked whether she thought homeless people had values or backgrounds similar to hers, Joyce responded: "I honestly don't know. I try to look past the stereotypes that they don't have any skills or ambition; however, I don't know enough about them to formulate my own decision. I definitely think that some of the homeless people get screwed by the system." In answering the same question posed to Joyce, Alisa stated: "It's hard to identify the similarities and differences because I don't want to base this answer on stereotypes. Perhaps we are similar in wanting to provide a good life for our families and different in the resources we have in obtaining help when tragedy occurs, like education, jobs skills, and family support."

Despite some alternative senses of charity that may underscore structural issues such as access to educational opportunities or wage differentials, the dominant sense of charity is not based on an empathetic connection to homeless people's experiences. Rather, the status-maintenance model of charity has widespread cultural support. Interactions between homeless and housed people find the homeless struggling to appear deserving while the housed try to filter out the virtuous from the unworthy. Homeless people attempt to get money or housing by appearing needy, reputable, and appreciative of help. In the process they may misrepresent themselves, sometimes because housed people operate with definitions of the acceptable poor that do not converge with the lived experiences of homeless people.

Indeed homeless people insist that they change only pieces of their pasts to fit into an identity housed people have created for them. Homeless women in this study attempt to represent themselves as "situationally homeless," based on definitions of the deserving poor reflected in shelter eligibility criteria and personal interactions with nonhomeless people. To fit into the category of acceptable poor, they often have to engage in misrepresentation.

They hide some of the reasons for their homelessness and emphasize others. Since housed people expect a single-issue explanation for homelessness—especially from those whom they define as the deserving poor—women seeking shelter, help from charitable institutions, or aid from individuals quickly learn how to reconstitute themselves to appear eligible for assistance.

Housed people, even those with no direct or formal connection to the homeless, have significant power to shape conceptions of homelessness. Through the exercise of creating and reifying notions about homelessness and homeless people, housed people address the often unspoken—although widely shared—ideas that homeless people are variously weak (although deserving) victims, lazy, criminal, irresponsible, and racial others. Although a number of people spoke of near misses with homelessness or precarious housing situations, few housed people perceive that much overlap exists between the housed and the homeless population. Homeless people are constructed as the "other," as outsiders from mainstream society[32] and therefore as part of a distinctly different—and inferior—stratum of society.

f   o   u   r

MEANINGS AND MYTHS OF HOMELESSNESS
Homeless Women Speak

Homeless and housed people often espouse similar stereotypes about the homeless. It is a common argument among many homeless and housed people alike that most of the homeless are responsible for their situations, that they have chosen their own fates.[1] Both groups generally rely on the notion that homeless people are deviants to explain homelessness. But at the same time, each homeless woman in this study invariably argues that she does not fit the stereotypes.[2] In this sense shelter residents' interviews differ from those of housed people. Homeless interviews often reveal tensions and conflicts as each woman attempts to reconcile her sense that she could not control the circumstances that precipitated her homelessness with the general cultural rebuke of the homeless for their "deviant lifestyles."

Individual shelter residents often emphasize their differences from other homeless people or from the label *homeless* itself; as many as two-thirds of the women in this study refuse to identify themselves as "homeless." Homeless women distance themselves from other shelter residents through a number of strategies. They may claim that others became homeless because they lack a work ethic, are lazy, or prefer to receive welfare rather than work. They may conjecture that other shelter residents became homeless because of uncontrolled drug or alcohol use. Or they may point to their own class status or education to distinguish themselves from other homeless women. White women may use whiteness to symbolize their deservingness and to mark Latina or African American women as automatically unworthy of assistance.

But struggles between classifications of the deserving and undeserving poor comprise just one aspect of shelter residents' construction and definition of homelessness. Indeed cultural definitions of the term *homeless* are layered with multiple ideological and material connotations. Listening to homeless women discuss and explain homelessness suggests that to call a person homeless conveys much more about her than the fact that she simply lacks housing. In fact, it implies something about her connection to others, her ability to operate as an independent adult, and her value system.

"THEY THINK WE'RE NOT PART OF EVERYDAY LIFE": HOMELESSNESS AND MEANINGS OF HOME

Cultural meanings of homelessness are shaped in part by meanings of "home," which signifies more than simply an edifice.[3] It is already clear that homeless people are often constructed as lazy, dependent, and passive; the relationship of homelessness to home adds more layers to cultural views of the homeless. Most important, when home is defined as a source of comfort and stability and as providing the essential basis for healthy human development, homeless people come to be seen as fundamentally different from the rest of us.[4] Homeless people's ability to live the way they do is often used as proof that they are different, ill, and by some estimates lacking certain feelings, desires, or needs considered key to a definition of humanness.

Although the ideology of home may operate in ways different from, or in addition to, the ways homelessness is represented, meanings of home reverberate through meanings of homelessness. Homelessness, then, is not ideologically a simple lack of home, but the concept of home does influence the ways people think about homelessness. For example, in their interviews with homeless women in Britain, Sophie Watson and Helen Austerberry found that although 30 percent of the women interviewed did not define the shelter or place where they currently lived as home, they also did not define themselves as homeless.[5] Watson and Austerberry noted that the "difficulty of drawing a line between having a home and being homeless" results from the myriad meanings of home: "This difficulty is further compounded when discussing women's homelessness, because the sexual division of labour in this society implies a specific domestic role for women, and thus a specific meaning of the home."[6]

Many homeless women speak to the characterization of home as a place of origin or as a "fountainhead," noting that "home" is constructed as necessary to create the next generation, to have a wholesome, healthy, or "normal" beginning. To be correctly formed, this discourse suggests, one must be attached to other people through (preferably) the nuclear family but must also be connected to a place. Home is integral to the life cycle of a fully developed person. The person without a home will lack a "nest" in which to evolve and as a result will go out into the world missing important lessons others have learned, lacking complete moral and social maturation. The children of homeless adults cannot mature correctly, then, because their parents do not provide a space for them to learn responsibility and morality. In this sense discourses of home and homelessness are tied to the culture of poverty thesis.

Angela, a resident of the Lighthouse, defined a homeless person as one who is isolated and without family support in response to a question about whether she currently considers herself homeless: "For a while there I did because I didn't have my family supporting me. When a person feels like they're no good, they feel like they're homeless." Angela's conception of homeless people as displaced, or rootless, was echoed by Julie: "When we got evicted . . . the sheriff was there and arrested my husband; he said we had an hour to get out. I was ready to just take everything I could carry and *become nobody*. I was ready to give up."[7] To Julie, a homeless person who lives on the street, as she and her husband and daughter did for a day until they were accepted into the Family Shelter, "becomes nobody," simply disappearing into a zone of the displaced.

Ann, a Lighthouse resident, believes homeless people are often seen as "less than human": "A lot of people don't consider homeless citizens because they don't have a home, they think we're not part of everyday life, like you're scum. Society looks at you like you're nothing, but you're somebody who has potential." Jersy Kosinski has suggested that "homelessness . . . means less-than-home. It presupposes somehow that one ought to have a home and that, therefore, a homeless person is somehow deprived of something that some other people may take for granted."[8] Moreover, as Ann's comments imply, the homeless person is seen as personally deprived of the moral or social development that "normally" would make one demand housing; she is somehow less than human because she *can* live without a home. This view of homelessness resonates with Erin, who wishes housed people would not label her as a "separate species."

The cultural significance of ownership or access to private space also impacts the experience and interpretation of what it means to be homeless. Access to private space in the form of "home" signifies the passage into adulthood, particularly newfound independence and control over one's life. Thus homeless women sometimes feel their reliance on relatives, friends, or shelters for housing implies a failure to operate as a fully grown adult. Gloria indicated that her loss of independence and loss of control are difficult aspects of her homelessness. She experienced these losses both while she stayed with her brother after she and her children were evicted and when she lived at a homeless shelter:

> From the moment I was evicted I considered myself homeless. Living with my brother did not make me feel any better because it was not my own place. Being homeless meant you didn't make the rules, you didn't come first, and that maybe you weren't a worthy person. . . . I felt a little relief when we got to the Ministry [shelter] because it was our own room, where I could make the rules, fix the place up. When you're homeless you're controlled by a whole lot of factors, just that you're sitting in someone's chair.

Gloria's self-reported "loss of self-esteem" over her enforced dependence on others illustrates the contention that "home" is connected to a sense of autonomy, particularly for women. Although the assumption that women will set up their own family homes once they get married or "settle down" with a partner ignores the realities of many low-income families, lesbian and gay families, extended families, and postmodern or nontraditional family forms that are statistically most prevalent in U.S. society,[9] it nevertheless maintains enough cultural legitimacy to affect understandings of homelessness. And although it is financially difficult or even impossible for many women in this study to do so, women like Gloria speak to the pressures to maintain private space.

Despite the fact that Gloria found the shelter in some aspects a better alternative than staying with her brother, the shelter is a weak approximation of the privacy of home. Many homeless shelters do not allow residents privacy or autonomy regarding personal lifestyle choices and, moreover, encourage staff regulation and surveillance of residents. Leslie Kanes Weisman points out the implications of such regulation on the possibility that a shelter will provide substitute housing that approximates a home:

> Sleeping arrangements are dormitory-like with little or no privacy. Few visitors are permitted, and when they are there is no place to entertain them, be they a relative, friend, or lover. This suggests that homeless people do not need privacy, self-expression, friendships, and sexual relations, or at least that these needs should not be taken seriously. Perhaps this explains why housing for the homeless is referred to as "shelter," meaning a roof over your head, rather than "home," which implies autonomy and emotional as well as material support.[10]

Shelter residents often note the loss of dignity, status, and independence associated with homelessness. Diane, a resident of the Family Shelter, explained: "I felt like a failure when I had to go to shelter. I felt like I let the kids down, disrupted their home of five years." Although most women report that the caseworkers at homeless shelters are generally less empathetic than those at battered women's shelters, Diane felt more respected at the Family Shelter than at a domestic violence shelter where she had previously resided. She equates shelter living, and thereby homelessness, with a loss of independence and resulting forced degradation: "They help you here without making you feel homeless. It's not like [the domestic violence shelter] where they check on you after curfew, they look in your room with a flashlight. I think it's a control thing."

The gendered nature of adult independence also surfaced in the interviews, with some women noting that cultural lessons fail to emphasize economic and personal autonomy for women. A number of women in the shelters mentioned that they had never been "on their own" before and were frightened by the pressure to support themselves and their children. Lisa believed her fear of independence led to her history of abusive relationships as well as to homelessness:

> Women are not prepared to be self-contained, self-sufficient units. Women go from Daddy to hubby—I never had the feeling of being a totally independent person. . . . I'm finally coming to the point where self-sufficiency doesn't seem like second-best. [Before] I thought that if you're gorgeous enough, you will get a man who wants to do everything for you. Now I think that it's desirable to be fully functioning, balance my own budget, whether I'm with someone or not. I had to stop wanting a Prince Charming.

Lisa noted that she used to believe that if she maintained independent financial reserves, it would be a "slam" to the man with whom she shared a relationship. After leaving her fiancé and living for two years in rented rooms, sleeping on an office floor, and living in a shelter, she has begun to value relationships based on what she terms a "healthy separateness."

Like Lisa, Betsy sees her homelessness as the end result of being afraid to "be on my own and take care of myself": "A lot of the reason why I'm homeless is 'cause I always had someone take care of me. When it came time to take care of myself, I didn't know how." Although Betsy had been on her own since age fifteen, supporting herself through sex work and as a relief driver for truckers, she does not believe her creative solutions to homelessness as a teenager are proof that she was independent: "There was always someone else there. I may have been taking care of them, but it seemed like they were taking care of me." A crucial difference for Betsy in her current situation is that she is now responsible for three young children, whereas in her teenage years she had only herself to feed and shelter.

Not all homeless women extend their critiques of the meanings and causes of homelessness to an examination of their own gendered expectations that a man will take care of them. Further, they do not necessarily link their homelessness to their past financial dependence on a male partner. In part this results from the fact that many women worked outside the home and contributed to a family wage. Others, however, assume that it is natural for a man to support his family, even though they may be aware of the difficulties inherent in doing so. Thus some women continue to think of their male partners as the primary wage earners or as more responsible for the economic situation of the family, regardless of the amount of money each adult contributes.

For women, homelessness has another connotation that is also dependent on the meanings of home. Their disconnection from the domestic sphere means homeless women do not have access to one of the most important traditional markers of femininity. Despite the fact that the social construction of "woman" is tied up with a lifestyle significantly different from their own, many women in the shelters strive to maintain a connection to traditional signs of femininity. One of the ways this plays out is in the constant conflict over the question of who is a "good mother." Shelter residents expend enormous energy focusing on this issue; by contrast, debates about whether the men in the shelter are good fathers never surface. Apparently, men's connection to the traditional norms of masculinity are not tied to their ability to father but probably have more to do with their failure as providers. The stakes are high for women, however, since mothering becomes one of the few traditionally female markers available to them.

Shelter residents accuse one another of failing to supervise their children correctly, of having too many children, or of having "lost control" over their charges. For example, Diane, a resident of the Family Shelter, echoes the claims of many women when she accuses other shelter residents of being "bad mothers." She laments that one mother feeds her children "too much candy" and other "junk food," creating more stress for others at the shelter since her children are "hyperactive" as a result. Diane also blames women residents because their children hit other children, swear, and disobey adults. And she argues, as other homeless women do, that misbehaving children have taught her own kids bad habits they did not display before entering the shelter. Similarly, Angela derides "mothers [at the Ministry shelter] who wouldn't clean their kids or comb their own hair" and appreciates the fact that at the Lighthouse "they make people be clean." Erin has much the same criticism for mothers at the Family Shelter, whom she refers to as "street people," and states that their "kids were not taken care of, they were dirty, no one was watching their kids, they were neglected."

It is assumed—even by homeless women—that homeless children are missing much of what is necessary for healthy emotional and physical development. In part this has to do with images of home as integral to rearing children and the belief that homeless children must be missing out on important life lessons. Homeless women are also aware that their children are at higher risk for low birth weight as infants, for chronic physical disorders, and for developmental delays and that they are likely to fall behind their peers educationally.[11] They accuse one another of bad parenting based on their knowledge of statistics that show that children, once homeless, have such difficulties and because of cultural pressures to provide a domestic haven. Although the latter reason has less material basis, it is no less consequential for beliefs about shelter residents to which both the homeless and nonhomeless subscribe.

"I'M NOT A TYPICAL HOMELESS PERSON": DISTANCE AND DISASSOCIATION

In addition to homelessness being defined in part by its relationship to home, homeless people provide a key to the ideological meanings of homelessness through their attempts to distance themselves from the category "the homeless."[12] Just as women living in battered women's shelters fashion their identities by defining themselves against the traits stereotypically associated with the homeless, women in homeless shelters try to distance themselves from other homeless women. In particular, homeless women in Phoenix argue that they are not lazy, mentally ill, drug addicted, or "different" from housed people. They often base such arguments on implications or straightforward assertions that most other homeless people do fit the stereotype.

In their interviews with homeless people in Austin, David Snow and Leon Anderson found a similar attitude: "A substantial proportion of the identity talk we recorded was consciously focused on distancing from other homeless individuals, from street and occupational roles, and from the caretaker agencies servicing the homeless. . . . This distancing technique manifested itself in two ways among the homeless: disassociation from the homeless as a general social category, and disassociation from specific groupings of homeless individuals."[13] Snow and Anderson describe "categorical distancing" as homeless people's insistence that they are different from the "typical" homeless person, in particular that they are more interested than other homeless people in finding housing and employment. Others disparaged the homeless people who used social service agencies or stayed at shelters as "institutionally dependent."

Similarly, two-thirds of the women in Phoenix homeless and domestic violence shelters reported that they do not consider themselves to be part of the homeless. A few women maintained that to label themselves homeless would lead to depression and a concomitant difficulty finding the energy to persevere in their attempts to secure housing. Other women, even if they do not express their need to reinvent their identities for fear of depression, may in part need to separate themselves from the homeless label for similar reasons. Susan, a fifty-nine-year-old white woman at People in Transition, avoids thinking about whether she is homeless: "When I start thinking about that I get depressed, and I can't deal with depression. . . . Some people lose their jobs; when you lose a job, you lose hope and get depressed. A lot of times you get so depressed with your situation, you feel like you can't do anything—then you can't."

Rita, a mother of three who is living at the Family Shelter with her husband and children, argued that she is unlike other shelter residents because she and her husband have jobs and do not use drugs. When asked whether she considers herself to be homeless, Rita's response indicates that her capacity to continue working and to find housing without feeling overwhelmed depends upon her mental separation from others at the shelter:

> I don't feel like we are [homeless]. I just feel like we're taking a vacation-type thing. If I keep looking at myself as homeless, I'll get negative and not want to do anything. I get depressed. I feel bad that my kids aren't in a regular home, but it's better than living in a car. I can't let myself—I get depressed a lot anyway, so I can't let myself be negative.
>
> A lot of people choose to be here because they're too busy doing drugs. They want a free ride so they can get more drugs. I've met drug addicts that try to be homeless so they can get more money for drugs. . . . I feel we're different than people here. We're working. We use this place as a last resort. We tried other places but couldn't afford it, where other people come here right away—three months of free rent for them.
>
> JW: Have you met people like that here?
>
> Rita: I don't really associate with people here, so I don't know.

Although both Rita and Susan give voice to the overwhelming depression that afflicts some people living in shelters, in other ways their understandings of homelessness diverge considerably. Rita argues that most homeless people have themselves to blame for their situations, whereas Susan points primarily to unemployment and underemployment as the underlying causes of homelessness.

Indeed Susan articulates the class boundaries of homelessness more clearly than most shelter residents, pointing to the impact of poverty on the likelihood of becoming homeless. She refers to the ways her class position limits her options both to support herself and to contend with the financial difficulties inherent in her daily existence.[14] Arguing that "people don't realize there are complications to getting out of the shelter—you need a job, an apartment," Susan ties her homelessness to her previous history as a low-wage worker. Her ability to grapple with these "complications" is circumscribed by low wages and a low-income housing shortage and, in Susan's case, employers' hesitation to hire an older worker.

Susan talked about the ways her class status has affected her materially and emotionally throughout her life and prior to entering a shelter: "When I went to night school to get my GED [general equivalency] diploma, I told a woman there I worked in a laundry, and that was too low class for her. If you don't work in an office, people treat you bad. If you don't have a certain status, you're beneath that individual. Some people can't quite swallow manual laborers—it's like, 'you're not educated; is this the best you can do?'" Even while others looked down on her for the work she did, in the past Susan's attempts to find jobs other than manual labor were stymied. When she contacted an employment agency to help her find a higher-paying job after she left her husband a number of years ago, Susan found they saw her only as a manual laborer. Despite her attempts to move into work that offered opportunities for advancement, Susan recalled, "The employment office would throw laundry work at me." Susan empathizes with homeless people even while refusing to label herself homeless, pointing to the structural pressures affecting low-wage workers as an explanation for homelessness.

Women's claims that they do not consider themselves homeless are often coupled with a rejection of other homeless people because they are lazy, addicted to drugs, and taking advantage of the system. If others in the shelter would make a concerted effort, many homeless women argue, they would soon be able to move into their own housing.[15] These women join housed people in stereotyping homeless people while separating themselves into what many argue is a small group of the deserving poor. Women with vastly different experiences and reasons for being in the shelter make a similar point—they see structural reasons for their own homelessness and behavioral reasons for many others' homelessness.

A white mother of two, Michelle has been diagnosed with schizophrenia and has been clean for three years from a former addiction to speed. Michelle defined herself as homeless when, prior to coming to the shelter, she was living in a motel and in the park with her children. Now that she is living at the Family Shelter, she no longer considers herself homeless. She refuses a specific homeless identity she associates with "shelter people":

> There are two classes of people here: people who lost their places 'cause they lost jobs—they're one paycheck away from homelessness. Then there are people here who were doing drugs and didn't give a shit. I put myself above drug addicts who do drugs in front of their kids. My kids never saw me do drugs. . . . My kids aren't like others here who are street kids and . . . have been in and out of shelters—they're shelter people. The parents put the stress on the kids; they know too much for kids. My kids aren't like that, but they're learning this behavior here, hitting other kids.

Notwithstanding Michelle's attempts to differentiate herself from "shelter people," however, she was one of the few women interviewed who had lived in another shelter—albeit six years ago—prior to her stint in the Family Shelter. She is both a self-described drug addict and mentally ill. She supports herself and her children primarily through disability and welfare payments. Yet she emphasizes a certain mind-set that distinguishes her from "shelter people," primarily citing her strong parenting skills and attachment to work as proof that she conforms to the other "class" of people at the shelter: "I want to get out of the system; it drives me crazy to live on welfare. I like to work."

Other homeless residents speak in like manner about a class of "shelter people" to illustrate the differences between themselves and others at the shelter. They define *shelter* or *street people* as those who move from one shelter program to another, who are streetwise—with literal experience living on the street or simply belonging to a milieu characterized by drug and alcohol use, irresponsible sexuality, and criminal activity. As Michelle's comments suggest, however, a street person can be identified based on his or her lifestyle or, alternatively, through a certain perceived mind-set. Even if Michelle's behaviors or experiences conform to the shelter person lifestyle, then, she can still use the identity as a foil to demonstrate her superior morality or more judicious way of conducting herself at the shelter. She is not a shelter person because she lacks the street mind-set; she places worth on work, manners, and well-behaved children.

Similarly, Frances uses the street person identity as a tool to establish that her own value system is preferable to that of others at the shelter. Frances is a former heroin user and self-defined twenty-year alcoholic who lived in several shelters and mental wards before coming to People in Transition. But she contrasts herself with the homeless person who values street smarts, who is happily dependent upon welfare, and whose objective is to remain in a shelter or somehow on public support. Although she has plenty of experience in shelters and halfway houses, Frances emphasizes her seeming naïveté and trusting personality:

> It's a completely different world down here [at the shelter], and it's very hard for people who haven't been on the streets. I think I can loan money to people, but they look at me like I'm a sucker, not like it's an act of kindness. They'll even steal your toilet paper. It's just so hard to get used to if you've been out of this world for a while. . . . I'm a little different than some here 'cause I want to go off welfare and be a productive member of society. Everyone else here just wants a free handout; they think you can live this way. . . . I don't think of myself as homeless 'cause I've got a roof over my head. I guess I am, though, because I don't have my own freedom.

Frances's assertion that she does not consider herself to be homeless because the shelter provides a "roof over her head" belies the content of her foregoing comments. A roof over the heads of others at People in Transition cannot, for Frances, erase the smear of "homeless" that defines them. Other women's comments echo this tension between, on the one hand, characterizing homelessness in the barest terms—as simply lacking a roof over one's head—and, on the other hand, calling up ideological meanings of homelessness that extend far beyond the essential question of whether one is physically sheltered.

Kristen provides another example of these competing senses of homelessness. She responded to a question about whether she considers herself homeless with a literal interpretation: "Only when I was in my car. I didn't when I was staying in shelters because I had some place to go, a roof over my head." Here home is simply a building to keep out the elements, and homelessness is the lack of such shelter. When Kristen described others at the Lighthouse, however, she used homelessness to signify laziness, amoral sexuality, and welfare dependence:

> People I've seen here have become homeless through their own choosing; they can stay with their friends. I had no choice. . . . For other people it's avoidable. But everyone who's homeless at one time or another had a better choice—a lot chose drugs and alcohol over money for an apartment. . . . A lot of people feel they can get a lot of charity—people feel sorry for them. A lot of these people have become baby factories and want the state to take care of them. I'm different because I had to protect my child, get her somewhere warm.

Kristen's peers at the shelter are not allowed the same values that would lead them to protect their children at any cost; rather they are "baby factories," giving birth capriciously. Kristen argues that, unlike others, she entered the shelter only as a last resort and only because she had a responsibility to her child. She uses her decision to stay at the Lighthouse as evidence of her superior values and as equally sure proof that other Lighthouse residents lack values.

Another Lighthouse resident, Ann, makes a similar argument by emphasizing her "Christian values." Although at one point in the interview Ann commented that homeless people enter shelters because they want to "better themselves," she repeatedly returned to her Christian upbringing to differentiate herself from other residents: "I think I'm a lot different than a lot of people here. A lot of people here aren't trustworthy; they spread rumors. A lot of people don't like to obey the rules. . . . I was raised differently than people here—I'm a strict Christian. Most of the people here weren't raised Christian." In the context of Ann's history, however, the meaning of "strict Christian" is elusive. She claims to have stolen money and merchandise to purchase drugs, admits to having cheated on her husband on six different occasions, and has spent time in jail.

As in the case of Ann's assertion that she lives by a superior set of values, the life choices and experiences of some homeless women call into question their differentiation vis-à-vis other residents. The terms *homeless* and *street person* become, in a sense, meaningless in this context because so many women argue that such labels cannot be applied to them. Even if their past experiences include drug use, sex work, criminal activity, or a prior shelter stay, many of the women interviewed use some aspect of their histories or personalities to suggest that they are different from other homeless women. The characteristics many people use to describe the undeserving street person or shelter person could easily be applied to Frances or Ann. Both of them, however, find some basis to assert their deservingness, which in essence translates to their distance from the label *homeless*.

The actual material past of a shelter resident may affect the success of her use of narratives of difference, but even so, women with significantly diverse material circumstances make startlingly similar claims to difference. Both Lisa and Magdalena individually describe themselves as "not a typical homeless person," using very similar language to set themselves apart. Yet their life experiences and material circumstances before entering a shelter were dissimilar, and indeed Magdalena approximates Lisa's definition of a "typical" homeless person.

When Lisa discussed homeless shelter life, she maintained "I'm totally atypical of the people who are here" because she is college educated, "white, middle-class, and articulate." Lisa stated that she felt ashamed about having to enter a shelter, whereas others "seemed blasé about being there. They were still trying to live a dysfunctional lifestyle—sneaking out to drink. [They] partied their way into their situation, they have a couple kids out of wed-lock—there's a logical connection to why they're homeless." By contrast, Lisa characterized her homelessness as "out of her control" and, like Kristen, asserted that she chose to enter the shelter out of concern for her children and the belief that she needed to "do anything" to give them "food and a roof over their heads."

In discussing her experiences at the shelter, Lisa repeatedly mentioned her desire to become a spokesperson for homeless people, thereby placing herself in a different category than other shelter residents. Lisa's contention that she would like to help other homeless women and welfare recipients enables her to separate herself from them: "How many people who are on welfare speak English as their first language? How many are educated and articulate enough to talk about homelessness issues?" By assuming that home-less women need a spokesperson with her qualifications, Lisa differentiates herself from other shelter residents and homeless people in general based on her class, race, and ethnicity. Although most of the women in the Family Shelter are white (the racial makeup of the shelter reflects in part the large percentage of both housed and homeless whites in Phoenix), she mentions her whiteness as code for including herself in the ranks of the deserving poor. Her whiteness becomes evidence of her status as an atypical homeless person and an endorsement for her argument that her homelessness occurred for reasons out of her control, not as a result of "partying" or having children out of wedlock. Moreover, Lisa uses ethnicity and race to signify class position. She uses her college education and language skills to establish her middle-class credentials but further relies on her "not Latina" and "not African American" identity to shore up her claim to middle-class status.

Magdalena, a resident of Rose's House, also argues that she is not a typical homeless person, yet she fits much of Lisa's description of a characteristic homeless person. Magdalena recently emigrated to the United States from Cuba, and her English is limited. She states that she has never worked and possesses few skills. Lisa uses her status as "white, middle-class, and articulate" to define herself against Magdalena, who is Latina, low-income, a welfare recipient, and an unmarried mother. At the same time, Magdalena attempts to define herself against other homeless people by pointing to her boyfriend's violence as the reason she is homeless: "I'm not a typical homeless person. If I don't want to be with [my boyfriend], I have to get my own place. I became homeless just to get away from him. If I work out things for myself, I won't be homeless." Magdalena stresses the difference between herself as a battered woman, who seeks shelter because of the actions of someone else, and a "real" homeless person, who, Magdalena argues, becomes homeless as a result of either her own actions or events within her control.

Although Magdalena and Lisa may share similarities with one another and with others at domestic violence and homeless shelters, each declares herself distant from the homeless identity. In reality, both sought shelter because they left abusive partners, realized they could not find high-paying work, and could not support themselves and their children on the money from welfare benefits. Rather than stress those commonalties, they individualize the reasons for homelessness and blame homeless people for their own conditions. Magdalena relies on her position as a battered woman who is a brave "survivor" for leaving her relationship and who is not to blame for her current circumstances to establish that she is not representative of most homeless people. Lisa uses references to class, race, and ethnicity to substantiate how atypical a homeless person she is.

A number of other white homeless women also rely on racial categories to establish their distance from other homeless people. Notwithstanding the fact that the majority of shelter residents in Phoenix are white, some white women constructed Latina or African American women as the only "real" homeless women. White women could then claim they did not fit the profile of addicted, criminal, or lazy homeless women simply—or primarily—because of their whiteness. Denise, a white resident of Rose's House, entered the shelter after she lost her job and a family member forced her to leave the apartment they shared. Denise described how her problems began when she contracted a skin infection on her face and was fired from her job as a waitress. Since she worked in close vicinity to the kitchen where food was prepared, the restaurant manager believed the infection posed a health hazard to customers. Denise did not have enough money to go to a doctor to have the infection treated and had difficulty finding another job because her skin did not clear up on its own.

After she was evicted Denise stayed with various acquaintances, sleeping on the floor at each place for a few days until she had worn out her welcome and was asked to move on. Although Denise called battered women's and homeless shelters trying to find any place with an opening, her current residency in a battered women's shelter allows her to assume an identity in opposition to that of homeless people. In response to a question about whether she had ever stayed in a homeless shelter before coming to Rose's House, Denise stated that she had not and used the opportunity to argue that she *could not* stay at such a shelter: "I would stay in a campground if I had a tent or sleep in a construction site rather than stay in a shelter with those people."

Denise related a previous experience at a free clinic to describe the differences between herself and homeless people. She assumed that the rest of the clinic clientele was homeless, although many could be precariously housed, in a financial position similar to her own at the time: "We waited for four hours. We were the only white people there—it was a bunch of Hispanics and Indians. It was really horrible and dirty in there—kids running all over, bothering people. I would never let my kids do that. I have no patience with stupid people. They should be given an IQ test before they're given the opportunity to breed." Here low-income and Latino or Native American are automatic markers of homelessness, whereas white is the marker of "not homeless," even if one is indigent. Denise identifies people of color with homelessness in much the same way she labels them unhygienic and "stupid," having children irresponsibly and lacking parenting skills. Her list includes many of the characteristics social workers are hired to fix in the underclass, specifically in homeless people at the shelters. For Denise, Latinos and Native Americans are by definition more likely to be the "real" homeless, and she uses their perceived differences to construct a homeless identity in opposition to her own.

Like Denise and Lisa, other white women also associate homelessness with people of color to establish the otherness of both identities. Janet, a Family Shelter resident, mentioned both her race and her class in response to a question about what circumstances led her to the shelter. She slipped back and forth between a discussion of her homelessness and welfare recipients, intermingling the two and using both as contrasts for her own identity: "My family was upper-middle-class. I'm a regular person. I come from a regular home. . . . When I went on welfare the first time I saw all these people, dirty, drug addicts, working the system, not a lot of white people. I had to leave the office because I was crying." For Janet, a person who is homeless is by definition not a "regular" or "normal" person but a racially other person who "works the system," relying on welfare rather than working to support herself. Janet uses her whiteness to support her claims to an "upper-middle-class" background. By conflating the race or ethnicity of blacks, Latinos, and Native Americans with an "underclass" identity, Janet, like Denise, can make whiteness a marker of automatic exclusion from such an identity.

The fact that references to the omnipresent "welfare queen" may be read as code for African American women has been much discussed, but the volume and acerbity of charges of system dependence and laziness directed toward the Latino population in Phoenix indicate that a variation of the "welfare queen" concept extends to them as well. Sylvia, a case worker at La Casa battered women's shelter, contends, "There is a lot of hatred and anger toward Latinos in Phoenix, probably due to our proximity to the border." Latinos endure numerous racial and class-based stereotypes. Indeed many housed whites categorize all low-income Latinos as lazy or as foreign interlopers taking advantage of a generous U.S. welfare system.

"SOMETHING BETTER FOR THEMSELVES AND THEIR KIDS": COMMONALITY AND CONNECTION

Although the majority of homeless women distance themselves from other shelter residents, a few women contend that homelessness results from unemployment, underemployment, and low-income housing shortages. Rather than echo and further develop an individualistic understanding of poverty and homelessness, these women insist on an explanation for homelessness that emphasizes the commonalties in the life experiences of low-income women. Their demands for a political response to homelessness that attends to the impact of structural economic issues on women's lives as opposed to individual homeless people's values sets them apart from other shelter residents and most housed people.

Gloria, an African American woman, framed her discussion of homelessness within the context of her experiences as one of the few previously middle-income women who lost housing. She did not, however, try to distinguish herself from others. Rather Gloria argued that her strong values made it possible for her to overcome the many obstacles to becoming stably housed and that such values are shared by other shelter residents:

> I think most people don't understand homeless people. Right now I'm a year from finishing my BA. I'm not a product of generations of welfare. Homeless people have varied backgrounds. They could be college graduates, and those are the ones who fall the hardest because they have farther to fall. They're used to a certain standard of living. I think [most homeless people] have the same values: strong work ethics, wanting a good education for your children, honesty, integrity. Those were the values I learned as a child, and they are the ones that got me through homelessness to where I am.

Gloria seems to best understand her own and other previously middle-income homeless people's experiences or reactions to homelessness, suggesting that middle-class people may "fall harder" than those accustomed to having less. She does not, however, extend that notion to argue that she has superior values when compared with other homeless women. Rather Gloria points to the commonalties in the value systems of homeless and housed people and to the prevalence of women's economic insecurity.

Like Gloria, Yvette concentrated on women's shared struggles to remain afloat financially. Yvette is a thirty-two-year-old African American resident of Rose's House. Although Yvette has little formal education, she has consistently worked at jobs that paid more than minimum wage—although sometimes only slightly more—such as positions as a day care provider and an administrative assistant. Her husband's salary was twice that of Yvette's, however, and without his help to support their children and given her refusal to apply for welfare benefits lest he access state records to locate her, she recognizes the insecurity of her financial situation. Yvette does not have enough money to pay a security deposit and the first month's rent on an apartment. Since she is unfamiliar with Phoenix, she also lacks employment contacts or friends:

> Being homeless myself sure does change your way of thinking about things. It sure is an eye-opener. I think everyone has the picture of a homeless person where it's the bag lady, and you feel sorry for her, but you cross the street so you don't have to give her money. Now I'd say there is no typical homeless person. You never know what's going to happen in your life. If you had told me I'd be in a shelter for domestic violence, I'd have said you must be crazy. Now if some homeless person asked me for money, I'd always give them some.

Unlike other shelter residents for whom becoming homeless created shame and generated attempts to distance themselves from other homeless people, Yvette's shelter experience enables her to empathize with others. She articulates the avoidance and pity that describe some housed people's approach to the homeless, as well as the changes in her own attitudes.

Likewise, Tracy, a white resident of the Family Shelter, exhibited empathy and refused to distance herself from other shelter residents. She suggested that a cultural emphasis on individual reasons for homelessness and disapproval of relying on public assistance sometimes dissuade women from seeking shelter:

> People think people are on the streets because of drugs and alcohol. It's not true. There are many reasons why people become homeless: they lost their jobs, couldn't make rent, women have abusive husbands. . . . Too many women have a hard time getting out of abusive relationships because they feel it's a put-down to ask for help, to go to a shelter. . . . Everyone who's here are here because they want to do something better for themselves and their kids.

Unlike Tracy, Yvette, and Gloria, most of their peers distance themselves from other shelter residents by insisting that they do not consider themselves homeless and that they are atypical of the homeless. Rather than recognize the shared factors that circumscribe the options available to them as well as to other low-income people, most homeless people advance the notion that each person is responsible for her own poverty or homelessness. They make this argument, however, in the context of also insisting that homelessness—especially their own—can be caused by economic restructuring or underemployment.

It is difficult to pinpoint why these three women and a few others respond to homelessness so differently from the majority of their peers. Their stories are not necessarily similar to one another or remarkably distinct compared with those of other shelter residents. Perhaps they are simply particularly introspective or empathetic people. Given the negative associations inherent in the term *homeless,* their refusal to distance themselves from other homeless people is more surprising than most shelter residents' attempts to appear deserving at others' expense. Gloria, for one, appears to have analyzed the issue of homelessness as it operates politically and perhaps possesses a less parochial outlook than other shelter residents. It is interesting that Latina and African American women empathize with other homeless people and try to avoid stereotypes in disproportionately large numbers in comparison to their overall representation in this study. Possibly because they are disproportionately poor and suffer discrimination based on race and ethnicity, Latina and African American women are well positioned to understand the structural conditions that shape homeless women's poverty.

CONCLUSION

Homeless women's active participation in constructing meanings for homelessness mitigates against an understanding of them as passive receptors of definitions of homelessness created elsewhere or as simply internalizing the stigma of homelessness. One should not interpret shelter residents' words as evidence that they are submissively accepting an ideology of homelessness defined by the nonhomeless; to do so ignores homeless women's contributions to creating meanings for poverty and homelessness.[16] It perceives them as somehow "outside" or on the fringes of society rather than as active participants in creating cultural meaning.

In claiming that most homeless women simply need to work harder and eschew their current deviant lifestyles to become housed, shelter residents rely on a myth of unlimited opportunities and vindicate rugged individualism as the answer to structural inequities. In fact, it should not be surprising that homeless women's understandings of homelessness tend to focus on individual failure or deviance, since they—like housed people—are shaped by the focus on individualism in the United States. Homeless women do, however, moderate an individualistic understanding of homelessness by placing themselves in the category of deserving poor. Thus each homeless woman provides some critique of capitalist economic structures by describing the process by which she became homeless. Homeless women place their personal experiences into a context of their histories as low-income members of the economy, pointing to the static nature of their income levels and limited opportunities for social mobility. In so doing, Phoenix women do analyze class positions (even if they refuse to extend their critique to the formation of class solidarity) by explaining how the "social class into which one is born has [a] major influence on where one ends up."[17]

Even as they participate in the production of meaning and are inherently part of symbolic contests over definitions of the homeless as deserving or undeserving poor, Phoenix shelter residents by and large do not attempt to claim or redefine a homeless identity. Rather homeless women generally work very hard to find some aspect of their histories, experiences, or personalities that will distance them from other homeless women. Their refusal to self-identify as homeless, and their participation in the construction of other shelter residents as undeserving, limits homeless women's resistance to negative portrayals of homeless people and to questions about homeless people's values and honesty. Further, distancing techniques that separate the homeless into a mass of those constructed as undeserving of assistance and a small group that is worthy of help make articulation of a self-conscious group identity almost impossible.

HOMELESS AND BATTERED WOMEN
Parallel Stories, Opposing Identities

Women's stories and comments have shown repeatedly the importance of domestic violence in understanding homelessness. Yet most research distinguishes between women who live in homeless shelters and those in domestic violence shelters. Likewise, the environments and programs the two types of shelters offer vary significantly, based on the idea that battered women need different services than homeless women do. By contrast, striking similarities exist in women's reasons for seeking emergency housing, regardless of the type of shelter they are in.[1] Women's stories challenge the usual distinctions drawn between battered and homeless women. Specifically, many women are low income and experience a history of abuse, primarily from partners. They define their principal need from shelters as housing assistance. Both battered women's and homeless shelters, then, are increasingly occupied by low-income, persistently poor, and precariously housed battered women.[2] The complex connection between battering and homelessness is rarely captured by the easy distinctions generally drawn between women identified either as battered or homeless.

Both kinds of shelters operate on the assumption that every woman easily fits into one—and only one—type of program because of different lived experiences. The experiences of battering and homelessness are understood to have little in common with one another. Thus programs geared toward battered women and those directed toward homeless women vary considerably in the importance given to housing and employment considerations, lifestyle and behavioral issues, and emotional state. In short, homeless shelters are concerned with economic stability and finding housing, whereas battered women's shelters are more likely to focus on counseling and mutual support to help women heal from abuse. Moreover, the shelter staff spends significant time and effort to discern whether women are appropriate for its shelter, based largely on the assumption that each woman is clearly *either* battered or homeless.

The battered and homeless woman identities are delimited by a range of "experiences and characteristics" that do not necessarily match women's lives.[3] Thus some women struggle to get a shelter to accept them because of staff members' beliefs that each woman should conform either to the identity *battered woman* or *homeless woman*. This chapter attempts to tease out "the material consequences of ideas," arguing that they "play a part in constructing what counts as 'real'":[4] shelters create and regulate the battered woman and homeless woman "types" by forcing women to mold their stories to meet the criteria associated with those identities. In this way constructed categories and identities affect the ways women present themselves to the shelters.

By focusing in particular on this process within the battered women's shelter, I repeat Donileen Loseke's question: "What must be subjectively apprehended about an individual woman in order to classify her as a battered woman?"[5] Sheltering women who fit the identity *battered woman* while refusing access to others both reflects and helps to create a concept of a "battered woman" distinctly different from that of a "homeless woman." In particular, it may support the representation of the battered woman as a helpless victim in need of emotional healing, self-esteem training, and physical safety.

Of course, it is not merely individual staff members or shelters that characterize battered and homeless women in such markedly different ways. The classifications the people in this study relied on reflect social policies that generally provide resources that are more generous, and less confined by negative judgments about deservingness, for battered women than they are for homeless women.[6] The irony, manifest in so many women's stories, is that although these labels assume distinct experiences associated with the two groups, the stories women tell barely differ.

BATTERED WOMEN'S AND HOMELESS SHELTERS: PHILOSOPHIES AND PROGRAMS

The divergent services and programs offered by domestic violence and homeless shelters are based on their different perspectives regarding what constitutes their residents' most pressing needs and problems. Loseke has pointed out that the rules and services in battered women's shelters are organized around a representation of the "battered woman type of person . . . a type of woman needing only a good environment encouraging self-help and peer support, a type of woman capable of self-determination, a type of woman seeking to achieve independence from abuse."[7] She describes the battered woman "ideal type" as

> A woman of any age, race, social class, or marital status who was in the social roles of wife and mother. Such a woman would want to leave . . . but she would be trapped within her continuing and brutal victimization by economic and emotional dependence, by friends and social service providers who refused to help, and by her traditional beliefs. Such a woman would be isolated from others, overwhelmingly fearful and emotionally confused; she would have little faith in herself.[8]

The battered woman identity, then, excludes all but the traditional, heterosexual wife and mother. She is passive, confused, and dependent on others; and battering (with its attendant emotional disorders) represents her only problem. This portrayal clearly differs from the representation of the lazy homeless woman as a manipulative, hardened drug user steeped in underclass pathology.

The creation of the battered woman ideal type takes place in a shelter system that primarily employs professional social workers. During the 1980s many battered women's shelters underwent a process of professionalization.[9] By the 1990s most shelters had revamped their programs or staffing to conform to the demands of funding sources by centralizing authority, emphasizing employees' formal credentials, and insinuating therapeutic techniques and language into daily interactions between the staff and battered women. Rose's House provides an example of a shelter organized on the professional model. At Rose's House, almost all employees are paid social workers. Only one woman is formerly battered, and she has a master's degree in social work. Only the director defines herself as a feminist. Not surprisingly, the techniques used to work with residents are shaped by the caseworkers' belief in maintaining "emotional distance" from shelter residents.[10] The professional relationship sets up battered women as "clients" dependent upon the expert knowledge of the caseworker, and the caseworker operates according to the values of professional distance, objectivity, and rationality.

Battered women's shelters facilitate a woman's separation from her abuser largely through psychological and emotional healing. One way to accomplish this is through a "closed" program. Two of the nine shelters in Phoenix have such programs, although Rose's House and La Casa do not. Such shelters dictate that women entering their programs remain on the premises—eschewing any contact with friends, employers, and especially their partners—for periods ranging from two days to two weeks.[11] Women must get a leave of absence from work, reschedule any appointments or meetings during that time, and generally upset their daily schedules. One woman called Rose's House wanting to transfer there from a shelter with a closed program, complaining that she had already missed one housing appointment she had scheduled in anticipation of leaving her husband and was in danger of missing more if she stayed at the shelter. Women who have been working on separating from their abusers even before calling a shelter, in particular by arranging for housing, find themselves forced to put practical considerations aside during the first days in closed programs.

Supporters of closed programs argue that a woman in a violent relationship, much like a drug addict or an alcoholic, is addicted to the relationship and needs a period of intense "in-patient" counseling to ensure her recovery. By mandating resident confinement for a period of time, closed programs strive to "break the addiction" to an abusive partner, suggesting that at the end of a few days or a week of intensive counseling a woman will be less likely to return to her partner. The rationale for canceling appointments for low-income housing or demanding that a woman miss work is the belief that a battered woman's most pressing need is for counseling, supported by the notion that women remain in abusive relationships primarily because of low self-esteem, co-dependence, or the fear of being alone. Although these psychological factors may affect a woman's decision about whether to leave her relationship, closed programs basically ignore the economic insecurity many Phoenix women factored into their decisions about their partners.

Likewise, even in programs that are not closed, women sometimes have to refuse jobs if they interfere with regularly scheduled group counseling meetings. In shelters for battered women—unlike the Lighthouse and the Family Shelter—issues of joblessness, underemployment, and lack of low-income housing are secondary. Many domestic violence shelter caseworkers support the notion that a woman's economic dependence must be addressed for her to meet her goal of living independently. Some shelters' lack of assistance with finding employment that pays a living wage, however, or shelters that interfere with women's jobs and attempts to find housing suggest little concern for economic considerations. As Kimberlé Williams Crenshaw has argued, the staff focuses on "what is in [women's] minds" rather than on "access to employment, housing, and wealth"[12] and in that sense can do a disservice to women.

In addition to closed programs, several other examples show how domestic violence shelters assist women emotionally rather than materially. First, the housing list women are given at Rose's House is out-of-date and confusing. It mixes listings for privately owned, nonsubsidized housing, public housing, and Section 8 apartments without clearly distinguishing among them. Few instructions are provided regarding how to contact the agencies or apartments or how to approach the application processes. Moreover, many phone numbers are no longer valid, and women waste valuable time tracking down new numbers or following up on housing leads that no longer exist. Worse, the staff receives little training on how to assist women with housing or how to interpret the list, so they are sometimes of little service to women often overwhelmed by the tasks ahead of them. One resident became so frustrated with the time wasted pursuing dead ends that she located a low-income housing organization that gave her an updated housing list. She copied the list and gave it to the staff, who restocked the packets new residents receive with the current, more comprehensive list.

In addition to the fact that women are expected to find their own housing, Rose's House does not employ a job developer to help them find work. Likewise, the shelter lacks a job bank, connections to potential employers, or résumé-building classes.[13] It is not surprising that the shelter has no money to support a more comprehensive approach to women's employment, since like most agencies Rose's House has a tight budget and is further circumscribed by the short time women stay at the shelter. Yet Rose's House also has some freedom to choose how to allocate funds, and the shelter makes choices based on program priorities. For example, the shelter funds counseling sessions three nights a week on the dynamics of abuse, arguing that using the money for women's emotional healing is consistent with the program's mission.

On the other hand, women describe homeless shelters as lacking sensitivity to issues of personal safety and emotional support; discussions of domestic violence simply do not take place. As a result, some women may feel victimized by the homeless shelter staff or policies, and others suggest that they deteriorate emotionally and mentally while at homeless shelters. Some homeless shelters are affiliated with counseling centers and can refer residents who request therapy or would seem to benefit from one-on-one counseling. Many of these agencies, however, do not provide free care, so counseling can represent a significant investment, even when agencies' fees are determined on a sliding scale. Homeless shelter caseworkers also counsel residents— usually informally, since their job descriptions tend to stress creating and maintaining the case plan and advocating for and referring the client to other agencies. In addition, caseworkers usually operate under considerable time constraints, given the number of clients they have, which circumscribes their ability to offer regular counseling.

Betsy was first a resident of a battered women's shelter and later transferred to the Family Shelter. She faults homeless shelters for their lack of counseling, indicating that the significant emotional support she received at the battered women's shelter not only helped her stay away from her husband but was instrumental in maintaining her sobriety. Once she was living at the homeless shelter, Betsy felt it was more difficult to persevere in her goals to live independent of her husband and to avoid drugs. For women like Betsy, the more confined atmosphere of a battered women's shelter—which in Phoenix tend to be located in converted houses—might contribute to their ability to stay sober. Opportunities for drinking or using drugs are more limited than they are in homeless shelters because space is more constricted, curfews are earlier, and an ethic of emotional sharing and mutual support encourages self-disclosure. Battered women's shelters, moreover, invite women to examine their fears of being alone in a way homeless shelters do not. More support exists for women like Betsy, who admits to being overwhelmed by the responsibility of living alone with her children.

In addition to differences in basic services, homeless shelters are less oriented toward a concern with how women's gender identities impact their experiences, and caseworkers are sometimes insensitive or misuse their positions in a way that harms women residents. Marta, for example, was pressured by Mark, the caseworker at the Family Shelter, to ask her estranged husband for money to help support their children. Marta had left her husband because he was abusive, and her subsequent search for low-income or subsidized housing was unsuccessful. Marta feared future financial instability if she tried to support herself and her five children on welfare benefits without housing assistance, but she did not want to return to her husband. She complained that Mark "was pushing her toward" her husband, since Mark had gone so far as to have Marta sign a contract making her continued residence at the shelter contingent on obtaining money from her husband. But he did not take account of the likelihood that money from her husband would come with strings attached. Marta argued that in exchange for the money, her husband would demand that she continue to see him, which she saw as the first step toward reestablishing the relationship. At the very least, then, such an arrangement would keep her connected to the person she had been trying to leave for years.

With at least a modest connection to feminist philosophy, it is doubtful that a battered women's shelter would push a resident back toward an abusive partner. To the contrary, at least in theory, Rose's House perceives a strong connection between financial and emotional dependence on a male partner and works to assist women to make decisions regarding intimate relationships uninfluenced by economic need. Homeless shelters, whose first priority is clearly financial stability, generally believe practically any arrangement should be pursued if it makes housing more attainable. Caseworkers indicate that they would prefer to ensure that all residents aspire to housing and employment arrangements that preclude the potential of homelessness in the future. For example, Marta's unstable marriage does not appear to hold the promise of permanence. But caseworkers also recognize that given most residents' employment skills and educational backgrounds, in concert with their other problems, such a scenario is rarely feasible. Moreover, without sensitivity to power differentials based on gender or a commitment to women's empowerment, they may subscribe to the belief that encouraging two-parent families and attaching women to men provides a key to ending women's poverty. When such an agenda is pursued, it rarely gives priority to women's safety or freedom or focuses on their roles within their relationships.

Tammy's experience with one of the large armory shelters for homeless people in Phoenix exemplifies how homeless shelters ignore the specificity of women's homelessness. Tammy had been living at a battered women's shelter in another Arizona city when her husband discovered her location and began to threaten her. The shelter helped Tammy relocate to Phoenix and arranged for her to stay at an armory shelter:

> They sent me to [the armory shelter], which they thought was a battered women's shelter. When they answer the phone they talk about all the programs, and it sounds like a battered women's shelter. [When I got there] they said I couldn't keep my stuff there, and I came in with a huge rolling suitcase. And you have to be out by six o'clock every morning. And when I get there they said, "You should know when you walk outside tomorrow morning, this is the most dangerous part of the city. Women get raped and robbed and beat up." And for a woman who's been battered, that's a terrible feeling. So I got on the phone in tears until I found Rose's House.

Tammy's experience suggests that a significant disparity exists between homeless and battered women's shelters, especially homeless shelters not designed specifically for families. Tammy had entered a shelter that did not provide storage space for its clients and was located, as many are, in a high-crime area that lacks job opportunities. Battered women's shelters are less likely to be met with the strong neighborhood opposition engendered by homeless shelters, which housed people assume will attract criminals and bring general chaos to their neighborhoods. As a result, battered women's shelters are usually smaller and located in residential areas; most are houses that do not look like shelters from the outside. At Rose's House, Tammy did not have to worry about her safety. She could look for a job without having to tote a suitcase and her other belongings with her. And she could enjoy more amenities, including a furnished house with a comfortable living room, access to a kitchen stocked with food, a laundry room on-site, and a private backyard.

A more blatant example of the consequences for women who enter a homeless shelter is apparent in an incident that occurred at People in Transition.

During the course of this study, Beth, the administrative assistant at the shelter, informed the staff that one of the caseworkers had tried to kiss her and was repeatedly asking her out despite her refusals. After some review, the shelter director reprimanded the caseworker in question and forced him to take a month off without pay, although he used his vacation time and received a paycheck during his suspension. It eventually surfaced that Sharon, along with several other residents, had been harassed by the caseworker as well. The director called each woman into his office to describe the incidents. The residents perceived, however, that the staff's primary concern revolved around finding out whether Beth had told the residents about her experience, not around whether the caseworker had actually harassed them. Further, the director, according to Sharon, did not try to ascertain whether the experience had aggravated her severe mental illness. Although women residents felt they were interrogated by the director with little concern for their well-being, the director did transfer women residents to another caseworker. The accused caseworker was allowed to return to his job, but he was limited to working with male clients only.

This is not to argue that an all-female staff is always sensitive to women's specific concerns or that women are not mistreated at battered women's shelters or by other women. Residents of battered women's shelters certainly complain that the staff sometimes regards them with suspicion, and they do not consistently receive the kind of help they want from the shelter. According to women's stories, however, battered women's shelters are more receptive to women's concerns regarding physical safety; are more knowledgeable about the specific, gendered abuse women may suffer; and are less apt to revictimize women in certain ways as a result. A few women find it comforting to be in the generally all-woman environments at Rose's House and La Casa because their personal experiences have created fear of men.

DEFINING THE BATTERED WOMAN:
DOMESTIC VIOLENCE SHELTER STAFF

Rose's House shelter staff works with a specific definition of domestic violence that assumes first and foremost that women need the shelter for physical protection. Caseworkers maintain that women are victims of controlling male violence and must hide from their husbands or boyfriends, who are likely to become more violent if they locate their partners. Other women, the staff asserts, need the shelter to work on their diminished self-esteem while finding housing and a job. Caseworkers believe domestic violence includes physical, emotional, verbal, and sexual abuse and in this sense recognize that all women seeking shelter do not necessarily need physical protection from their abusers. But physical safety remains the principal explanation for why women seek shelter. For example, some staff members argue that a woman who visits her abuser while she resides in the shelter—thereby proving that she is not in hiding from him and is not in severe physical danger—does not "really" need shelter. In other words, she is not a "real" battered woman.

Caseworkers additionally suspect that women who do not appear "helpless" might simply need housing from the shelter or might be lying about their experiences with abuse. Thus they expect battered women to be passive and dependent rather than angry or combative. Staff members may argue that sometimes to survive a woman has to develop a hardened exterior and become quick at protecting herself against others with verbal insults. These behaviors can to some extent be seen as defense mechanisms, then, even if used within the shelter setting. But they also assume that "real" battered women will perceive that the staff and other client members of the shelter community support them and will drop their tough facade relatively quickly once in the shelter.

The many women who primarily sought housing from the shelter were placed in a difficult situation by caseworkers' expectations of how a battered woman behaves. Although residents often appreciated the counseling and group support, many had entered the shelter because they had little money and no place to live. Residents hope the staff will focus on assisting them with housing and income matters, whereas the shelter emphasizes mandatory counseling and emotional issues; this mismatch creates frustration on both sides. Caseworkers complain of a dearth of "good clients," whereas battered women insist that the shelter is not doing enough to help them.

Caseworkers at battered women's shelters, then, play an important part in constructing the battered woman as a person in need of counseling and emotional support, as categorically different in many ways from a homeless woman. In selecting shelter clients, caseworkers actively base their decisions on whether women are the "battered woman type."[14] One of Rose's House caseworkers' primary jobs is to answer the crisis line. Women call looking for shelter, and if an opening is available, caseworkers screen the caller to see if she would be appropriate for the shelter. Caseworkers make much of their responsibility for screening out women who are "homeless," expending significant time and energy discussing with one another how to ascertain if a caller is a "real" battered woman. Unlike the lack of training new staff members receive on how to negotiate the housing list, considerable attention is paid to screening potential callers.

The shelter staff contends that battered women are best served within "therapeutic communities of women"; a "real" battered woman fits into such a communal living arrangement because she is likely to submit to its restrictions:

[A battered women is] defined in terms of her passivity, low self-esteem, other-directedness, fear, confusion, and helplessness. . . . We would anticipate that such a woman would be a good commune member since she would be highly attuned to others and try to please them. . . . Clearly, shelters are for this type of woman. They are specifically organized for her, they depend on her to want and need what the organization offers, they depend on her to become a good member of the shelter community of women.[15]

Being a "good member of the shelter community" entails above all sharing one's personal history with caseworkers and other clients without complaint or reservation, including revealing intimate details about past relationships. Disclosure is expected to take place in mandatory group therapy and through approaching caseworkers to request individual counseling. This notion of community is predicated on the assumption that women need and appreciate the shelter's focus on psychological well-being and on the idea that community will be shared in and sometimes overseen by the staff. The "good client" perceives the staff as working for her best interests and is willing to accept their counsel as correct even if it conflicts with her own ideas about how to conduct her life.

Staff members operate on the assumption that "real" battered women will approximate the "good client" image, including automatically subscribing to a certain version of community. Caseworkers often become frustrated with clients' level of mistrust and hostility toward them and the extent to which many residents do not perceive that the shelter community includes the staff. Although many shelter residents assert that caseworkers are compassionate and helpful, other residents perceive the staff—with their demands for personal information and criticism of women who refuse to participate in self-disclosure—as something of a malevolent presence. Staff members are to be tolerated because of the women's need for shelter but are not considered on a par with other residents as community members.

Some women do not accept a notion of the shelter as community even when it only includes other residents. Occasionally, women are accused of and sometimes caught stealing from each other or from the shelter. In addition, women complain constantly that other residents have avoided completing their assigned chores or are shirking their communal responsibilities and that particular women receive favored treatment from the staff. Residents also sometimes hoard toiletries or donated clothing, even though they know they are taking another woman's share. Not all women see the shelter as offering support and camaraderie but rather view residence there as an opportunity to benefit all they can from what they consider to be just another meddling social service agency. And given the paucity of material assistance available, especially the scarcity of low-income housing, residents may regard each other as competitors for scarce resources. This includes public or private subsidized housing, staff recommendations to transitional housing programs, extensions to remain at the shelter after thirty days, clothing, and chore assignments. Women in the shelter understand the need to be seen as deserving of help, and one way to achieve that is to define oneself against other shelter residents.

The concept of a supportive cooperative of women as the basis for a "therapeutic community" is also wrapped up in the representation of battered women as passive, frightened, and responsive to the counsel of knowledgeable caseworkers. Callers who become angry or hostile on the phone when put on hold or told there is no space in the shelter automatically raise doubts about their status as battered women. Their anger is grounds for not letting them into the shelter even when space does become available. Caseworkers fear such women will be sullen or explosive and therefore difficult to work with. In part this is a concern because the staff needs to maintain order, and caseworkers believe this requires that residents respect their authority. But they also suspect such women cannot be "real" battered women, and their exclusion from the shelter, in turn, feeds this belief. Because most of those who are admitted present themselves as docile and appreciative of the shelter's help, few residents challenge the construction of battered women as afraid, helpless, and innocent.

Once accepted into the shelter, some women reveal hostility toward other shelter residents or caseworkers that they managed to keep in check during their initial phone call and interview. These women, and even those whose response to the violence in their lives is defined primarily by animosity and bitterness, do not fit the image of a "good client." Women who appear driven by anger and not by fear or depression may be suspected of having something to hide, of having misrepresented their histories or the real reason they need shelter. Amy, a white caseworker at Rose's House, implied that battered women can be defined best by their "helplessness," commenting that she mistrusts one of the shelter residents and believes the woman has not revealed the whole story about why she sought shelter: "I know there's more to her story. I don't know what it is, but she's *not* completely helpless." The woman, however, had not claimed to be helpless and in fact, like most battered women, went to considerable lengths to indicate that she had fought back against the abuse in her life. Her self-presentation, though, did not correspond to the staff's expectations of a true battered woman, one who is docile and sweet-tempered.

This is not to argue that caseworkers want women to be depressed and submissive. Rather they understand their jobs as helping to empower women to move from a state of relative passivity—they have been unable to take action in their lives—to a state where, as Amy put it, they "take responsibility for their lives and figure out what they need to do for themselves." This is the way caseworkers define occupational success for themselves. Their sense of accomplishment on the job is based on the work they do helping passive women become more assertive. By narrowing their focus to working with passive, depressed women (rather than those who are angry), they are responding to institutional prerogatives they then reinforce through admissions policies.

Shelters are invested in maintaining an ideal type their programs are designed to serve, and in the constant practice of attempting to fit women into these socially constructed designations, they actually create battered and homeless woman types. Particularly for staffs at battered women's shelters, adhering to a characterization of battered women that ignores women's complicated histories and multiple social problems creates a constant battle between staff and clients or potential clients. Battered women try to approximate the ideal type to gain entrance into the shelter, whereas the staff endeavors to maintain the status of the battered woman by keeping certain women out. Once accepted, residents and staff struggle over client behavior, such as hostility and uncooperativeness, that conflicts with the characterization of battered women caseworkers seek to maintain. Arguably, a more expansive definition of the battered woman identity would modify staff members' expectations and limit the number of women defined as "bad clients." "Bad clients" are often suspected of hiding something, are accused of not being appreciative of the shelter's assistance, or are disparaged for rejecting caseworker advice regarding their lives. Once designated "bad clients," women are much less likely to be given an extension beyond thirty days and are generally regarded as troublemakers within the shelter setting.

In addition to caseworkers' definitions of occupational success, their orientation toward shelter residents is affected by the tendency for shelters to be underfunded and understaffed. Herbert Gans has noted that agencies that work with impoverished populations are often in financial need:

> Agencies from which the poor seek help must operate under more or less permanent triage conditions. One way of deciding who will be sacrificed in triage decisions is to assume that most clients cheat, use every contact with them to determine whether they are cheating, and exclude those who can be suspected of cheating. Since clients are of lower status than service suppliers and lack any power or influence over them, the suppliers can also vent their own status frustrations on clients.[16]

Rose's House staff labors under just the kinds of conditions Gans describes. In part, the necessity of defining a "battered woman" identity results from the institutional demands placed on caseworkers. Because the demand for shelter in Phoenix is much greater than the available space, Rose's House is almost always full. As a result, caseworkers have to turn away significant numbers of callers every day. The pressure on the staff to ensure that "real" battered women are assisted is underscored by the lack of shelter space available citywide. The assumption that most potential clients are misrepresenting themselves mitigates against the psychic toll on caseworkers when they have to turn so many women away. These pressures combine with their relatively low pay and status compared with other professionals. Staff members at Rose's House who have undergraduate degrees in social work can expect to be paid approximately $20,000 a year—too little given the stress they experience. Their work demands significant interpersonal interaction, and moreover, caseworkers are the targets of much of the frustration low-income shelter residents have built up toward social service agencies.

DEFINING THE BATTERED WOMAN: HOMELESS SHELTER STAFF

Whereas staff members at domestic violence shelters create a battered woman "type" that often does not reflect reality, homeless shelter staff tend to ignore the strong relationship between battering and women's homelessness. Thus they perceive homeless and battered women to have little in common. Some homeless shelter staff members insist that since battered women leave their housing "by choice," they cannot be considered homeless and should not be eligible for housing assistance and other programs designed for the homeless. Others are willing to address domestic violence as a cause of homelessness only insofar as it is an element of "underclass" pathology—including drug and alcohol use, broken families, and lack of a work ethic—that debilitates homeless people.[17] Still others simply disregard battering as a cause of homelessness. Thus despite Phoenix homeless advocates' and shelter directors' admissions that 60 to 80 percent of homeless women are victims of abuse, domestic violence is rarely cited among the primary causes of homelessness. When it is discussed, it is often perceived as a "special circumstance," one that cannot be generalized to an evaluation or understanding of homelessness in the aggregate.

In most cases homeless shelter directors and caseworkers do not mention battering as a reason for homelessness unless directly asked about its role. When pressed, shelter staff members might respond with a strong affirmation that battering is indeed an issue for homeless residents, but they then usually focus on the staff's struggles to keep women from returning to abusive relationships. For example, a caseworker from People in Transition did not include battering on a list of reasons people become homeless. When I asked him about it directly, the caseworker said, "Oh yes. It's definitely a big problem, but you know we have so many women who go back to the relationship, even when these guys do awful things to them. Then sometimes they come back here asking if they can reenter the shelter." Similarly, in discussing whether domestic violence ranked as a significant cause of homelessness for women, the director of a transitional housing program concentrated on the phenomenon of women who stay with abusive men. Although she suggested during the interview that as many as 80 percent of women in homeless shelters are victims of battering, the director primarily focused on a particular family who was accepted into her program. Once they became clients, the husband's violence against the wife escalated to the point that they were asked to leave. Although the wife was "given every opportunity to stay without him," she decided to leave as well.

Both staff members speak to an important problem. Their comments suggest that such programs should clearly address battering and offer assistance to clients. The greater significance, however, lies in their interpretation of battering as primarily a question about "why women stay"—an emphasis that places responsibility on women for the abuse, remaking it into an issue about women's emotional dependence and ignoring the complexity of the relationship between battering and women's homelessness. Neither staff person commented on their initial failure to include battering on the comprehensive list of reasons for homelessness they offered. Their descriptions of why women become homeless were fairly thorough—including women whose welfare grants are too small to cover rent and other expenses, those from other states who come to Arizona looking for work but run out of money before they find it, and those who suffer from substance abuse, family medical problems, mental illness, and physical handicap. Instead of interpreting the existence of battering as evidence that controverts distinctions between battered and homeless women's identities, they support the distinction by renegotiating the discussion of battering to one of family pathology and women's tendency to stay in such relationships.

The caseworkers also offer little information about why women return to their relationships, implying that it is primarily attributable to their emotional addiction to their partners. Women's interviews, despite caseworkers' unwillingness to address the issue, indicate that their reasons for returning to violent partners were much more complex. Adrian, Sandy, and Yvette are women who maintained some connection to abusive partners. The examination that follows of those connections and of the women's experiences while living in shelters offers revealing details about their decisions regarding their relationships.

Adrian, a white woman in her mid-forties, transferred to People in Transition from a local battered women's shelter where she had spent thirty days. Although she said she was happy at the battered women's shelter and enjoyed the counseling and emotional support, she does not like People in Transition. Adrian has been so uncomfortable with the organization of the shelter, especially the fact that the women's and men's sleeping quarters are in the same building, that she called her daughter to pick her up the day she arrived. Adrian's daughter never appeared. The daughter, in fact, has been generally unwilling to assist her; their strained relationship stems from Adrian's history of mental problems and methamphetamine use.

Although Adrian worked for five years at a local engineering firm where she made between $16,000 and $20,000 per year, she was fired a year ago after missing work repeatedly because of physical problems brought on by a car accident. Moreover, she cites "family problems" as having been central to her irregular commitment to her job in the year before she was fired. Adrian describes these problems as ongoing arguments with her mother and her own (adult) children centered around Adrian's attempts to make them believe her brother sexually molested her as a child and again in the recent past. And although she claims her drug use became heavy only after she was fired, it may also have been an important contributing factor.

After she was fired Adrian could no longer pay her rent, so she moved in with her then-friend Gary. Even though she disliked his violence toward her, Adrian intensified a fairly casual relationship with Gary because she thought she would otherwise have to sleep in the streets or at a homeless shelter. The couple began to use methamphetamines regularly. Eventually, they were evicted and stayed with Adrian's sister for one night, but the family would not tolerate Gary's violence and kicked the couple out. Adrian stayed with her sister's neighbor for three weeks: "He forced me to sleep with him or I couldn't stay there. I hated him; I despised him. No one in my family would help me. I went back to my boyfriend, who was living in a motel, because I didn't feel like I had any choice. I had nowhere to go."

So began a cycle of evictions, violence, and drug use that included several attempts to commit suicide. Adrian maintains that she returned to her relationship with Gary only after exhausting several options and feeling like she had nowhere else to turn: "I kept trying to leave him. I slept in my car one night, went to a shelter one night, and it was horrible. It was mostly street people. A lot of guys were there, and they just looked like bums." After Adrian's last suicide attempt she was taken to a hospital that released her to a battered women's shelter, and she says she has not used drugs for two months. Although she stated that she feels no emotional connection to her boyfriend and has experienced only relief at being away from him since her time at the battered women's shelter, Adrian returned to Gary for several days after entering People in Transition. She eventually reentered the shelter and has resigned herself to staying until she can secure housing on her own.

When Adrian left the shelter to return to Gary, the caseworker at People in Transition understood only that Adrian wished to reestablish her relationship. The caseworker recognized that the relationship was violent because of Adrian's previous stay at the domestic violence shelter. No doubt his interpretation of her leaving was much like the statement he made when pressed about the relationship of battering to women's homelessness, focusing on the question "why do women stay," or in this case, "why do they return to their relationships." Adrian, however, construes her attempt to return to Gary not as an effort to repair the relationship but as an escape from People in Transition, which she perceives as contributing to her further mental deterioration:

> I didn't have much choice when I came here. Everyone said I needed special care, but I came here and there's nothing. I'm almost back where I came from, except I'm not with my boyfriend and not on drugs. . . . While I was at [the battered women's shelter] I think I was better. Since I got here I've gotten more depressed. I feel like I'm not doing anything. It's not safe to walk down the street. I feel stuck here. The counselors at [the battered women's shelter] helped me a lot. They were real compassionate, willing to listen. I could relate to a lot of the women's problems—many had issues with domestic violence and drugs. I felt really safe there.

Unlike her feeling of safety at the other shelter, Adrian feels vulnerable both off the grounds of People in Transition and, because men and women share space, on the shelter grounds as well. She maintains that she cannot talk to her male caseworker and often skips meals to avoid interaction with the male residents.

Sandy, another People in Transition resident, also tells a story that calls into question some caseworkers' simplistic response when asked about the connection of battering and homelessness. Sandy's husband has beaten her ferociously and repeatedly. He is in and out of jail, and Sandy lives in fear of the next time he gets out and tracks her down, as he has done on several occasions. According to Sandy, he threatens and terrorizes her mother or other family members until they reveal her location. When he finds her, Sandy is too fearful not to resume the relationship, at least for the short term until she can escape again. Similar to Adrian's silence on the subject of her prior relationship, Sandy has not discussed with her caseworker her fear that her husband could locate her at the shelter and force her to leave with him. Domestic violence is not discussed by shelter caseworkers or addressed in the handouts or paperwork residents receive when they arrive. As a result, caseworkers would probably not interpret Sandy's leaving the shelter, should her husband find her, as the result of her fear. Rather they would see her as another example of those women who cannot live without their abusive partners.

Sandy's and Adrian's stories also suggest the pointlessness of listing domestic violence as yet another single-factor "cause" of homelessness. Adrian's lack of a job, drug use, precarious mental state, sexual abuse, and separation from her family surely contribute to her need for a shelter. Like Adrian,

Sandy also has a history of drug use and was asked to leave People in Transition when drugs were found in her belongings. The next time she visited the shelter Sandy had trouble focusing, and her speech was slurred. She had, however, arranged for housing by staying with a friend rent free in exchange for providing child care. Although she was temporarily off the street, her housing situation appeared rather precarious—particularly because it was contingent upon her caring for children, a job that in her present state she would have difficulty doing.

Yvette, an African American woman with three children, would also be included in statistics of those women who leave shelters to return to abusive relationships. Yvette left her husband in South Carolina and traveled across the country to Phoenix to minimize his chances of finding her. Her previous attempts at leaving had always ended in her husband locating her—one time because she stayed with relatives and another because she applied for welfare benefits for herself and her three children, and her husband's lawyer obtained the records and found her new address. Unlike the other times she had left, Yvette did not bring her children with her when she fled cross-country. With no idea where she would stay when she first arrived in Arizona, she feared subjecting her children to living on the streets if she could not find a shelter.

When Yvette found an opening at Rose's House, she immediately began to look for a job and housing so she could send for her children as soon as possible. She was under the impression that her husband "would never hurt the kids" and, since he had never spent much time taking care of them, that he would allow them to join her. Her primary concern was arranging for their move to Arizona without her husband learning her location. After she left, however, her husband threatened that she would never see her children again if she refused to return to him. She eventually decided to go back to her husband for a few months so she could save some money and, more important to her, take her children with her the next time she left.

DEFINING THE BATTERED WOMAN: DOMESTIC VIOLENCE SHELTER RESIDENTS

Shelter caseworkers are not the only ones interested in defining the battered woman. Battered women themselves also contribute to representations of their own experiences. Although they speak eloquently about the financial constraints that influence their decisions regarding their relationships, at the same time battered women often differentiate themselves from homeless women. Unlike those in homeless shelters, battered women can rely on an identity that names them victims of someone else's pathology. They also have access to the "survivor" persona, which helps describe them as potentially strong women. Although her partner's victimization undercuts her self-esteem, a "survivor" retains a core of mental and emotional soundness that in the right circumstances will flourish. Ann Jones has noted that "women who have lived through such violence, who know the immense daily expenditure of strength and attention and self-discipline it takes to survive, rarely identify themselves as 'victims.' They think of themselves as strong women who can somehow 'cope.'"[18] Although it could be argued as easily that the women in homeless shelters develop personal fortitude through their struggles to survive, they tend not to be constructed as survivors. Culturally, battered women are congratulated for turning to a shelter because leaving their relationships is seen as the defining first act in helping themselves, whereas those in homeless shelters are perceived to be lazy, turning to shelters as a way to live off the system.[19]

Phyllis, a fifty-five-year-old white resident of Rose's House, provides an example of how residents distinguish themselves from homeless women. She contends that homeless people seek shelter after they have allowed their financial and personal lives to deteriorate, whereas battered women are in shelters because they want to change their lives, which have been ruined by someone else: "I think I just ended up in this place through no fault of my own. . . . I've found so much caring here, we really support each other, we have that sister love." Kim, a white woman in her mid-forties and also a resident of Rose's House, responded similarly to a question about whether she considers herself to be homeless: "No, not really. I've always been very resourceful. . . . I've got friends who are battered women and come to shelters like this, but I don't know anyone who's been homeless. We're survivors, most of us. We've learned to be very strong and resourceful because of everything we've been through. Financially, it's a big hurdle. If you don't have a job or skills, then you've got a problem." Despite cultural narratives of domestic violence that historically have constructed battered women as "masochists"[20] and more current beliefs about battering that concentrate on its psychologically debilitating effects,[21] Kim constructs women who leave as courageous. Indeed she argues that battered women are stronger than other women specifically *because* they have experienced abuse.

Tammy, also a white resident of Rose's House in her early forties, echoes Kim's construction of battered women as survivors. In response to the question Kim was asked regarding whether she thinks of herself as homeless, Tammy asserted:

> No, and it's bizarre because I guess I have been [homeless], but when someone says homeless you just go "yuck"—I think of a bag lady. I guess since I've always been able to provide for myself, I just think of myself as in transition instead of homeless. I think there's probably a lot of people with mental and addiction problems that are homeless. I have a hard time with that issue because

I've always had work. But I don't know how people in homeless shelters do it: you have to be out by six o'clock in the morning, no place to leave your stuff, and the fear level. It must be terrible to someone's self-esteem. If places like [Rose's House] weren't available and I knew my only option was a homeless shelter, I would *not* have left my husband.

Tammy's comments speak to constructions of both the battered woman and the homeless woman. The battered woman is "in transition," a status that implies a strong connection to work and other markers of middle-class position. A homeless woman, on the other hand, is a "bag lady," mentally ill, addicted, and lacking a work ethic. Tammy tempers these identities, however, by recognizing the difficulties inherent in moving from the "in transition" phase to one of self-sufficiency for those staying in large armory-style homeless shelters. She transferred to Rose's House after one day in such a shelter.

Tammy's belief that homelessness is related to mental illness, drug use, or the lack of a work ethic is echoed by Latanya. She argues that "homeless people have different problems" than she has; they "have given up." She insists that "there is always a way out of homelessness" and that she would "work really hard to get out of it," something homeless people do not do. Likewise, María differentiates herself from homeless women, stating that homeless women "don't clean themselves, talk to themselves, don't want to work on their lives or change," whereas women in domestic violence shelters do want to better themselves.

Women who become homeless for reasons other than domestic violence display a similar desire to separate themselves from the homeless label, which conjures up the image of a bag lady for many of them as well. "Homeless" suggests a woman mentally ill or drug addicted, unwashed, helpless, and hopeless—a person mired in a permanent lifestyle rather than "in transition." Although the inclination to escape the designation is as strong for homeless women who are not battered, battered women claim an alternative status to homelessness more successfully, largely because they have recourse to the battered woman identity.

Yet in many women's experiences, battering and homelessness are not so distinct. In fact, several women gained entrance into a battered women's shelter only by consciously emphasizing certain past experiences and not others. Betsy, for example, was not accepted initially by Rose's House, in part because she had not defined her problem as domestic violence. She says now, "I didn't understand that was the issue." Rose's House accepted her only after another agency spoke with Betsy and intervened with the shelter on her behalf, characterizing her primary problem as a battering husband and her principal need as emotional support. She entered the shelter the following day and stayed there for the next six weeks. Prior to the intervention on Betsy's behalf, Rose's House had characterized her as homeless, a woman whose need for shelter was related to her poverty and use of drugs.

Similarly, a nurse at the hospital where Adrian stayed after a suicide attempt directed her to call domestic violence shelters and describe herself as a battered woman. At the outset, Adrian was calling both homeless and battered women's shelters, and she stated, "I just wanted to find somewhere to go. I didn't really know what the battered women's shelter was about, but when I called, they asked if I'd been abused and I said yes, plenty of times." Another agency helped Diane emphasize her past relationship—which was violent—as her primary problem, and as a result she was accepted into a domestic violence shelter. Although her battering relationship had ended five years prior to her eviction and present need for housing, the Head Start teacher at Diane's children's school prodded her to tell the shelter that domestic violence was her main problem.

Both Betsy and Adrian maintain that they had previously failed to realize they were battered women. Once accepted to the shelter, talking with the staff and participating in the counseling groups resulted in a change in their self-definitions. Even if they initially played along just to get into the shelter, both currently appear to accept wholeheartedly the battered woman identity. Diane, on the other hand, admits to some embarrassment that she relied on an experience with abuse that had taken place some time ago to gain entrance into the shelter. She did not change her self-definition as the other women did. Whereas Adrian and Betsy embraced the identity and began to think of themselves as inherently different from homeless women—or nonbattered women, for that matter—Diane self-consciously molded her story to fit the battered woman construction and related eligibility criteria without accepting the identity for herself.

Betsy's and Adrian's attempts to renegotiate the primary signifiers of their self-definitions from "homeless" or "drug addict" to "battered woman" are similar to the insistence of Phyllis, Kim, and Tammy that they are not like homeless women. In fact, most women in domestic violence shelters believe women who live at homeless shelters do not share their experiences. This widely shared belief by women in domestic violence shelters exists alongside the reality that many women—in both kinds of shelters—both experience violence and state that they stayed in relationships for fear of homelessness. As argued earlier, women in domestic violence shelters have an incentive not to recognize the relationship between abuse and homelessness, since battered women garner more public sympathy than homeless women do. And in the case of women without children in particular, the shelters available to battered women tend to be better funded and offer more amenities than homeless shelters.

One effect of creating separate categories for battering and homelessness is that most women in homeless shelters with some history of abuse, and even those who were initially in battered women's shelters, have no idea that other women at the shelter have lived through battering. This is the case at the Family Shelter even when several women with similar experiences are living in close proximity. With only twenty-six units, the Family Shelter is compact enough that residents usually become familiar with one another fairly quickly. Nevertheless, women both there and at Rose's House had perceptions of women in homeless shelters seriously at odds with what women revealed to me in private interviews. Neither Marta nor Betsy, for example, whose sojourns at the Family Shelter overlapped for a time, knew that the other woman had experienced battering and had come from Rose's House. Although their rooms were less than 500 feet from one another, Marta stated that "there are only two or three women" she knew who went to a homeless shelter after Rose's House. Because, as she put it, "many don't talk about domestic violence or their pasts," Marta did not realize that some current Family Shelter residents share much of her history. Betsy likewise stated that she "feels different" from other women at the Family Shelter because "most people aren't from domestic violence shelters."

Marta's and Betsy's reticence to speak to one another may grow out of the relative silence about domestic violence within the Family Shelter generally. A history of a battering relationship is not an admissions requirement, as it is at women's shelters, and women are not encouraged to discuss it. Mandatory life skills classes stress learning expertise in tasks like budgeting and interviewing for jobs, and these are the aspects of residents' lives the program tries to affect. Staff silence on abusive relationships supports the notion that battering is a separate issue from homelessness. Staff members send the message that even if battered women live at the Family Shelter, domestic violence is inappropriate as a primary concern for residents, who should be expending their energy on other aspects of their lives.

In addition to Betsy and Marta, Adrian, Ella, and a number of others first stayed at battered women's shelters and subsequently transferred to homeless shelters or transitional housing programs. It is nearly impossible to clearly define each of these women as either a "battered woman" or a "homeless woman." All have multiple reasons for the difficulty they experience remaining stably housed. Attempting to reduce their experiences to the one reason each sought shelter would only ignore complexity and ambiguity in favor of unilateral explanations that leave out the most interesting facets of their histories.

Deciding which type of shelter each woman fits into raises an equally difficult question. If the "battered woman type" is one who can clearly show how battering has affected her life—leading directly to her need to escape her present situation—Betsy certainly fits the description. She tried repeatedly to leave her husband because she could no longer live with his abusiveness, but the several alternatives she pursued, including staying with friends and family members, were not effective as long-term options. She required the support of Rose's House because of her income status and her need to support her three children. Yet Betsy also used drugs, a primary marker of "homeless woman" in public discourse and a practice rarely associated with battered women. Further, unlike the battered woman who appears to have no problem with her work ethic, Betsy was evicted repeatedly in part because neither she nor her husband worked consistently.

Likewise, Adrian's need for a shelter could be attributed to her drug use, which led to her losing the job she had held for five years and to her lackadaisical attitude toward finding a new one. She has traded sex for housing, been rejected by her family, and been evicted from her home. All these factors and events can be described as markers of "the homeless." On the other hand, Adrian attributes her job loss to a car accident that damaged her back and to a lack of medical insurance that might have paid for physical therapy to relieve her pain and allow her to continue to work. She needed a shelter because her boyfriend's violence had become too much for her to bear. His violence had also resulted in their being kicked out of a family member's home, thereby destroying a possible housing option for Adrian.

"I KNEW I DIDN'T WANT TO BE HOMELESS": WHY WOMEN STAY

Although women in domestic violence shelters attempt to distinguish themselves from homeless women, they are nevertheless acutely aware and fearful of homelessness. Many women attribute their decisions to remain in battering relationships to financial fears and insecurities, particularly the fear of homelessness. Like Michelle, they stayed with an abusive spouse because they considered homelessness a real possibility if they left. Michelle entered the Family Shelter in part to escape her abusive relationship with her second husband: "I stayed with my last husband for at least the last eight years of our marriage because I was afraid I couldn't make it on my own. . . . The only reason I moved out and got on welfare was because I saw the effect on my kids—my son was getting violent." Her anxiety about poverty and homelessness kept her in a relationship for years, and only her responsibility toward her children convinced Michelle that living on the street or in a shelter would be better than suffering the abuse. This was the case in part because Michelle perceives shelters, where she must live communally with strangers and abide by the many rules governing resident behavior, to represent an option barely more attractive than living on the street: "It's really hard to live in a shelter. It's absolutely the last choice. It's one choice above the street."

Likewise, Phyllis, a Rose's House resident, factored economic considerations into her choices to marry and then remain for varying periods with
three men, all of whom were abusive. Like Michelle, during all her marriages
she worked in low-wage occupations—as a laundromat attendant, a domestic
worker, and a cashier. Her fear of poverty and homelessness was a powerful
incentive to remain married until her anxiety about her child's safety provided the impetus for her to leave:

> I stayed with my second husband for financial reasons. He was an engineer. I
> grew up in poverty and swore that my child wouldn't. Then I found out he was a
> child molester. I got my daughter out of there, and I didn't have anything. I got
> two jobs. I worked in sales modeling at night and on a moving van during the
> daytime. I stayed with my third husband because I didn't have anywhere to go.
> The places I had to go are almost as bad as being with him. My brother [might
> have taken me in], but he's abusive to his kids.

Phyllis rejected the shelter option for many years, based on an early
experience with a homeless shelter:

> When my child was little, she was eight or nine, we had to get out of the house
> because the violence was so bad. We were in a homeless shelter that was like a
> prison. You didn't have a private bathroom, you had [open] stalls just like in a
> prison. You had to earn points by cleaning to get clothes that had been donated. I
> went back [to my husband] in a week. It was better than being there.

Phyllis finally decided to try Rose's House when the crisis counselor assured
her that the program did not resemble the shelter she had been in many
years ago. Like Michelle, Phyllis considered life in a shelter or on the street
unacceptable, leaving her with no other option but to stay in her relationship—at least for the short term.

Thus even though some women in domestic violence shelters attempt
to distinguish themselves from the homeless, their fears of and experiences
with homelessness cannot be ignored. Based on women's stories, whether a
woman finds housing in a battered women's shelter or a homeless shelter is
not always wholly contingent upon her experiences. Once accepted into a
shelter, however, she becomes labeled either a battered woman or a homeless
woman, and in the case of those in battered women's shelters, she often
begins to define herself based on that identity. The ideological rewards for
distinguishing herself from homeless women are manifold, yet the battered
woman identity retains its own negative connotations of dependence and
passivity and exists at the juncture of serious tension between "survivor" and
"victim" definitions.

CONCLUSION

Coupling an examination of shelters and an analysis of homeless and housed interviews reveals the tensions and links between the world of lived experiences and the creation of cultural constructs. Homeless and housed interviews expose the interplay between the process of becoming homeless and the complex, often contradictory perceptions of homelessness articulated by both homeless and housed people. Moreover, the environments and regulations of homeless and battered women's shelters provide the specific framework for women's experiences of homelessness; they are central to interpretations of homelessness. Shelter organization both reflects and encourages particular understandings of why people become homeless and which services will help them most. Likewise, cultural beliefs about why people become homeless have a significant effect on the kinds of solutions to homelessness that are pursued. Thus it has been necessary to investigate the multiple and sometimes inconsistent meanings of homelessness reflected in these many sources.

THE SHELTER "INDUSTRY" AND THE MAKING OF IDENTITIES

In their philosophies, programs, and daily operations, shelters help to newly formulate and to cement already existing notions of the "battered woman" and "homeless woman" identities. Shelters, like antipoverty and social service agencies of various kinds, operate with particular categories of need, as well as categories of persons meeting the definition of one in need.[1] Angela Tretheway has argued that "organizations . . . are political because they are primary sites of identity formation in contemporary life."[2] Her contention points to the ways the shelter system is fundamental to constructing not only homelessness but also homeless women. Thus the kinds of assistance offered to and withheld from homeless and battered women in Phoenix shelters can be directly linked to the ways homelessness and domestic violence—and homeless and battered women—are defined in contemporary political discourse.

In homeless shelters the staff focuses on providing housing and employment assistance within the context of defining homelessness as, at least in part, a behavioral problem. Social workers have been given primary responsibility for "fixing" the homeless through surveillance and control of deviant lifestyles, toward the ultimate goal of economic self-sufficiency. Staff members commonly understand the residents as "cases" to which an "expert" responds using professionalized methods. The surveillance and control of resident activities, combined with attempts to "know" residents through constant demands for personal information, suggest that homeless women will become housed only through invasive monitoring and discipline. Shelter caseworkers often patronize residents, believing the caseworker—not the homeless person—can best determine how a resident should live her life, what sort of choices she should make about how to support herself financially, and what caused her to become homeless.

Although battered women's shelters share some practices with homeless shelters, they also differ. Battered women's shelters sometimes engage in monitoring and surveillance of residents but are less wed to punitive measures and social control than homeless shelters are. Rather they provide individual and group counseling and a safe harbor from physically violent mates. If monitoring and other invasive tactics are used, it is often in the context of attempting to distinguish the "real" battered woman from imposters, those for whom battering is not the primary reason for seeking shelter. The "real" battered woman, it is perceived, needs and appreciates the focus on psychological and physical healing; assistance with employment and housing is clearly secondary.

These shelter practices reflect particular beliefs about homelessness and battering and about homeless and battered women. Homeless people are constructed as part of a lazy, irresponsible, addicted, or criminal underclass; homelessness stems from individual decisions and choices or from psychological problems ranging from low self-esteem to mental illness. The few homeless people defined as deserving assistance are expected to be docile and appreciative of help. The assumption of docility, of course, is much more widely applied to battered women, who are variably defined as passive, fearful, and traditional, or as strong survivors. Although a dominant discourse on both homelessness and battering may exist, multiple and conflicting representations of homeless and battered women abound.

Evidence for competing constructions of homelessness is apparent in the everyday workings of the shelters. Indeed the homeless shelter system appears to be organized around sometimes clashing convictions and goals: shelters must counteract the dysfunctional lessons homeless people have learned about life, yet changes occurring in the national and even the international economy—which neither the staff nor residents can control—are also responsible for homelessness. Thus mandatory deadlines for job seekers and drug and alcohol tests for those returning to the shelter after hours compete with staff advocacy to obtain better housing and employment opportunities. Structural issues compete with a lack of personal foresight and individual effort as explanations for homelessness.

INDIVIDUALISM OR SPECIALISM?

Perhaps the most central contradiction, one that most confounds those interested in providing alternatives to the current shelter system, lies in the question of how homeless services should be organized. The majority of staff people in both homeless and domestic violence shelters have difficulty addressing the interdependence of homeless women's problems, particularly the relationship between battering and homelessness. Although advocates affirm that 60 to 80 percent of women are homeless as a result of domestic violence, homeless shelters like the Lighthouse refuse to accept battered women, and domestic violence shelters like Rose's House create separate categories for homeless and battered women. Moreover, homeless shelters may be insensitive to the needs of battered women and may lack secure locations and support groups. Domestic violence shelters, on the other hand, often do not offer employment or housing assistance, concentrating primarily on counseling. Closed programs may even sabotage women's attempts at self-sufficiency by mandating that they cancel housing appointments and miss work for a period of time when they first enter the shelter.

If women become homeless as a result of intersecting factors—including battering, poverty, and low-income housing shortages—they are most likely to gain economic security when services are individualized. That is, each person would benefit most from a package of services targeted to her specific needs. Homeless women currently living in emergency shelters often assert that they need such individualized services that take into account their specific reasons for becoming homeless. They argue that an individualized approach, focusing on services identified by the homeless woman, would not only help her become economically self-sufficient but would also combat cultural beliefs that homeless people are to blame for their situations. Moreover, homeless women insist that despite the general public acceptance of single-issue explanations for homelessness—such as mental illness, drug addiction, welfare dependence, or teenage pregnancy—homelessness should be understood as an outgrowth of poverty. Thus drug addiction, eviction, and low wages should be addressed simultaneously as they relate to poverty.

The question about how shelter services should be constituted, then, is a question about how homeless programs reflect and further circumscribe cultural understandings and representations of homelessness. This suggests a serious quandary: individualizing services may lead to a focus on the homeless person herself. In essence, to target and shape services that address an individual's distinct needs, the individual herself becomes the locus of inquiry and correction. The fact that both homeless and housed low-income people are affected by the structural conditions and economic circumstances contributing to homelessness is lost. Emphasizing the individual's particular set of experiences might, in this sense, support rather than undercut emergency shelters' tendency to focus on individualized psychological and behavioral explanations for homelessness. Thus it would also endorse shelters' attempts to regulate and correct individual homeless women and ensure that social control remains a predominant objective of shelters.

PLAYING TO THE (HOUSED) PUBLIC

The complexity of shelter objectives and staff philosophies can also be traced to the ways homelessness resonates with the public. Interviews with the housed suggest that homelessness may operate as a symbol for people's anxieties over both their personal economic stability and the viability of the U.S. economy. The existence of homelessness in every major city calls into question widely held beliefs about limitless social and economic opportunities. For many, such opportunities, along with a commitment to work and personal independence, are of central importance to a definition of what it means to be a U.S. citizen. Because homeless people are increasingly visible, they provide a perpetual reminder of the numbers of people who do not fulfill the image of productive citizen.

Housed people construct the homeless in various ways. Many emphasize that homeless people are not to be trusted, that they are dishonest and engaged in various scams designed to swindle housed people out of their hard-earned money. Other housed people deride the "homeless lifestyle," defined as living for the moment, engaging in irresponsible and wasteful spending, and depending on welfare and other forms of charity. Paramount is the homeless woman's denial of personal responsibility for her circumstances. As Linda—a housed person—contends, personal responsibility separates the housed from the homeless: "I see a lot of this as lack of personal forethought and responsibility in terms of education, drug and alcohol abuse, and a lack of desire, [the idea] that someone will pick up the pieces for you." Thus homelessness is explained largely as a difference between the homeless and the housed in terms of mentality and drive.

The fact that homeless shelters' philosophies and programs reflect this set of beliefs suggests in part that homeless shelters are responding to the directives of the housed rather than to those of homeless people. Certainly, homeless women are not consulted for their expertise about how to solve the problem of homelessness, and their criticisms of the shelter system are often interpreted as complaints stemming from laziness or deviant thinking associated with the underclass. Yet homeless women speak eloquently about the ways shelter programs could be reconstituted to meet their needs. In particular, they bemoan the fact that to get help they must appear to meet constructed categories of need that do not reflect their lived experiences.

This situation is complicated by many homeless women's refusal to identify with homelessness or to link themselves with other homeless people. Indeed their point of view about homelessness does not necessarily differ from that of housed people. The attempt to disassociate oneself from homelessness extends to a rejection of the label *homeless* for two-thirds of the women interviewed. This is not surprising, as most homeless women believe that to be defined as deserving of assistance they must negotiate a way around the stigmatized identity *homeless*. Perhaps it makes more sense, in this context, to locate homeless women's critiques of homelessness and the shelter system in each individual's telling of her own story. A homeless woman who disparages other shelter residents will simultaneously articulate the interweaving of multiple problems—mostly structural economic issues—to explain her own homelessness.

SOLUTIONS TO HOMELESSNESS: EMPLOYMENT AND HOUSING

When women in both domestic violence and homeless shelters describe how shelters might better assist them, they often point to their need for low-cost housing and better-paying, more reliable employment. At the same time, shelters for homeless families that define themselves as mandatory work programs are gaining increasing favor with both the housed public and funding agencies. The growing emphasis on mandatory work rules in many homeless shelters has its counterpart in work requirements that provide the central organizing principle for welfare reform. Indeed approaches to both the homeless and those receiving welfare benefits, particularly cash aid, have become increasingly similar. One transitional housing program in Phoenix describes its objective as "breaking the welfare cycle." And homeless shelters that mandate work as a central component of their programs argue that without rules that force clients to find employment by a certain time, homeless people will simply while away their three months at the shelter—an argument that owes much to the lazy "welfare queen" image.

Clearly, this does not represent the focus on employment most homeless women have in mind. They complain that even the job training programs with the best reputations are not designed to create significantly different employment options for their clients. Homeless women want assistance that improves their training and makes them eligible for jobs that pay a living wage. They speak to the significant barriers that exist to finding well-paid employment—contentions supported by academic research.

A significant body of research criticizes the assumption that jobs are available for low-skilled workers and that those jobs pay enough to provide financial stability.[3] Several studies show that real wages for low-skilled, minimally educated workers have decreased significantly since the mid-1970s. Even the substantial numbers of such workers who maintain a strong connection to the labor force rarely make enough to rise above the poverty line.[4] In discussing welfare reform, William Gorham points to the deterioration of the low-wage job market that has deeply affected homeless people at Phoenix shelters: "The job market may well have enough jobs for the majority, perhaps most, of the nation's current welfare recipients. But these jobs do not typically pay enough for a family to become self-sufficient. In addition, a considerable group, perhaps 20 percent or more, do not have the capacity to find and hold even a low-paying job in the regular labor market."[5]

Homeless shelters—in particular those that define themselves as work programs—must address such job market realities, as well as the limited capabilities of a portion of the homeless population, if they are to provide real assistance to shelter residents. Moreover, as the jobs available to the least educated people become increasingly concentrated in the service sector, it is also important to consider the stories of people like Janet and Betsy, who blame their homelessness on their husbands' disinterest in working steadily. Service-sector employment—which offers minimal opportunity for advancement, intellectual stimulation, or the psychological rewards of doing well at a job one cares about—holds little appeal for many of the people interviewed.

Another issue to consider is the growing tendency for transitional housing programs to define themselves as work programs, just as short-term shelters do. Several high-profile transitional housing programs in Phoenix make full-time employment the only option for their residents, asserting that full-time employment is the key to a new "lifestyle" that will move people out of homelessness. If residents are in school or job training, these programs point out, they will be unable to save money and establish credit—important facets of long-term economic stability. If transitional housing programs become work programs across the board, however, using education and training to move homeless people into more profitable sectors of the economy becomes a much more improbable solution to homelessness. The homeless women accepted by these transitional housing programs will have to continue to work in the same low-paying jobs they were eligible for before entering the program—few of which offer a living wage, health benefits, or opportunities for advancement.

In addition to mandatory work programs, homeless women also speak to the drawbacks of relying on emergency, short-term shelters as the primary policy response to homelessness; rather, they favor longer-term transitional housing programs. Transitional housing programs usually charge residents one-third of their incomes for rent—a significantly lower percentage than most low-income families pay in the private housing market—and they couple housing assistance with multiple opportunities for other kinds of financial help. Some match clients with a housed family that may assist them with driving to job interviews, locating used furniture, and purchasing household appliances. Even if none of this extra attention exists, families argue that they benefit immensely from having one or two years—rather than three months—to pursue job training and education, find work, and save money.

It is also important to remember, however, how variable the organization and structure of transitional housing programs can be. People in Transition and the Endowment for Phoenix Families (EPF) provide two examples of transitional housing programs that differ in their philosophical approaches to residents, the kind of housing they make available, and the rules for and expectations of residents. Most transitional programs more closely approximate EPF in terms of the intensive, one-on-one assistance they offer, as well as in their reliance on single-family homes and apartments to house their clients.

Findings from People in Transition raise questions about the efficacy of longer-term programs. Despite a notion prevalent among many observers of homelessness that longer-term transitional programs ensure more client success than three-month emergency shelters do, interviews and participant observation suggest that merely giving homeless women a longer time to become financially stable may not be helpful unless support services are offered as well. Particularly for mentally and physically disabled homeless women like those at People in Transition, adding several months or even a year to their shelter time may not result in more people becoming stably housed. In fact, many People in Transition residents experienced depression and a growing sense of futility while living there, which they attributed to their repeated failures at addressing the issues that initially led to their homelessness. Many are like Susan, who wanted to find work but had difficulty because of her advancing age and the shelter's location in a dilapidated part of the city.

Even more detrimental to Susan were the lackadaisical caseworkers who spent little time with the residents, did not work with other agencies on most people's behalf, and created few relationships with prospective employers.

These and the many other descriptions of homelessness and critiques of shelters woven throughout this book suggest that homeless women have much to contribute to policy debates about homelessness. If given a chance, many can provide articulate and probing analyses. In reevaluating the shelter system, the first step must be to decouple homelessness from a notion of deviance so that homeless women's resistance to the current shelter system—and their criticisms and ideas about how to better structure shelters—will not automatically be dismissed as meaningless complaints from the undisciplined underclass.

NOTES

INTRODUCTION

1. I use the terms *shelter industry* and *shelter system* somewhat interchangeably. The term *shelter industry* in the title and throughout the book comes from Jennifer Wolch, "Review of *Tell Them Who I Am: The Lives of Homeless Women*, by Elliot Liebow," in *Urban Geography* 16:2 (1995): 178–188.

2. Similarly, Jodi Cohen studied the way impoverished clients at a soup kitchen construct meanings for poverty. See Jodi R. Cohen, "Poverty: Talk, Identity and Action," *Qualitative Inquiry* 3 (March 1997): 71–92.

3. Although some of the people with whom participant observation took place refused an in-person interview or were too mentally unstable to participate, interaction occurred over a long enough period that some of those people appear in the book. Any quoted material, however, comes from the interviews.

4. Michael B. Katz, *The Undeserving Poor: From the War on Poverty to the War on Welfare* (New York: Pantheon, 1989), 5.

5. Phyllis L. Baker notes the importance of using multiple methods to ensure more comprehensive and reliable ethnographic findings. Phyllis L. Baker, "Doin' What It Takes to Survive: Battered Women and the Consequences of Compliance to a Cultural Script," *Studies in Symbolic Interaction* 20 (1996): 76.

6. See, for example, Deborah R. Connolly, *Homeless Mothers: Face to Face with Women and Poverty* (Minneapolis: University of Minnesota Press, 2000).

7. Ibid., 133.

8. Much has been written about whites' incorrect assumption that African American women are the primary beneficiaries of welfare; likewise, welfare has become associated with blacks in political discourse. See, for example, Kenneth J. Neubeck and Noel A. Cazenave, *Welfare Racism: Playing the Race Card against America's Poor* (New York: Routledge, 2001); Jill Quadagno, *The Color of Welfare: How Racism Undermined the War on Poverty* (New York: Oxford, 1994); Karen Seccombe, Delores James, and Kimberly Battle Walters, "'They Think You Ain't Much of Nothing': The Social Construction of the Welfare Mother," *Journal of Marriage and Family* 60 (November 1998): 849–865.

9. The in-depth interviews consisted of open-ended questions about a woman's social history and her perceptions about homelessness. Because of the open-ended nature of the interviews, each one varied slightly and sometimes significantly from the next. For example, I would begin by asking a woman what series of events led her to the shelter, and she would recount what she considered to be her story of homelessness. I added some questions after a number of different homeless women had repeatedly (and individually) brought up the same issue. Specifically, the questions asking whether a woman considered herself to be homeless and whether she regarded herself as mostly similar to or different from the other people in the shelter were added after several weeks of interviewing.

10. James A. Holstein and Jaber F. Gubrium, *The Self We Live By: Narrative Identity in a Postmodern World* (New York: Oxford University Press, 2000), 103.

11. Aihwa Ong, *Spirits of Resistance and Capitalist Discipline: Factory Women in Malaysia* (Albany: State University of New York Press, 1987).

12. Joseph Gusfield, *The Culture of Public Problems: Drinking-Driving and the Symbolic Order* (Chicago: University of Chicago Press, 1981).

13. Most interviews were conducted either in person or over the phone, although in the interest of time a number of people filled out questionnaires. They contained the same questions used in the in-person interviews.

14. For examples of ethnographic studies of women's homelessness, see Connolly, *Homeless Mothers*; Elliot Liebow, *Tell Them Who I Am: The Lives of Homeless Women* (New York: Free Press, 1993); Stephanie Golden, *The Women Outside: Myths and Meanings of Homelessness* (Berkeley: University of California Press, 1992); Jonathan Kozol, *Rachel and Her Children: Homeless Families in America* (New York: Fawcett Columbine, 1988).

15. See, for example, Carol Stack, *All Our Kin: Strategies for Survival in a Black Community* (New York: Harper and Row, 1974); Elliot Liebow, *Tally's Corner: A Study of Negro Streetcorner Men* (Boston: Little, Brown, 1967); Mitchell Duneier, *Slim's Table: Race, Respectability, and Masculinity* (Chicago: University of Chicago Press, 1992).

16. See Joanne Passaro, *The Unequal Homeless: Men on the Streets, Women in Their Place* (New York: Routledge, 1996); Rob Rosenthal, *Homeless in Paradise: A Map of the Terrain* (Philadelphia: Temple University Press, 1994); David Wagner, *Checkerboard*

Square: Culture and Resistance in a Homeless Community (Boulder: Westview, 1993); Golden, *The Women Outside*.

17. Sherry B. Ortner, "Ethnography among the Newark: The Class of '58 of Weequahic High School," in *Naturalizing Power: Essays in Feminist Cultural Analysis*, ed. Sylvia Yanagisako and Carol Delaney (New York: Routledge, 1995), 257–258.

18. E.g., Peter H. Rossi, *Down and Out in America: The Origins of Homelessness* (Chicago: University of Chicago Press, 1989); Robert C. Coates, *A Street Is Not a Home: Solving America's Homeless Dilemma* (Buffalo: Prometheus, 1990); Christopher Jencks, *The Homeless* (Cambridge: Harvard University Press, 1994).

19. Peter Marcuse, "Neutralizing Homelessness," *Socialist Review* 18 (1988): 88.

20. Wagner, *Checkerboard Square*, 5; Charles Hoch and Robert Slayton, *New Homeless and Old: Community and the Skid Row Hotel* (Philadelphia: Temple University Press, 1989).

21. Attempts to categorize the homeless are often accompanied by estimates of the number of those homeless. The pervasive emphasis on counting the homeless seems to distance "us" from "them." "They" become nothing more than a policy problem needing to be "fixed," which based on an ongoing and sometimes acerbic debate over the numbers gains more or less funding and importance as a public issue. The focus, then, becomes the debate over the numbers rather than the homeless people themselves.

22. Connolly, *Homeless Mothers*, 36.

23. Talmadge Wright, *Out of Place: Homeless Mobilizations, Subcities, and Contested Landscapes* (Albany: State University of New York Press, 1997); Wagner, *Checkerboard Square*; Steven Vanderstaay, *Street Lives: An Oral History of Homeless Americans* (Philadelphia: New Society, 1992).

24. See David A. Snow and Leon Anderson, *Down on Their Luck: A Study of Homeless Street People* (Berkeley: University of California Press, 1993).

25. Both Wagner's *Checkerboard Square* and Snow and Anderson's *Down on Their Luck*, for example, offer nuanced ethnographies of life on the street and in armory shelters.

26. Constance A. Nathanson, *Dangerous Passage: The Social Control of Sexuality in Women's Adolescence* (Philadelphia: Temple University Press, 1991), 12–14.

27. Elizabeth Huttman and Sonjia Redmond, "Women and Homelessness: Evidence of Need to Look Beyond Shelters to Long-Term Social Service Assistance and Permanent Housing," *Journal of Sociology and Social Welfare* 19 (December 1992): 89–111; Theresa Funiciello, *Tyranny of Kindness: Dismantling the Welfare System to End Poverty in America* (New York: Atlantic Monthly, 1993).

28. Lee Rainwater, "A Primer on American Poverty: 1949–1992," Institute for Research on Poverty, University of Wisconsin–Madison, n.d., 1.

29. For a discussion of shelter workers' participation in constructing an identity for the "battered woman," see Donileen R. Loseke, *The Battered Woman and Shelters: The Social Construction of Wife Abuse* (Albany: State University of New York Press, 1992), 71–94.

30. See Huttman and Redmond, "Women and Homelessness," for another study that surveys staff members in both homeless and domestic violence shelters. For other

discussions about the relationship between homelessness and domestic violence, see
Joan Zorza, "Woman Battering: A Major Cause of Homelessness," *Clearinghouse Review* 25:4 (1991): 421–429; Lee Ann Hoff, *Battered Women as Survivors* (New York:
Routledge, 1990); Marjorie Bard, *Organizational and Community Responses to Domestic Abuse and Homelessness* (New York: Garland, 1994). See also Wagner, *Checkerboard Square*; Doug A. Timmer, D. Stanley Eitzen, and Kathryn D. Talley, *Paths to Homelessness: Extreme Poverty and the Urban Housing Crisis* (Boulder: Westview, 1994); Jan L.
Hagen, "Gender and Homelessness," *Social Work* 32 (July–August 1987): 312–316.

31. Hagen, "Gender and Homelessness," 313.

32. Statistics from the Office of the Chief Economist, Department of Labor. Cited
in David E. Sanger, "The Last Liberal (Almost) Leaves Town," *New York Times*,
January 9, 1997, A9.

33. Allen T. Dupree, *Poverty and Income Trends: 1999* (Washington, D.C.: Center
on Budget and Policy Priorities, 2000), 85.

34. Ibid., 51.

35. Ibid., 52.

36. Ibid., 13–15.

37. Ibid., 15.

38. U.S. Department of Commerce, Bureau of the Census, *Poverty in the United States: 1992.* Current Population Reports, series P60, no. 185 (Washington, D.C.: U.S.
Government Printing Office, 1993), 6; Dupree, *Poverty and Income Trends*, 17. See also
Diana Pearce, "The Feminization of Poverty: A Second Look," paper presented at the
American Sociological Association meeting, San Francisco, August 1989.

39. Eugene T. Lowe, *A Status Report on Hunger and Homelessness in America's Cities: 2000* (Washington, D.C.: U.S. Conference of Mayors, 2000), 50.

40. Several studies have argued that despite cultural beliefs to the contrary, class
structure in the United States is fairly immobile. Mark Robert Rank argues that parental educational, occupational, and financial achievements limit children's educational
and occupational opportunities. Thus the class system is relatively stagnant. And Jay
MacLeod cites quantitative studies that indicate that the class of one's family of origin
has a significant effect on social location such that, in general, class structure changes
little from one generation to another. See Mark Robert Rank, *Living on the Edge: The Realities of Welfare in America* (New York: Columbia University Press, 1994); Jay
MacLeod, *Ain't No Makin' It: Leveled Aspirations in a Low-Income Neighborhood* (Boulder: Westview, 1987).

41. Lowe, *Status Report*, 82.

42. Institute for Children and Poverty, *Ten Cities: A Snapshot of Family Homelessness Across America, 1997–1998* (New York: Institute for Children and Poverty, 1998), 7.

43. Lowe, *Status Report*, appendix.

44. Ibid.

45. Leslie Kanes Weisman, *Discrimination by Design: A Feminist Critique of the Man-Made Environment* (Urbana: University of Illinois Press, 1992), 73.

46. Rank, *Living on the Edge*; see also Rossi, *Down and Out in America*.

47. Hoch and Slayton, *New Homeless and Old*.

48. Stephen Metraux and Dennis P. Culhane, "Family Dynamics, Housing, and Recurring Homelessness among Women in New York City Homeless Shelters," *Journal of Family Issues* 20:3 (1999): 373.

49. Battered women voiced similar concerns in Baker's study. See Baker, "Doin' What It Takes to Survive."

CHAPTER ONE

1. Zorza, "Woman Battering," 421.

2. Bassuk and Rosenberg's study comparing homeless and low-income housed women found that 41 percent of the homeless women willing to answer a question about domestic violence had been in a relationship in which they had been battered. Twenty percent of the housed women had been battered. Ellen L. Bassuk and Lynn Rosenberg, "Why Does Family Homelessness Occur? A Case Control Study," *American Journal of Public Health* 78:7 (July 1988): 785. See also Timmer, Eitzen, and Talley, *Paths to Homelessness*; Elaine R. Fox and Lisa Roth, "Homeless Children: Philadelphia as a Case Study," *Annals of the American Academy of Political and Social Science* 506 (1989): 146.

3. Kimberlé Williams Crenshaw, "Mapping the Margins: Intersectionality, Identity Politics, and Violence against Women of Color," in *The Public Nature of Private Violence: The Discovery of Domestic Abuse,* ed. Martha Albertson Fineman and Roxanne Mykitiuk (New York: Routledge, 1994), 95–96.

4. All names and identifying background information have been changed to protect participants' anonymity.

5. Lee Bowker, "A Battered Woman's Problems Are Social, Not Psychological," in *Current Controversies on Family Violence,* ed. Richard Gelles and Donileen Loseke (Newbury Park: Sage, 1993), 155; Linda Gordon, *Heroes of Their Own Lives: The Politics and History of Family Violence* (New York: Penguin, 1988).

6. Susan Schechter, *Women and Male Violence: The Visions and Struggles of the Battered Women's Movement* (Boston: South End, 1982), 232–233.

7. National Coalition for the Homeless, *The Un-Balanced Budget: The Impact of the Congressional Budget on Homelessness* (Washington, D.C.: National Coalition for the Homeless, 1995), iii.

8. Dupree, *Poverty and Income Trends.*

9. House Committee on Ways and Means, 106th Congress, *Green Book.* Washington, D.C.: Congressional Research Service, 2000, tables 7.8, 7.9.

10. Iris J. Lav and Edward B. Lazere, *A Hand Up: How State Earned Income Tax Credits Help Working Families Escape Poverty* (Washington, D.C.: Center on Budget and Policy Priorities, 1996), 7.

11. House Committee on Ways and Means, 106th Congress, *Green Book,* table 7.7.

12. Ibid.

13. Kathryn Edin and Christopher Jencks, "Welfare," in *Rethinking Social Policy: Race, Poverty, and the Underclass,* by Christopher Jencks (New York: HarperCollins, 1993), 206–220.

14. Ibid., 208.

15. Ibid., 210.

16. Cushing Dolbeare and Tracy L. Kaufman, *Out of Reach: Why Everyday People Can't Find Affordable Housing* (Washington, D.C.: Low Income Housing Information Service, 1995), 4.

17. Ibid.

18. Quigley and colleagues argue that the "availability and pricing of housing" explain much about the dynamics of homelessness. See John M. Quigley, Stephen Raphael, and Eugene Smolensky, "Homeless in America, Homeless in California," *Review of Economics and Statistics* 83:1 (2001): 37. See also Timmer, Eitzen, and Talley, *Paths to Homelessness*; Liebow, *Tell Them Who I Am*; Meredith Van Ry, *Homeless Families: Causes, Effects, and Recommendations* (New York: Garland, 1993); Jennifer Wolch and Michael Dear, *Malign Neglect: Homelessness in an American City* (San Francisco: Jossey-Bass, 1993).

19. The American Housing Survey is sponsored by HUD and conducted by the U.S. Bureau of the Census. The national survey provides statistics on housing conditions and affordability, with data collected every other year. Additional data for a selected forty-seven metropolitan areas are collected approximately every four years.

20. Cushing Dolbeare, "Perspectives on Renter Income and Affordable Units." Washington, D.C.: National Low Income Housing Coalition, September 8, 2001.

21. Jennifer G. Twombly et al., *Out of Reach 2001: America's Growing Wage-Rent Disparity* (Washington, D.C.: National Low Income Housing Coalition, 2001), 39.

22. Marcuse, "Neutralizing Homelessness." See also Rossi, *Down and Out in America*; Hoch and Slayton, *New Homeless and Old*.

23. Marcuse, "Neutralizing Homelessness," 75.

24. Interview with Terry Cook, Homeless Programs coordinator, City of Phoenix, March 10, 1995.

25. Paul A. Leonard and Edward B. Lazere, *A Place to Call Home: The Low Income Housing Crisis in 44 Major Metropolitan Areas* (Washington, D.C.: Center on Budget and Policy Priorities, 1992), 18.

26. Edward B. Lazere, *In Short Supply: The Growing Affordable Housing Gap* (Washington, D.C.: Center on Budget and Policy Priorities, 1995), 2. Low-income renters are defined as families with incomes below $10,000, which was slightly above the poverty line in 1989. Low-cost units are those renting at less than 30 percent of the poverty level, or $250 per month in 1989.

27. Dolbeare, "Perspectives on Renter Income."

28. Because of the growing number of low-income households and the decline in private nonsubsidized low-rent housing since the mid-1970s, the federal government needed to augment the number of households receiving subsidized housing each year simply to ensure that the shortfall in low-cost apartments did not expand. In fact, the federal government did continue to provide aid to additional households every year. These programs saw a cut in the rate of growth, however, reducing the average number of new families assisted from 290,000 each year from 1977 through 1980 to an average of 76,000 each year from 1981 to 1993 and 66,000 in 1994. See Jencks, *The Homeless*, 96; Lazere, *In Short Supply*, 20.

29. Jencks, *The Homeless*, 95.

30. Lowe, *Status Report*, 88. The Section 8 certificate and voucher programs are tenant-based rental housing subsidies for low-income families administered by HUD. Eligible recipients conduct their housing search in the private housing market and rent a privately owned apartment or house from an owner who agrees to participate in the program. Recipients generally pay 30 percent of their incomes for rent, and the remainder is paid by HUD. Under the voucher program a different basis is used for determining subsidies that can result in the household paying more or less than 30 percent of its income for rent. To be eligible for either program, a household's income must be 50 percent or less of the median income in its area. Approximately 1 million households received certificate assistance nationwide in 1994, and 294,000 received voucher assistance.

31. Lazere, *In Short Supply*, 20.

32. Lowe, *Status Report*, 88.

33. Ibid., 88–89.

34. Ibid., 90.

35. Jennifer Daskal, *In Search of Shelter: The Growing Shortage of Affordable Rental Housing* (Washington, D.C.: Center on Budget and Policy Priorities, 1998), 21.

36. Jencks, *The Homeless*, 42.

37. I did not ask women directly whether they had used drugs or believed drugs or alcohol had contributed to their homelessness. Rather I would ask them why they had sought shelter, and the eight women who spoke about drug use broached the subject themselves.

38. Sandra Sue Butler, "Listening to Middle-Aged Homeless Women Talk about Their Lives," *Affilia* 8:4 (winter 1993): 390.

39. A Philadelphia study on homeless families found that "60.0 percent had lived with others immediately before entering the shelter." See Fox and Roth, "Homeless Children," 146.

40. Peter Marin, "Helping and Hating the Homeless: The Struggle at the Margins of America," *Harpers* (January 1987): 42; italics mine.

41. Ibid., 42–43.

42. Ellen L. Bassuk, Lenore Rubin, and Alison Lauriat, "Is Homelessness a Mental Health Problem?" *American Journal of Psychiatry* 141 (December 1984): 1548.

43. Bassuk and Rosenberg, "Why Does Family Homelessness Occur," 785.

44. Ibid., 786–787.

45. Marcia B. Cohen and David Wagner, "Acting on Their Own Behalf: Affiliation and Political Mobilization among Homeless People," *Journal of Sociology and Social Welfare* 19 (December 1992): 28–29.

46. Ibid., 37.

47. In her study of the history of family violence, Linda Gordon notes that one family investigated by a social service agency told agency employees they had no living relatives, "a claim as likely as not to have been false, considering that clients usually did not wish to give such information to investigators." Gordon, *Heroes of Their Own Lives*, 120.

48. Donileen Loseke emphasized this point in her review of the manuscript.

CHAPTER TWO

1. For a similar point, see Huttman and Redmond, "Women and Homelessness," 97; Weisman, *Discrimination by Design*, 78.

2. Wolch, "Review of *Tell Them Who I Am*," 180. See also David A. Snow and Michael Mulcahy, "Space, Politics, and the Survival Strategies of the Homeless," *American Behavioral Scientist* 45:1 (2001): 149–169.

3. Michel Foucault, *Discipline and Punish: The Birth of the Prison*, trans. Alan Sheridan in 1977 (New York: Pantheon, 1978, 2d ed. [New York: Vintage, 1995]); Paul Rabinow, ed., *The Foucault Reader* (New York: Pantheon, 1984), 17; Holstein and Gubrium, *The Self We Live By*.

4. Foucault, *Discipline and Punish*, 184.

5. Ibid., 172.

6. Ibid., 187.

7. Ibid., 191.

8. Nathanson, *Dangerous Passage*, 223.

9. Matthew Crenson suggested further examination of these ambiguities and in general encouraged analysis of the contradictions inherent in shelter programs.

10. Hoch and Slayton briefly mention the "bind of treating and even creating dependence in the name of independence." See Hoch and Slayton, *New Homeless and Old*, 226.

11. See also Marin, "Helping and Hating the Homeless," 47.

12. Foucault, *Discipline and Punish*; Rabinow, *Foucault Reader*.

13. Lisa Ferrill, *A Far Cry from Home: Life in a Shelter for Homeless Women* (Chicago: Noble, 1991), 73.

14. Foucault, *Discipline and Punish*, 172.

15. Weisman, *Discrimination by Design*, 78.

16. Hoch and Slayton, *New Homeless and Old*, 225.

17. This quote by Eleanor Leacock was stated in the context of critiquing the culture of poverty thesis. Leacock, quoted in Katz, *The Undeserving Poor*, 39.

18. Ibid., 237–238.

19. Some women stated that they had been reluctant to seek housing in an emergency shelter for fear of violence from other shelter residents.

20. Ferrill's experiences with mentally ill homeless women attest to the difficulties staff may encounter in working with them as shelter residents and point to the staff's reliance on rules to remain consistent in their treatment of mentally ill women (Ferrill, *A Far Cry from Home*, esp. 97). With the exception of People in Transition, however, Phoenix family shelters generally avoid accepting seriously mentally ill women or men.

21. Since most shelters consistently have more requests for shelter than they can manage, caseworkers want to know as soon as possible when a current resident plans to leave. Sometimes residents simply do not return to the shelter in the evening, leaving their clothes and other personal belongings in their rooms. Some call to verify that they do not wish to remain at the shelter, whereas others never contact staff again. The caseworkers' obligation to maintain current information on bed availability translates

to stern warnings or automatic eviction for curfew violations. If, however, a resident is late only once, at most shelters she can usually count on her bed still being available when she returns.

22. Interview, director, the Lighthouse, December 5, 1994.

23. Interview, caseworker, the Family Shelter, August 31, 1994.

24. Before calculating one-third of a family's income, EPF subtracts the cost of necessities such as food and utilities. The remainder comprises the "income" from which EPF takes one-third.

25. P. Phillip Tan and Ellen Ryan, "Homeless Hispanic and Non-Hispanic Adults on the Texas-Mexico Border," *Hispanic Journal of Behavioral Sciences* 23:2 (2001): 241.

26. For a similar point, see Crenshaw, "Mapping the Margins," 107; Loseke, *The Battered Woman and Shelters*, 198, n. 4.

27. Crenshaw, "Mapping the Margins."

28. Tan and Ryan, "Homeless Hispanic and Non-Hispanic Adults," 247.

29. Interview, caseworker, Community Housing, August 23, 1994.

30. J. Okely, quoted in Angela Tretheway, "Resistance, Identity, and Empowerment: A Postmodern Feminist Analysis of Clients in a Human Service Organization," *Communication Monographs* 64 (December 1997): 281–301.

31. James C. Scott, *Weapons of the Weak: Everyday Forms of Peasant Resistance* (New Haven: Yale University Press, 1985), 29.

32. Ibid.

33. Frances Fox Piven and Richard A. Cloward, *Poor People's Movements: Why They Succeed, How They Fail* (New York: Vintage, 1977), 5.

34. Scott, *Weapons of the Weak*, 29–31.

35. Hoch and Slayton, *New Homeless and Old*, 208.

36. Michael Gismondi, quoted in Paula L. Dressel and Jeff Porterfield, "Beyond an Underclass: An Essay on Up-Front Politics," *Journal of Sociology and Social Welfare* 20 (March 1993): 39. See also Tretheway, "Resistance, Identity, and Empowerment."

37. Ferrill, *A Far Cry from Home*, 124.

38. Funiciello, *Tyranny of Kindness*, 124. See also Tretheway, "Resistance, Identity, and Empowerment." For a discussion of the historical professionalization of female social workers, in particular the adherence to values of "objectivity and rationality," see Daniel J. Walkowitz, "The Making of a Feminine Professional Identity: Social Workers in the 1920s," *American Historical Review* 95:4 (October 1990): 1051.

39. Hoch and Slayton, *New Homeless and Old*, 208.

40. This section has been influenced by conversations on the topic of professionalization with Julie Lindberg.

41. Debora Paterniti notes that the relationships between staff and residents in a chronic care facility are similarly circumscribed. See Debora A. Paterniti, "The Micropolitics of Identity in Adverse Circumstances," *Journal of Contemporary Ethnography* 29 (February 2000): 93–119.

42. In her study of a social service agency, Angela Tretheway found that clients similarly criticized and resisted the idea that the social worker is the only expert. See Tretheway, "Resistance, Identity, and Empowerment."

43. In Aihwa Ong's study of women factory workers in an industrializing rural Malaysian town, she found little "coherent articulation of exploitation in class or even feminist terms." Rather the women resisted in fragmented, individualized ways what they perceived to be inhumane treatment that threatened their "moral status." Ong, *Spirits of Resistance,* 196. See also Paterniti, "Micropolitics of Identity."

44. Tretheway, "Resistance, Identity, and Empowerment."

CHAPTER THREE

1. Hoch and Slayton, *New Homeless and Old,* 203–204; Wagner, *Checkerboard Square,* 4–5. See also Mark J. Stern, "The Emergence of the Homeless as a Public Problem," in *Housing the Homeless,* ed. Jon Erickson and Charles Wilhelm (New Brunswick, N.J.: Center for Urban Policy Research, 1986), 113–123.

2. Hoch and Slayton, *New Homeless and Old,* 208.

3. Wagner, *Checkerboard Square,* 5.

4. See Passaro, *The Unequal Homeless,* 2.

5. Coates, *A Street Is Not a Home,* 60.

6. Seccombe, James, and Walters, "They Think You Ain't Much of Nothing."

7. Coates, *A Street Is Not a Home,* 60.

8. Center for the Study of Policy Attitudes, *Fighting Poverty in America: A Study of American Public Attitudes* (Washington, D.C.: Center for the Study of Policy Attitudes, 1994), 13–16.

9. Lars Eighner, *Travels with Lizbeth* (New York: St. Martins, 1993), 4–5.

10. Karen Dugger, "Social Location and Gender-Role Attitudes: A Comparison of Black and White Women," in *Race, Class and Gender: Common Bonds, Different Voices,* ed. Esther Ngan-Ling Chow, Doris Wilkinson, and Maxine Baca Zinn (Thousand Oaks, Calif.: Sage, 1996), 34. See also bell hooks, *Ain't I a Woman?* (Boston: South End, 1981); Joyce Ladner, *Tomorrow's Tomorrow: The Black Woman* (Garden City, N.Y.: Doubleday, 1971).

11. Mary S. Larabee, quoted in Mimi Abramovitz, *Regulating the Lives of Women: Social Welfare Policy from Colonial Times to the Present* (Boston: South End, 1996), 318–319.

12. Ibid.

13. Jersy Kosinski, "Interview with Jersy Kosinski," in *Beyond Homelessness: Frames of Reference,* ed. Benedict Giamo and Jeffrey Grunberg (Iowa City: University of Iowa Press, 1992), 39.

14. Sherry Ortner finds in her interviews with Jewish and Italian American housed people in New Jersey that many "implicitly identify specific groups with specific class positions as if the class positions were essences of the groups." See "Ethnography among the Newark," 267.

15. Wagner discusses the therapeutic model as used by social service agencies. See *Checkerboard Square,* 176.

16. Richard Campbell and Jimmie L. Reeves, "Covering the Homeless: The Joyce Brown Story," *Critical Studies in Mass Communication* 6 (1989): 33.

17. Stern, "The Emergence of the Homeless"; Golden, *The Women Outside,* 122.

18. Wagner argues a similar point. See *Checkerboard Square,* 176.

19. See Eric Lott, *Love and Theft: Blackface Minstrelsy and the American Working Class* (New York: Oxford University Press, 1993).

20. Ruth Rosen, "The Female Generation Gap: Daughters of the Fifties and the Origins of Contemporary American Feminism," in *U.S. History as Women's History: New Feminist Essays,* ed. Linda K. Kerber, Alice Kessler-Harris, and Kathryn Kish Sklar (Chapel Hill: University of North Carolina Press, 1995), 323–324.

21. Ibid.

22. Golden, *The Women Outside,* 135.

23. Ibid., 216–217.

24. Ibid., 8.

25. As Brackette Williams points out, "ideological precepts structure our conceptualization of charity, giving, begging, working, and taking." Brackette Williams, "The Public I/Eye: Conducting Fieldwork to Do Homework on Homelessness and Begging in Two U.S. Cities," *Current Anthropology* 36:1 (February 1995): 30.

26. Stern, "Emergence of the Homeless," 118. See also Gareth Stedman Jones, *Outcast London* (London: Oxford University Press, 1971).

27. Ibid.

28. Williams, "The Public I/Eye," 37.

29. Lowe, *Status Report,* 50.

30. See also Snow and Anderson, *Down on Their Luck,* 201–202.

31. Marcel Mauss, quoted in Stern, "The Emergence of the Homeless," 118.

32. This language is taken from Donileen Loseke's review of the manuscript.

CHAPTER FOUR

1. Amy L. Poulin, "Lower Than a Snake's Belly: The Role of Stigma in the Oppression of Sheltered Homeless Families." Ph.D. diss., University of Utah, Salt Lake City, 1992.

2. Seccombe and colleagues and Cohen found similar dynamics among welfare mothers and soup kitchen clients, respectively. See Seccombe, James, and Walters, "They Think You Ain't Much of Nothing"; Cohen, "Poverty."

3. Sophie Watson, with Helen Austerberry, *Housing and Homelessness: A Feminist Perspective* (Boston: Routledge and Kegan Paul, 1986); Passaro, *The Unequal Homeless.* Thanks to Sue Hemberger for encouraging me to explore this line of inquiry.

4. Watson and Austerberry, *Housing and Homelessness.* See also Campbell and Reeves, "Covering the Homeless," 21, 27–28.

5. Watson and Austerberry, *Housing and Homelessness,* 92.

6. Ibid., 104. See also Passaro, *The Unequal Homeless.*

7. Emphasis mine.

8. Quoted in Giamo and Grunberg, eds., *Beyond Homelessness,* 32.

9. Judith Stacey defines postmodern families as those fitting into one or more of these forms: single parenthood, cohabitation, two-earner households, and extended kinship networks. Judith Stacey, *Brave New Families: Stories of Domestic Upheaval in Late Twentieth Century America* (New York: Basic, 1990).

10. Weisman, *Discrimination by Design*, 78.

11. Fox and Roth, "Homeless Children," 147–148. See also Kozol, *Rachel and Her Children*, 30, 82–87.

12. I take the terms *distance* and *disassociation* from David A. Snow and Leon Anderson, "Identity Work among the Homeless: The Verbal Construction and Avowal of Personal Identities," *American Journal of Sociology* 92 (May 1987): 1348–1349 and from Snow and Anderson, *Down on Their Luck*, 215.

13. Snow and Anderson, *Down on Their Luck*, 215; also Snow and Anderson, "Identity Work among the Homeless."

14. Donna M. Budani, review of Jean Calterone Williams, "Domestic Violence, Poverty, and Housing: The Narratives of Homeless Women," for *Gender and Society*, January 22, 1996.

15. Poulin also found that homeless people in shelters tended to distinguish themselves from others in the shelter and did not refer to themselves as homeless. See Poulin, "Lower Than a Snake's Belly," esp. 182–187.

16. Holstein and Gubrium, *The Self We Live By*, 32.

17. MacLeod, *Ain't No Makin' It*, 20.

CHAPTER FIVE

1. Huttman and Redmond surveyed staff in both homeless and domestic violence shelters. See Huttman and Redmond, "Women and Homelessness."

2. Battering is, of course, not just about economics. Men may batter and women may stay in relationships for social or cultural reasons. Some women who enter Phoenix battered women's shelters want the safety and counseling the shelter affords to deal with the emotional fallout both from having been in *and* from having left their relationships.

3. For a discussion of the experiences and characteristics associated with battered women, see Loseke, *The Battered Woman and Shelters*.

4. Liz Kelly, Sheila Burton, and Linda Regan, "Beyond Victim or Survivor: Sexual Violence, Identity and Feminist Theory and Practice," in *Sexualizing the Social: Power and the Organization of Sexuality*, ed. Lisa Adkins and Vicki Merchant (London: Macmillan, 1996), 78.

5. Loseke, *The Battered Woman and Shelters*, 4.

6. I thank Donileen Loseke for pointing this out in her review of the manuscript.

7. Loseke, *The Battered Woman and Shelters*, 61–62.

8. Ibid., 28.

9. Schechter, *Women and Male Violence*.

10. Ferrill, *A Far Cry from Home*, 124.

11. Loseke states that the shelter she studied mandated a three-day minimum stay with no outside contact.

12. Crenshaw, "Mapping the Margins," 95–96.

13. This is based in part on funding constraints. When the shelter received a new grant during the course of this study, it contracted with a jobs program that provided some assistance to residents through weekly on-site visits. Residents complained, how-

ever, that the main objective of representatives from the organization was to help women match their skills to an occupation, but many are already knowledgeable about the limited kinds of employment for which they qualify.

14. Loseke, *The Battered Woman and Shelters*, 4.

15. Ibid., 38.

16. Herbert J. Gans, *The War against the Poor: The Underclass and Antipoverty Policy* (New York: Basic, 1995), 68.

17. Alice Baum and Donald Burnes, *A Nation in Denial: The Truth about Homelessness* (Boulder: Westview, 1993).

18. Ann Jones, *Next Time She'll Be Dead: Battering and How to Stop It* (Boston: Beacon, 1994), 83.

19. Fine indicates that women she has interviewed in domestic violence shelters often refuse the label *battered woman* as well, understanding the label to describe a woman who is helpless or who did not fight back. See Michelle Fine, "The Politics of Research and Activism: Violence against Women," in *Violence against Women: The Bloody Footprints*, ed. Pauline B. Bart and Eileen Geil Moran (Newbury Park: Sage, 1993), 282.

20. Florence Hollis, *Women in Marital Conflict: A Casework Study* (New York: Family Service Association of America, 1949).

21. Lenore Walker, *The Battered Woman* (New York: Harper and Row, 1979); Walker, "The Battered Woman Syndrome Is a Psychological Consequence of Abuse," in *Current Controversies on Family Violence*, ed. Richard J. Gelles and Donileen Loseke (Newbury Park: Sage, 1993), 133–153.

CONCLUSION

1. Donileen R. Loseke, "Constructing Conditions, People, Morality, and Emotion: Expanding the Agenda of Constructionism," in *Constructionist Controversies: Issues in Social Problems Theory*, ed. Gale Miller and James A. Holstein (New York: Aldine de Gruyter, 1993), 207–214.

2. Tretheway, "Resistance, Identity, and Empowerment," 281. See also Foucault, *Discipline and Punish*.

3. See, for example, Demetra Smith Nightingale, "Welfare Reform: Historical Context and Current Issues," in *The Work Alternative: Welfare Reform and the Realities of the Job Market*, ed. Demetra Smith Nightingale and Robert H. Haveman (Washington, D.C.: Urban Institute, 1995), 2.

4. Ibid., 9.

5. William Gorham, "Foreword," in *The Work Alternative: Welfare Reform and the Realities of the Job Market*, ed. Demetra Smith Nightingale and Robert H. Haveman (Washington, D.C.: Urban Institute, 1995), xi.

BIBLIOGRAPHY

Abramovitz, Mimi. *Regulating the Lives of Women: Social Welfare Policy from Colonial Times to the Present.* 2d ed. Boston: South End, 1996.

Arizona Community Action Association. *Poverty in Arizona: A Shared Responsibility.* Phoenix: Arizona Community Action Association, 1994.

Baker, Phyllis L. "Doin' What It Takes to Survive: Battered Women and the Consequences of Compliance to a Cultural Script." *Studies in Symbolic Interaction* 20 (1996): 73–90.

Baker, Susan Gonzalez. "Gender, Ethnicity and Homelessness: Accounting for Demographic Diversity on the Streets." *American Behavioral Scientist* 37 (February 1994): 476–504.

Bard, Marjorie. *Organizational and Community Responses to Domestic Abuse and Homelessness.* New York: Garland, 1994.

Bassuk, Ellen L., and Lynn Rosenberg. "Why Does Family Homelessness Occur? A Case Control Study." *American Journal of Public Health* 78:7 (July 1988): 783–788.

Bassuk, Ellen L., Lenore Rubin, and Alison Lauriat. "Is Homelessness a Mental Health Problem?" *American Journal of Psychiatry* 141 (December 1984): 1546–1550.

Baum, Alice, and Donald Burnes. *A Nation in Denial: The Truth about Homelessness.* Boulder: Westview, 1993.

Bowker, Lee. "A Battered Woman's Problems Are Social, Not Psychological." In *Current Controversies on Family Violence*, ed. Richard Gelles and Donileen Loseke, 154–165. Newbury Park: Sage, 1993.

Butler, Judith. *Gender Trouble: Feminism and the Subversion of Identity*. New York: Routledge, 1990.

Butler, Sandra Sue. "Listening to Middle-Aged Homeless Women Talk about Their Lives." *Affilia* 8:4 (winter 1993): 388–409.

Campbell, Richard, and Jimmie L. Reeves. "Covering the Homeless: The Joyce Brown Story." *Critical Studies in Mass Communication* 6 (1989): 21–42.

Center for the Study of Policy Attitudes. *Fighting Poverty in America: A Study of American Public Attitudes*. Washington, D.C.: Center for the Study of Policy Attitudes, 1994.

Coates, Robert C. *A Street Is Not a Home: Solving America's Homeless Dilemma*. Buffalo, N.Y.: Prometheus, 1990.

Cohen, Jodi R. "Poverty: Talk, Identity and Action." *Qualitative Inquiry* 3 (March 1997): 71–92.

Cohen, Marcia B., and David Wagner. "Acting on Their Own Behalf: Affiliation and Political Mobilization among Homeless People." *Journal of Sociology and Social Welfare* 19 (December 1992): 21–39.

Connolly, Deborah R. *Homeless Mothers: Face to Face with Women and Poverty*. Minneapolis: University of Minnesota Press, 2000.

Crenshaw, Kimberlé Williams. "Mapping the Margins: Intersectionality, Identity Politics, and Violence against Women of Color." In *The Public Nature of Private Violence: The Discovery of Domestic Abuse*, ed. Martha Albertson Fineman and Roxanne Mykitiuk, 93–118. New York: Routledge, 1994.

Daskal, Jennifer. *In Search of Shelter: The Growing Shortage of Affordable Rental Housing*. Washington, D.C.: Center on Budget and Policy Priorities, 1998.

Davis, Liane V., Jan L. Hagen, and Theresa J. Early. "Social Services for Battered Women: Are They Adequate, Accessible, and Appropriate?" *Social Work* 39:6 (November 1994): 695–704.

Dolbeare, Cushing. "Perspectives on Renter Income and Affordable Units." Washington, D.C.: National Low Income Housing Coalition, September 8, 2001.

Dolbeare, Cushing, and Tracy L. Kaufman. *Out of Reach: Why Everyday People Can't Find Affordable Housing*. Washington, D.C.: Low Income Housing Information Service, 1995.

Dressel, Paula L., and Jeff Porterfield. "Beyond an Underclass: An Essay on Up-Front Politics." *Journal of Sociology and Social Welfare* 20 (March 1993): 27–46.

Dugger, Karen. "Social Location and Gender-Role Attitudes: A Comparison of Black and White Women." In *Race, Class and Gender: Common Bonds, Different Voices*, ed. Esther Ngan-Ling Chow, Doris Wilkinson, and Maxine Baca Zinn, 32–51. Thousand Oaks, Calif.: Sage, 1996.

Duneier, Mitchell. *Slim's Table: Race, Respectability, and Masculinity*. Chicago: University of Chicago Press, 1992.

Dupree, Allen T. *Poverty and Income Trends: 1999*. Washington, D.C.: Center on Budget and Policy Priorities, 2000.

Edin, Kathryn, and Christopher Jencks. "Welfare." In *Rethinking Social Policy: Race, Poverty, and the Underclass*, by Christopher Jencks, 206–220. New York: HarperCollins, 1993.

Eighner, Lars. *Travels with Lizbeth*. New York: St. Martins, 1993.

Enchautegui, María E. *Policy Implications of Latino Poverty*. Washington, D.C.: Urban Institute, 1995.

Erickson, Jon, and Charles Wilhelm. *Housing the Homeless*. New Brunswick, N.J.: Center for Urban Policy Research, 1986.

Ferrill, Lisa. *A Far Cry from Home: Life in a Shelter for Homeless Women*. Chicago: Noble, 1991.

Fine, Michelle. "The Politics of Research and Activism: Violence against Women." In *Violence against Women: The Bloody Footprints*, ed. Pauline B. Bart and Eileen Geil Moran, 278–287. Newbury Park, Calif.: Sage, 1993.

Foucault, Michel. *Discipline and Punish: The Birth of the Prison*. 2d ed. Trans. Alan Sheridan. New York: Pantheon, 1978. [New York: Vintage, 1995].

———. *The History of Sexuality, Vol. 1*. New York: Random House, 1978; reprint, New York: Vintage, 1990.

Fox, Elaine R., and Lisa Roth. "Homeless Children: Philadelphia as a Case Study." *Annals of the American Academy of Political and Social Science* 506 (1989): 141–151.

Fraser, Nancy, and Linda Gordon. "Contract versus Charity: Why Is There No Social Citizenship in the United States." *Socialist Review* 22:3 (1992): 45–68.

———. "A Genealogy of Dependency: Tracing a Keyword of the U.S. Welfare State." *Signs* 19 (winter 1994): 309–336.

Funiciello, Theresa. *Tyranny of Kindness: Dismantling the Welfare System to End Poverty in America*. New York: Atlantic Monthly, 1993.

Gans, Herbert J. *The War against the Poor: The Underclass and Antipoverty Policy*. New York: Basic, 1995.

Gelles, Richard J., and Donileen Loseke, eds. *Current Controversies on Family Violence*. Newbury Park, Calif.: Sage, 1993.

Giamo, Benedict, and Jeffrey Grunberg, eds. *Beyond Homelessness: Frames of Reference*. Iowa City: University of Iowa Press, 1992.

Golden, Stephanie. *The Women Outside: Meanings and Myths of Homelessness*. Berkeley: University of California Press, 1992.

Gordon, Linda. *Heroes of Their Own Lives: The Politics and History of Family Violence*. New York: Penguin, 1988.

———. *Pitied but Not Entitled: Single Mothers and the History of Welfare*. New York: Free Press, 1994.

Gorham, William. "Foreword." In *The Work Alternative: Welfare Reform and the Realities of the Job Market*, ed. Demetra Smith Nightingale and Robert H. Haveman, xi. Washington, D.C.: Urban Institute, 1995.

Gusfield, Joseph. *The Culture of Public Problems: Drinking-Driving and the Symbolic Order*. Chicago: University of Chicago Press, 1981.

Hagen, Jan L. "Gender and Homelessness." *Social Work* 32 (July–August 1987): 312–316.

Hoch, Charles, and Robert Slayton. *New Homeless and Old: Community and the Skid Row Hotel.* Philadelphia: Temple University Press, 1989.

Hoff, Lee Ann. *Battered Women as Survivors.* New York: Routledge, 1990.

Hollis, Florence. *Women in Marital Conflict: A Casework Study.* New York: Family Service Association of America, 1949.

Holstein, James A., and Jaber F. Gubrium. *The Self We Live By: Narrative Identity in a Postmodern World.* New York: Oxford University Press, 2000.

hooks, bell. *Ain't I a Woman?* Boston: South End, 1981.

House Committee on Ways and Means, 106th Congress. *Green Book.* Washington, D.C.: Congressional Research Service, 2000.

Huttman, Elizabeth, and Sonjia Redmond. "Women and Homelessness: Evidence of Need to Look Beyond Shelters to Long-Term Social Service Assistance and Permanent Housing." *Journal of Sociology and Social Welfare* 19 (December 1992): 89–111.

Institute for Children and Poverty. *Ten Cities: A Snapshot of Family Homelessness across America, 1997–1998.* New York: Institute for Children and Poverty, 1998.

Jencks, Christopher. *The Homeless.* Cambridge: Harvard University Press, 1994.

———. *Rethinking Social Policy: Race, Poverty, and the Underclass.* Cambridge: Harvard University Press, 1992; reprint, New York: HarperCollins, 1993.

Jones, Ann. *Next Time, She'll Be Dead: Battering and How to Stop It.* Boston: Beacon, 1994.

Katz, Michael B. *The Undeserving Poor: From the War on Poverty to the War on Welfare.* New York: Pantheon, 1989.

Kelly, Liz, Sheila Burton, and Linda Regan. "Beyond Victim or Survivor: Sexual Violence, Identity and Feminist Theory and Practice." In *Sexualizing the Social: Power and the Organization of Sexuality,* ed. Lisa Adkins and Vicki Merchant, 77–101. London: Macmillan, 1996.

Kerber, Linda K., Alice Kessler-Harris, and Kathryn Kish Sklar, eds. *U.S. History as Women's History: New Feminist Essays.* Chapel Hill: University of North Carolina Press, 1995.

Kosinski, Jersy. "Chance Beings." In *Beyond Homelessness: Frames of Reference,* ed. Benedict Giamo and Jeffrey Grunberg, 31–49. Iowa City: University of Iowa Press, 1992.

Kozol, Jonathan. *Rachel and Her Children: Homeless Families in America.* New York: Fawcett Columbine, 1988.

Ladner, Joyce. *Tomorrow's Tomorrow: The Black Woman.* Garden City, N.Y.: Doubleday, 1971.

Lav, Iris J., and Edward B. Lazere. *A Hand Up: How State Earned Income Tax Credits Help Working Families Escape Poverty.* Washington, D.C.: Center on Budget and Policy Priorities, 1996.

Lazere, Edward B. *In Short Supply: The Growing Affordable Housing Gap.* Washington, D.C.: Center on Budget and Policy Priorities, 1995.

Leonard, Paul A., and Edward B. Lazere. *A Place to Call Home: The Low-Income Housing Crisis in 44 Major Metropolitan Areas.* Washington, D.C.: Center on Budget and Policy Priorities, 1992.

Liebow, Elliot. *Tally's Corner: A Study of Negro Streetcorner Men*. Boston: Little, Brown, 1967.

———. *Tell Them Who I Am: The Lives of Homeless Women*. New York: Free Press, 1993.

Loseke, Donileen R. *The Battered Woman and Shelters: The Social Construction of Wife Abuse*. Albany: State University of New York Press, 1992.

———. "Constructing Conditions, People, Morality, and Emotion: Expanding the Agenda of Constructionism." In *Constructionist Controversies: Issues in Social Problems Theory*, ed. Gale Miller and James A. Holstein, 207–214. New York: Aldine de Gruyter, 1993.

Lott, Eric. *Love and Theft: Blackface Minstrelsy and the American Working Class*. New York: Oxford University Press, 1993.

Lowe, Eugene T. *A Status Report on Hunger and Homelessness in America's Cities: 2000*. Washington, D.C.: U.S. Conference of Mayors, 2000.

MacLeod, Jay. *Ain't No Makin' It: Leveled Aspirations in a Low-Income Neighborhood*. Boulder: Westview, 1987.

Mahoney, Martha R. "Victimization or Oppression? Women's Lives, Violence, and Agency." In *The Public Nature of Private Violence: The Discovery of Domestic Abuse*, ed. Martha Albertson Fineman and Roxanne Mykitiuk, 59–92. New York: Routledge, 1994.

Marcuse, Peter. "Neutralizing Homelessness." *Socialist Review* 18 (1988): 69–96.

Marin, Peter. "Helping and Hating the Homeless: The Struggle at the Margins of America." *Harpers* (January 1987): 39–49.

Mead, Lawrence M. *The New Politics of Poverty: The Nonworking Poor in America*. New York: Basic, 1992.

Metraux, Stephen, and Dennis P. Culhane. "Family Dynamics, Housing, and Recurring Homelessness among Women in New York City Homeless Shelters." *Journal of Family Issues* 20:3 (1999): 371–396.

Nathanson, Constance A. *Dangerous Passage: The Social Control of Sexuality in Women's Adolescence*. Philadelphia: Temple University Press, 1991.

National Coalition for the Homeless. *The Un-Balanced Budget: The Impact of the Congressional Budget on Homelessness*. Washington, D.C.: National Coalition for the Homeless, 1995.

Neubeck, Kenneth J., and Noel A. Cazenave. *Welfare Racism: Playing the Race Card against America's Poor*. New York: Routledge, 2001.

Nightingale, Demetra Smith. "Welfare Reform: Historical Context and Current Issues." In *The Work Alternative: Welfare Reform and the Realities of the Job Market*, ed. Demetra Smith Nightingale and Robert H. Haveman, 1–13. Washington, D.C.: Urban Institute, 1995.

Ong, Aihwa. *Spirits of Resistance and Capitalist Discipline: Factory Women in Malaysia*. Albany: State University of New York Press, 1987.

Ortner, Sherry B. "Ethnography among the Newark: The Class of '58 of Weequahic High School." In *Naturalizing Power: Essays in Feminist Cultural Analysis*, ed. Sylvia Yanagisako and Carol Delaney, 257–273. New York: Routledge, 1995.

————. "Resistance and the Problem of Ethnographic Refusal." *Society for Comparative Study of Society and History* 37:1 (January 1995): 173–193.

Passaro, Joanne. *The Unequal Homeless: Men on the Streets, Women in Their Place.* New York: Routledge, 1996.

Paterniti, Debora A. "The Micropolitics of Identity in Adverse Circumstances." *Journal of Contemporary Ethnography* 29 (February 2000): 93–119.

Pearce, Diana. "The Feminization of Poverty: A Second Look." Paper presented at the American Sociological Association meeting, San Francisco, August 1989.

Piven, Frances Fox, and Richard A. Cloward. *Poor People's Movements: Why They Succeed, How They Fail.* New York: Vintage, 1977.

Poulin, Amy L. "Lower Than a Snake's Belly: The Role of Stigma in the Oppression of Sheltered Homeless Families." Ph.D. diss., University of Utah, Salt Lake City, 1992.

Quadagno, Jill. *The Color of Welfare: How Racism Undermined the War on Poverty.* New York: Oxford University Press, 1994.

Quigley, John M., Stephen Raphael, and Eugene Smolensky. "Homeless in America, Homeless in California." *Review of Economics and Statistics* 83:1 (2001): 37–51.

Rabinow, Paul, ed. *The Foucault Reader.* New York: Pantheon, 1984.

Rainwater, Lee. "A Primer on American Poverty: 1949–1992." Madison: Institute for Research on Poverty, University of Wisconsin–Madison, n.d.

Rank, Mark Robert. *Living on the Edge: The Realities of Welfare in America.* New York: Columbia University Press, 1994.

Rosen, Ruth. "The Female Generation Gap: Daughters of the Fifties and the Origins of Contemporary American Feminism." In *U.S. History as Women's History: New Feminist Essays,* ed. Linda K. Kerber, Alice Kessler-Harris, and Kathryn Kish Sklar, 313–334. Chapel Hill: University of North Carolina Press, 1995.

Rosenthal, Rob. *Homeless in Paradise: A Map of the Terrain.* Philadelphia: Temple University Press, 1994.

Rossi, Peter H. *Down and Out in America: The Origins of Homelessness.* Chicago: University of Chicago Press, 1989.

Rousseau, Ann Marie. *Shopping Bag Ladies: Homeless Women Speak about Their Lives.* New York: Pilgrim, 1981.

Russell, Betty G. *Silent Sisters: A Study of Homeless Women.* New York: Hemisphere, 1991.

Schechter, Susan. *Women and Male Violence: The Visions and Struggles of the Battered Women's Movement.* Boston: South End, 1982.

Scott, James C. *Weapons of the Weak: Everyday Forms of Peasant Resistance.* New Haven: Yale University Press, 1985.

Seccombe, Karen, Delores James, and Kimberly Battle Walters. "'They Think You Ain't Much of Nothing': The Social Construction of the Welfare Mother." *Journal of Marriage and Family* 60 (November 1998): 849–865.

Sidel, Ruth. *Women and Children Last: The Plight of Poor Women in Affluent America.* New York: Penguin, 1987.

Snow, David A., and Leon Anderson. *Down on Their Luck: A Study of Homeless Street People.* Berkeley: University of California Press, 1993.

————. "Identity Work among the Homeless: The Verbal Construction and Avowal of Personal Identities." *American Journal of Sociology* 92 (May 1987): 1336–1371.

Snow, David A., Leon Anderson, and Paul Koegel. "Distorting Tendencies in Research on the Homeless." *American Behavioral Scientist* 37 (February 1994): 461–475.

Snow, David A., and Michael Mulcahy. "Space, Politics, and the Survival Strategies of the Homeless." *American Behavioral Scientist* 45:1 (2001): 149–169.

Stacey, Judith. *Brave New Families: Stories of Domestic Upheaval in Late-Twentieth-Century America*. New York: Basic, 1990.

Stack, Carol. *All Our Kin: Strategies for Survival in a Black Community*. New York: Harper and Row, 1974.

Stedman Jones, Gareth. *Outcast London*. London: Oxford University Press, 1971.

Stern, Mark J. "The Emergence of the Homeless as a Public Problem." In *Housing the Homeless*, ed. Jon Erickson and Charles Wilhelm, 113–123. New Brunswick, N.J.: Center for Urban Policy Research, 1986.

Tan, P. Phillip, and Ellen Ryan. "Homeless Hispanic and Non-Hispanic Adults on the Texas-Mexico Border." *Hispanic Journal of Behavioral Sciences* 23:2 (2001): 239–249.

Timmer, Doug A., D. Stanley Eitzen, and Kathryn D. Talley. *Paths to Homelessness: Extreme Poverty and the Urban Housing Crisis*. Boulder: Westview, 1994.

Tretheway, Angela. "Resistance, Identity, and Empowerment: A Postmodern Feminist Analysis of Clients in a Human Service Organization." *Communication Monographs* 64 (December 1997): 281–301.

Twombly, Jennifer G., Cushing N. Dolbeare, Nancy Ferris, and Sheila Crowley. *Out of Reach 2001: America's Growing Wage-Rent Disparity*. Washington, D.C.: National Low Income Housing Coalition, 2001.

U.S. Department of Commerce, Bureau of the Census. *Poverty in the United States: 1992*. Current Population Reports, series P60, no. 185. Washington, D.C.: U.S. Government Printing Office, 1993.

U.S. General Accounting Office. *Homelessness: McKinney Act Programs and Funding through Fiscal Year 1993*. Washington, D.C.: U.S. General Accounting Office, 1994.

Van Ry, Meredith. *Homeless Families: Causes, Effects, and Recommendations*. New York: Garland, 1993.

Vanderstaay, Steven. *Street Lives: An Oral History of Homeless Americans*. Philadelphia: New Society, 1992.

Wagner, David. "Beyond the Pathologizing of Nonwork: Alternative Activities in a Street Community." *Social Work* 39 (November 1994): 718–727.

————. *Checkerboard Square: Culture and Resistance in a Homeless Community*. Boulder: Westview, 1993.

Walker, Lenore. *The Battered Woman*. New York: Harper and Row, 1979.

————. "The Battered Woman Syndrome Is a Psychological Consequence of Abuse." In *Current Controversies on Family Violence*, ed. Richard J. Gelles and Donileen Loseke, 133–153. Newbury Park: Sage, 1993.

Walkowitz, Daniel J. "The Making of a Feminine Professional Identity: Social Workers in the 1920s." *American Historical Review* 95:4 (October 1990): 1051–1075.

Watson, Sophie, with Helen Austerberry. *Housing and Homelessness: A Feminist Perspective*. Boston: Routledge and Kegan Paul, 1986.

Weisman, Leslie Kanes. *Discrimination by Design: A Feminist Critique of the Man-Made Environment*. Urbana: University of Illinois Press, 1992.

Williams, Brackette. "The Public I/Eye: Conducting Fieldwork to Do Homework on Homelessness and Begging in Two U.S. Cities." *Current Anthropology* 36:1 (February 1995): 25–51.

Wolch, Jennifer. "Review of *Tell Them Who I Am: The Lives of Homeless Women*, by Elliot Liebow." *Urban Geography* 16:2 (1995): 178–188.

Wolch, Jennifer, and Michael Dear. *Malign Neglect: Homelessness in an American City*. San Francisco: Jossey-Bass, 1993.

Wright, Talmadge. *Out of Place: Homeless Mobilizations, Subcities, and Contested Landscapes*. Albany: State University of New York Press, 1997.

Zorza, Joan. "Woman Battering: A Major Cause of Homelessness." *Clearinghouse Review* 25:4 (1991): 421–429.

INDEX